LINCOLN HALL WITH
SUE FEAR

FEAR
NO BOUNDARY
ONE WOMAN'S AMAZING JOURNEY

Lothian
BOOKS

To young people—be the people you want to be

A LOTHIAN BOOK
An imprint of Hachette Livre Australia Pty Limited
Level 17, 207 Kent Street, Sydney NSW 2000
www.hachette.com.au

Copyright © Lincoln Hall and Sue Fear 2005

First published 2005

This edition published 2006

'Risk' is a modified version of a poem attributed to Janet Rand.

All rights reserved. No part of this publication may be reproduced, stored in a retrieval system or transmitted in any form by any means without the prior permission of the copyright owner. Enquiries should be made to the publisher.

**National Library of Australia
Cataloguing-in-Publication data**

Hall, Lincoln, 1955- .
 Fear no boundary : the road to Everest and beyond.

 Rev ed.
 ISBN-13 970 0 734409 76 8.
 ISBN-10 0 7344 0976 1.

 1. Fear, Sue. 2. Women mountaineers - Australia - Biography. 3. Mountaineering - Everest, Mount (China and Nepal). I. Title.

796.522092

Cover design by Christabella Designs
Text design by Mason Design
Typesetting by Cannon Typesetting
Digital production by Bookhouse, Sydney
Printed in Australia by Griffin Press

RISK

To laugh is to risk appearing a fool.
To weep is to risk appearing sentimental.
To reach out to another is to risk involvement.
To expose your feelings is to risk rejection.
To place your dreams before the crowd is to risk mockery.
To love is to risk not being loved in return.
To go forward in the face of overwhelming odds is to risk failure.
But risks must be taken, because the greatest risk of all is to risk nothing.
The person who risks nothing, does nothing, has nothing and is nothing.
She may avoid suffering and sorrow, but she cannot learn, she cannot feel, she cannot change, she cannot grow and she cannot love.
Chained by certainty, she is a servant.
Only the person who risks is truly free.

Read at Sue's Memorial Service on 7 June 2006
by Rebecca Fear, Sue's eldest niece

FOREWORD
by Gabi Hollows

The true mountaineer, like the poet, is born not made.

Freda du Faur, *The Conquest of Mount Cook*

'Sue Fear! What kind of name is that?' demanded Fred Hollows. Those were the very first words that my late husband Fred uttered to Sue when they met in his office, some seventeen years ago. At the time, Fred was Chairman of the Division of Ophthalmology at the Prince of Wales Hospital and an Associate Professor at the University of New South Wales, as well as being an experienced (though modest) mountaineer. His playful introduction left even brave Sue trembling in her boots! So began our family's long-lasting friendship with Sue Fear.

It was a great thrill for me to be invited by Sue to be one of the first people to read her book, *Fear No Boundary*. It is an enjoyable task to read each line as Sue talks, walks and stage-manages each step of her epic journey through her childhood and early years living in St Ives (sharing the same childhood stomping grounds as Australian mountaineer Freda du Faur, who in 1913 became the first woman to summit Mount Cook) with parents Joan and Ron, and two brothers, John and Grahame.

These early fun-loving experiences were where Sue fell in love with the idea of adventure, where she dreamed of far away places, not knowing that the next phase of her life would be to visit, revisit, and conquer many of them. With such wonderful achievements, Sue's story is truly amazing.

As the first Australian-born woman to have climbed so many mountains (including four of the world's fourteen peaks higher than 8000 metres), her ultimate experience was to climb Mount Everest on 31 May 2003—fifty years, almost to the day, that Tenzing Norgay, a Nepalese Sherpa, and Edmund Hillary, a young New Zealand mountaineer, summitted Mount Everest on 29 May 1953. (It was also a big week for me—I was born on 21 May 1953!)

Sue's book deserves to be a classic, along with other tales of tremendous journeys to Everest, including Lincoln Hall's *White Limbo*, our dear friend Tim Macartney-Snape's *Sea to Summit* and Sorell Wilby's *Beyond the Icefall*. The most precious account of this conquest is Edmund Hillary's own *Nothing Venture, Nothing Win*. His observations still ring true today, and offer all of us inspiration:

> Even the mediocre can have adventures, and even the fearful can achieve. In a sense, fear became a friend.

As I travelled along with Sue on her story, I could not help but hear, echoing in my brain, the many times that our strong but sensitive Fred quoted Rudyard Kipling's 'The Female of the Species':

> When the Himalayan peasant meets the he-bear in his pride,
> He shouts to scare the monster, who will often turn aside.
> But the she-bears thus accosted rends the peasant tooth and nail.
> For the female of the species is more deadly than the male.

Sue always remains focused and determined, and with this book shares her knowledge that the female of the species is, indeed, more deadly than the male. I admire Sue for her greatness and courage, but most of all for the respect and grace she shows towards her Nepali friends, Sherpa guides, sponsors, family, friends, fellow climbers, trekkers and 'summiteers'.

As fearsome as she can sometimes seem on the outside, Sue is a wonderfully unselfish and wise person, who has a keen awareness of the hopes of others. Sue respects everyone's dreams of climbing Mount Everest, and doesn't just consider her own goals. Her disappointment at an unsuccessful summit attempt was admirably kept aside while her happiness for fellow climbers returning triumphantly to base camp shone through. As Sue says in these pages, 'It was about them, not me.' That's just so Sue.

As I write this foreword, I sit here at Farnham House in Randwick looking up at Sue's pride and joy — one of her 'little treats' from that momentous day at the summit of Mount Everest, captured in the magnificent poster printed by Australian Geographic. It is, of course, one of those 'pocketed little rocks' for our family to share and to go with her goggles, which she so kindly donated for auction for the Fred Hollows Foundation and that I proudly obtained.

Thank you Sue for reminding me of Fred's words: 'Remember, she's a good woman, that Sue Fear.' We are all so proud of you Sue — and I know Fred would be too.

Gabi Hollows
Farnham House
31 May 2005

FOREWORD

by Greg Mortimer

You have to take your hat off to someone with a distinctive walk. It makes you sit up and take notice. Sue Fear has a very distinctive walk. She moves on the balls of her feet and springs on her toes with shoulders slightly hunched forward, like a mountain cat, maybe a snow leopard. Her small frame propels with deliberate intent.

I first saw that walk in Adaminaby, in the Australian ski fields, in 1985. It belonged to a self-deprecating, beautiful woman who described herself as a bit of a boofhead. It has developed since then. Now her idea of a big day out is to climb to the top of Mount Everest. She did it. She just went out and did it. And the walk has got stronger.

Having done that, and having travelled the world to climb other great mountains, she has taken the even more frightening step of walking that dangerous fine line between exposing her heart and maintaining the inner privacy, the deeply buried pool of secrecy that helps a mountaineer survive. She has let us in.

Sometimes reading these words I felt shock. What does she mean by 'date rape'? What does she gain from telling us about a relationship that never was on Makalu, and the almost fatal foolishness of forgetting a headtorch? Why exactly does she expose herself so? As you read this book you come to understand her reasons. On those desperate climbs you can hide nothing about yourself from yourself. Sue remembers what it was like up there, above 8000 metres, despite the dense fog that settles on your brain — how non-essential everything is, except survival;

how openness and clarity form the key; how tenuous life is on the highest of highs, but also how sweet, even when you are so close to your own demise.

On Everest, Sue found the Mother Goddess of the Earth—Chomolungma—and was smiled upon.

Greg Mortimer
(first Australian to climb both
Mount Everest and K2)
Blue Mountains
May 2005

CONTENTS

Preface x
Acknowledgements xiv

1 Africa 1987 1
2 Finding the path 33
3 To heaven and hell 53
4 For whom the bell tolls 79
5 Learning my ABCs 99
6 Shaken, not stirred 133
7 Down but not out 159
8 Summit fever 183
9 Ms Everest 225
10 Gasherbrum 2004 243

Epilogue 255
Postscript 262
Glossary 270

PREFACE

Stories of Mount Everest are full of drama and myths, and it seems that almost everyone who goes there writes a book. After my own success on the mountain, I found that I wanted to share my experiences as well, but in my book I wanted to cover more than my climb to that famous summit. I certainly felt that the northern spring of 2003 was an interesting time to record events on Everest because it was the fiftieth anniversary of the first ascent by Edmund Hillary and Tenzing Norgay. It was especially interesting for me because I was there, at grips with all the challenges, fears, hopes and joys that are part of the climb. At the same time, I was aware that a woman's perspective as a climber is not often heard, and I wanted to tell that story, from my own personal viewpoint at least.

I regard myself as a regular kind of person who happened to hit upon a particular purpose in life that led me away from the ordinary. From my happy suburban upbringing on the north side of Sydney, my life has unfolded in a way I would never have predicted, and by pottering along and giving things a decent shot I have found myself at the heart of some unusual events. This is my first chance to share them with people in a way that is more than a glimpse, and it allows people to link the pieces together so that the outcome of Sue Fear on the summit of Everest does not seem so illogical after all.

The writing of this book was no easy feat, and I expect that is the case for everyone's first book. So many people told me I had to write a

PREFACE

book about my experiences that I felt I had no option but to take on the challenge. The prospect excited me, and I was very keen to get started. However, other people were asking me to do other things in the flush of excitement after my success, and as a result the book kept hovering around me as an ungraspable idea. The prospect of writing my story felt like climbing another Everest all over again. How would I be able to capture the mood of the different periods in my life, or the essence of events on big mountains? Success on a mountain invariably involves a team of some sort, and a perceptiveness at recognising your strengths, weaknesses and available time …

And so I decided to make the book a team effort. I contacted Lincoln Hall, mountaineer and author, with three mountaineering books among his six published titles. Not only did Lincoln share my passion for mountains but, like me, he had a long history in the adventure travel business. And so began a different kind of journey. It has been a long process, but rewarding for us, and hopefully for our readers as well.

As you can imagine, the book took me back to places and times that varied from memorable to intense and joyous; quite a journey in itself but a necessary one. I feel Lincoln has captured this in a way I don't think I could have achieved, and one that is for all readers rather than just mountaineers.

Both of us are still passionate about climbing, travel and guiding, so the synergy was right for this project. And we definitely had more laughs than angst in getting this together.

Sue Fear

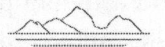

When Sue called to ask if I would like to write her book, I was both delighted and dismayed. I was delighted because it was a confluence of my loves—my love of writing, of the intense magic of climbing itself, and of the intoxicating landscapes of Nepal, Tibet, and South America, where most of the action takes place. My dismay at Sue's invitation was nothing more than the feeling I have every time

I contemplate writing another book. Books are like mountains in that they are all-consuming from the first stage to the last.

Obviously I accepted the invitation, and the mountain of pages has been laid to rest. It has been a great process working with Sue. She is a natural storyteller, and my main problem was that of having too many hours of interviews on tape, as we delved deep into the details of everything we discussed. I was as much to blame as Sue, with my constant questions endeavouring to discover obscure details, feelings and motivations, as well as the precise sequences of events. Although I have known Sue for twenty years through the crossing of our paths in the industry of adventure travel, it is only with the book that we have become firm friends.

Like Sue, I have very strong bonds with my Sherpa friends, and deep respect for their Tibetan Buddhist approach to life. In many ways it was a perfect book for me to write as I also had a thorough knowledge of Mount Everest, which included climbing to 8350 metres during the first Australian ascent of the mountain in 1984, when our small team climbed a new route on the North Face without oxygen. I felt Everest's daunting presence then, humbled by its power as a symbol before we even arrived at its base. I was excited about the opportunity to write about Everest again, in its current, much more popular context. My first book was a personal account of Everest in a year when there were only two expeditions on the Tibetan side of the peak. Nineteen years later, Sue shared that same side of the mountain with eighteen other expeditions, two film crews broadcasting live telecasts, and a shantytown of shops at Base Camp. It was a different place altogether, and I enjoyed discovering it fully in this unfamiliar guise. More importantly, I welcomed the opportunity to present mountaineering—on Everest and elsewhere—through a woman's eyes.

What I did not expect as we put the book together were the dramatic adventures that preceded Sue's Himalayan climbs. I was frequently startled by the hurdles Sue had to face in this predominantly male domain. When I had all these stories on tape, I knew we had a remarkable story to tell. I am glad that it was my job to shape the telling of it, and present the nuances, because I know that had it been left to Sue, the tale would have been told in her understated way, with herself in the background. This is an untenable position when you are writing about yourself, and could be one reason why she found it impossible to get started on the book.

The approach I decided to take was to present the book through two perspectives — Sue's and that of an observer or narrator. Sometimes the distinction in content between the two voices is blurred — such as when Sue reflects on events — but in general Sue's chapters are personal and immediate, while the narrator's are analytical, descriptive and detached. All aspects are necessary to portray fully the many dimensions of Sue's life.

Although Sue is happy to talk amongst her friends and family, when she steps into the mountaineering community at large she prefers to let her actions speak louder than her words. Could it be that she wants to be judged on what she does, and not on what she says, because too many mountain men have presumed that her presence on the slopes of a mountain was as an accessory to some other spunky mountaineer? Or is it that she feels all of us would be happier if we spent less time on the pros and the cons, the who did this and the who did that, and more time exploring what life is really about? These are some of the questions I had to ponder for myself, and I am not going to provide you with easy answers. Instead, you will have to read on.

Lincoln Hall

ACKNOWLEDGEMENTS

Many people spoke to me about writing a book, but it was Margaret Gee who was most persistent and who ultimately galvanized me into action. The months ticked by. It was only when I was talking with Margaret about how hard it was for me to make a start that the idea arose of asking Lincoln Hall to handle the writing. Lincoln was living in Singapore at the time, so when Margaret became our agent she also found herself coordinating the two of us, and the project. Most importantly she found us a perfect publisher. It is true to say that without Margaret there would have been no book.

At Lothian Books it was Sydney-based Averill Chase who first saw that we had an exciting story to tell. She recognized that the excitement was as much about presenting a woman's perspective on being an adventurer as it was about the adventures themselves. Averill steered the book to completion, not only by extending deadlines but also by providing narrative direction.

When the manuscript made it to Melbourne, Sharon Mullins oversaw the editing process, eager to see the book in final form so that she could give a copy to her mother, a keen trekker. Owen Salter was a patient and thorough editor, perfect for the job because of his lack of knowledge about mountaineering. He brought a fresh eye to the manuscript and drew our attention to any assumed knowledge that may have made some passages unclear to readers. Owen was diligent in highlighting discrepancies in dates and spellings, patiently passing all but the most minor changes back to us for approval or elaboration.

ACKNOWLEDGEMENTS

He also applied his skill to the occasional clunky sentence, ensuring that the narrative read smoothly.

On the writing side, I would like to thank my family, starting with my mother and father who only saw my story as I lived it, not in written form. Huge thanks for the love and support of my brothers Grahame and John, who only have minor roles in the book but continue to have major roles in my life. The past few years would not have been possible without them.

I am also grateful to the many people who read relevant sections of the manuscript and provided comments. These include Colin Chaplin, my partner on climbs in Peru and Tibet, and John Maraz from the Makalu 2 expedition (who was seriously ill for two years following the climb—and probably during it, which may explain why such a competent outdoor person had to struggle so hard at every stage of the climb). From the Everest expedition I would like to thank Russell Brice, Mark Whetu, Tryntje Young and Tony Kelly, not only for commenting on relevant passages and supplying me with facts when my diary was short on detail, but for their friendship.

Many of my closest friends are not mountaineers, and therefore don't feature prominently in the book. However, they are very prominent in my life. One exception is my mention in the book of Megan Harris (née Hammond), who allowed me to make her wedding public. Sue Badyari is also mentioned in places, but her contribution to my success on Everest needs an extra acknowledgement here.

And, of course, I would like to thank my sponsors, without whom some of the adventures in the book would never have happened. They include the Australian Geographic Society, Mountain Designs, World Expeditions, Highland Expeditions in Nepal, the Radisson Hotel in Kathmandu, Oakley Musashi and Icebreaker.

I would also like to thank Lincoln's family, Barbara Dylan and Dorje, who were supportive of his absence from their lives during much of the writing of the book.

Sue Fear

1

AFRICA 1987

When the aircraft touched down on the tarmac at Nairobi airport, I was already emotionally exhausted, even though my adventure had barely begun. After an enforced dawdle through Kenyan customs and immigration, I made my way to the baggage hall where the first suitcases, trunks and backpacks were starting to appear on the baggage carousel. I stood there blankly, not feeling ready to come to terms with the dramatically different way of life that was Africa.

A man's voice said in excellent English, 'Did you have a good flight?'

I did not think the question was directed to me, but the distinctly English voice among the African accents made me turn. A man in flight crew uniform was smiling at me.

'Yes, I did have a good flight,' I said. 'But then I would have been happy with any kind of flight. I was just so pleased to get on the plane.' I explained that in Bangkok I had been frantic with worry because I had presented my ticket at the Pakistan International Airlines counter only to be told that my connecting flight to Kenya was overbooked and I would have to catch the next flight—a full week later.

'I never have that problem because I'm a pilot. Your pilot, in fact.'

'I'm sure you've had other problems. But until now I've never had anything go wrong with any of my travels.'

Admittedly, I had only travelled on organised tours before, both those run by the travel agency for which I worked and special tours arranged to familiarise travel professionals with particular destinations.

'I was devastated,' I continued. 'If you're the pilot from that PIA flight, you should tell the ground staff and the reservations people to get their act together. I only got here by arguing and arguing. I told them I was a young woman travelling alone with nowhere to stay and I needed to be on this plane. End of story.'

He nodded sympathetically. 'Sounds like you need a drink,' he said. 'May I buy you one? Or perhaps dinner tonight. I know some great places here.'

Okay, I thought, *my pilot is seeking some entertainment for the evening.*

'Thanks,' I said, 'but when I get my bags I'm going to meet an Australian friend. He'll be waiting for me at the hotel.'

'Which hotel?'

'The New Stanley.'

He looked at me for a moment then said, 'Okay, every taxi driver knows the Stanley. Enjoy Nairobi.'

With a nod of his head and another smile he picked up his bag and headed towards the exit. I wondered if it was a compliment to be propositioned by a pilot. Perhaps he thought so, with his fancy uniform and the big jet he flew.

Outside the airport I was besieged by many Africans wanting me to take a taxi into town for US$45. I looked in my guidebook and saw I could catch the local bus a short walk down the road from the airport for 10 shillings, which was about US$1. This was my first awareness of how easy it could be to get ripped off. However, what I didn't realise was that by skimping on costs in this way I could also be risking my safety. I already felt that I stood out as a bit clean cut and 'fresh' to it all.

When I got to the hotel an hour later, I realised why the pilot had paused before speaking when I mentioned the hotel's name. I was a twenty-four year old backpacker, very casually dressed, and any observer would have guessed I was a budget traveller. The New Stanley was one of the ritziest hotels in town, not the sort of place where I was likely to have booked a room. He must have thought this was my method of saying, 'See you later — much later.'

In a way it was, but what I had said was true. I had arranged to meet Clive at this hotel. When he had come to my desk in the Australian Himalayan Expeditions office in Sydney some months earlier, I had processed his booking and then told him I would be on his African tour as well. He was a nice guy with a sense of humour who liked my idea of arriving in Nairobi early in order to climb Mount Kenya, and so we agreed to tackle the mountain together. I had selected this particular trip from the many marketed by our company because its 105-day, cross-continent itinerary included the Ruwenzoris—Africa's famous Mountains of the Moon—and an ascent of Mount Kilimanjaro. The real highlight would be Kilimanjaro, but it would be a great bonus if I could manage a walk across Mount Kenya's equatorial glaciers or climb one of its peaks.

Despite the arrangement I had made with Clive in Sydney, there was no sign of him anywhere in the New Stanley. We had agreed to meet on this day in the hotel's Thorn Tree Café, and if we did not cross paths here then we would leave messages for each other on the notice board. I checked, but there was no letter for me. His flight was before mine so I was now at a bit of a loss. This must have showed because after my sixth circuit of the lobby a man asked me if I was okay. He introduced himself as Richard, adding that he was working in Kenya with the Catholic Relief Mission.

Once again I found myself explaining my circumstances, that I had just arrived that day and was looking for my friend, who was meant to meet me here at the hotel. Richard nodded sympathetically, then said that he had a room. If I liked, I could leave my bags there and have a rest or a sleep until my friend showed up. He seemed like a nice man so I accepted his offer. We took my rucksack up to his suite, which was very luxurious and well beyond what I would ever spend on a hotel.

I did not feel like resting, though, so Richard offered to show me around. We walked through the streets, but as it was late afternoon he suggested I come on a tour with him next day. He was new to town and was keen to go to Lake Naivasha and Lake Nakuru to see the pink flamingos and hippos and other African wildlife exotica. It sounded great so I decided to tag along. We booked at the tour desk and I got a shock when I was asked to hand over US$100 for my ticket. At the beginning of an open-ended trip I had just blown two weeks' budget. I comforted myself with the thought of the amazing sights I would see the next day.

However, I did not have to wait until then for amazing sights.

When we returned to the New Stanley that night there was still no message from Clive. I had virtually dismissed him by that stage, anyway. We went up to Richard's room and very quickly I realised where he was coming from. I had begun to suspect that he might ask me to sleep with him, and that he would feel embarrassed when I said no. I was only half right. I totally underestimated what might happen to me. I came out of the bathroom and he was sitting on the side of the bed with no clothes on at all. Outwardly I remained unflustered and focused on the fact that I had something wrong with my camera. He offered to fix it, with the camera in his lap.

I thought, *Is this the missionary position or what? I have nowhere to go. I know nobody. I'm in trouble here. What have I done?*

The situation was obvious. I had a totally naked, beige kind of religious guy wanting to make up for his abstinence with me. He effectively raped me that night, completely caught me off guard with his smooth talk. Date rape, call it what you will. I was really shocked but too scared to say anything.

Shaken to my core but deeply tired, I managed to sleep. In the morning I did not know what to think or feel, but I was determined not to be crushed by the experience. I was telling myself, *So what? He's not important*, but I could not really believe my own words. The only thing to do was to act out those words, and prove that they were more than a protective mantra. The lake tour was booked and I did not want to make myself feel even more used by abandoning what I had already paid for. If I did so, Richard would not only have taken advantage of me, but would also have made me waste my money. I steeled myself to face the day ahead as planned.

The tour was good—the pink flamingos in their hundreds were

amazing, the hippos extraordinary and the landscape dramatic—but the up-market older crowd who comprised the tour was mostly oriented round hotel rests and meals. Lunch was at a fantastic hotel on the lake, and I swam off some of my angst. I proved to myself that my mind could still push my body hard, and that my body was in good shape.

Meanwhile, a bevy of black waiters were bossed around the tables on the terrace by white managers. Porters and doormen were treated similarly in the lobby. It was at this hotel that I first became aware of the wide gap between whites and blacks. I was shocked that in this modern era the blacks were expected to be so servile to whites. My own violation had been a one-off, yet these Kenyans suffered indignity every day of their lives.

We returned to Nairobi and went for dinner with two other couples at the Karen Blixen Museum Restaurant. I turned up in green track pants, a red-checked flannel shirt and sneakers because those were the clothes that I had. When I packed back in Australia, I decided that a truck trip across Africa, which was the basic format of my tour, did not warrant smart outfits. At least what I wore was spotlessly clean. We walked in and were directed to an area for drinks, although I did not drink alcohol at that time. We were 'interviewed' about our choice of meal. I could not believe the process or the prices. I was uncomfortable; I do not like being beholden to people who have covered my costs. I could see now that Richard had planned everything long before we had gone back to the hotel. But I had not seen it coming because he was so mild-mannered.

His friends were good people. One of them said to me, 'Richard's a really nice bloke. I've known him for a long time.'

I demurred. 'I'm not so sure about that.'

'Oh, yes. He's got a good heart.'

Clearly she did not know what I knew. *He may have had a good heart*, I thought, *but it has nothing on the power of his lust.*

Back at the hotel, I was filled with foreboding. The rooms at the New Stanley were several hundred dollars a night, so there was no way I could afford to take a room for myself. I did not know where else I could go. It was late at night, and if I went looking for another hotel I might end up in an even worse situation. I thought, *I'll get through this one more night and then I'll go to a youth hostel.* So I eased myself into the other side of the bed as late as possible with all my clothes on. Richard got the message. I wondered what I could have been thinking the night before to let myself get so badly compromised.

I got up early, swam at the pool and enjoyed my last lavish breakfast at the hotel. I got through the meal without too much chit-chat with Richard. I just wanted to get the hell out of there without appearing to feel that way.

When I was out in the fresh air, finally on my own again, suddenly I had a feeling of space. Questions came flooding in. What had I been doing? Why didn't I read the danger signs? What signals had I been putting out? Two men were after me within two hours of my arrival in the country. At least the pilot had been polite and direct, but Richard had been so manipulative. He had preyed on me, and the scariest part was that I had had no idea of what had been on his mind from the beginning.

A few weeks earlier I had resigned from my job with Australian Himalayan Expeditions because I needed a change. And a change was certainly what I was getting. The fact that I had allowed the situation with Richard to develop to crisis point was a sign of how much I needed some lessons from the world at large.

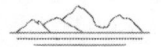

For several years I had worked in reservations for AHE. I discussed clients' needs, explained the nature of their destinations, and told them what to expect as a daily routine. I also watched a man whom I had trained get promoted above me and earn almost twice as much as I was paid. I had been on several treks to Nepal so I had a good feel for this type of holiday. I had no official role on any of the treks—there was always a designated leader whose job was to keep both the program on track and the clients well and happy—so I had been sheltered by the structured nature of the holiday. Back in the Sydney office, I found there was very little adventure in my job and I was always farewelling people who were heading off to exotic places. Work procedures were routine. Life was interesting enough with my weekend work as a ski and raft guide, but not challenging. I found my challenges in triathlons, not at work. I asked if there were opportunities to work in 'operations' or to become a guide but nothing was suggested. The only advice was that I take off to Tasmania to look for work. I would not do this because it may well have led to nothing.

I felt I had served a fair apprenticeship so I decided it was time to take action. My plan was to go and see the world, and work it out on the way.

So here I was in Africa, thoroughly shaken after less than forty hours on the continent. I told myself, 'You need to stand on your own two feet, and you need to be much more aware of what is going on around you. You're in the big wide world now, a very long way from home.' My one-way ticket was from Sydney to Nairobi, and from here I was to take an overland truck heading to London—the opposite direction to home. Where I had grown up, people had behaved in decent and respectable ways. I now saw that I should never assume that others held those same values. My approach should be to regard everyone as guilty until proven innocent. And if that seemed too harsh, then at least I had to be mindful of the potential of every situation. I had to be aware that everything is not always as it seems.

When I got to the youth hostel I found that it was a good place, clean, comfortable and well organised. I did not like Nairobi much. It was very busy, and with a lot of harassment. Even in the hotel, sales touts would call and chase me with a constant 'Mama safari?' There were lots of rich tourists in safari garb, a social niche which did not do much for me. At night the place did not feel safe. There were people lurking away from the streetlights, and police were on patrol in the parks and the streets. The youth hostel was situated a bit out of town, and I was very happy to be away from the unsavoury aspects of Nairobi.

By chance I bumped into someone at the hostel who had just climbed Mount Kenya from the Chogoria side. He told me that this was the route by which I must climb the mountain as the regular Naro Moru route was like a big bog and uninteresting to boot. I felt that my luck had changed. He helped me plan a program for that route, and I felt good about tackling it by myself. The next day I went to the market, bought a mug and some food, and then set off on my own. By this stage I had given up looking for Clive, part of my new stance of self-reliance.

I caught the local bus out of Nairobi, and with a couple of changes arrived at the village of Chogoria, over 200 kilometres and a good day's travel to the north. I got off and started walking up the trail towards the Mount Kenya National Park. It was quite a remote place, but the thought did not enter my mind that being alone exposed me to risks—until one of the locals passing by said 'Hello', then turned around and began to follow me up the hill. Instantly I began to worry about being robbed, or worse, especially as there was no one else around. He kept his distance, but I was relieved when we approached the gate of the park and I saw there was an official in attendance. My relief was transformed to dismay when the gatekeeper informed me that I could not continue on my own. During this brief exchange the man who had been following me disappeared. It was a case of swapping one problem for another.

In Australia I often walked carefree through national parks by myself, and had presumed I could do the same here in wildest Africa. I had not even considered the implications of being alone so I had no Plan B to implement. There was no possibility of resolution now that it was late in the afternoon. And I knew water was hard to find on this route. I had no choice but to stay the night, in the hope that something would happen in the morning. The problem with this plan was that there was no accommodation. My only option was a small concrete hut where I presumed an attendant waited during the day to check traffic in and out of the park. On the other side of the road was another hut where the gatekeeper lived.

When darkness fell I rolled out my foam mat and sleeping bag on the concrete floor in the hut and went to sleep. I was glad to be alone, and glad to be a long way from Richard. I woke up just before dawn and was startled to see the gatekeeper inside the room, two metres away from where I lay. He just stood there with his bright white eyes; I could see little else in the black. I was absolutely terrified. Nothing happened, and he did not utter a word. Maybe he had been guarding me; maybe he was just bored. Other possibilities I did not even want to think about.

Very soon there came the roar of a big truck chugging up the road, heralding daylight. It was a lorry full of Africans going up the hill to fetch firewood. I was still frightened from having woken up with the gatekeeper staring at me, and I made a decision instantly. I thought, *I'm not hanging around here.* I jumped into the back of the truck with my rucksack and the Africans. There were about ten of them, and they all had machetes. As we drove off, the gatekeeper called out to me that I would not be able to go up the mountain alone.

The men in the back of the truck did not seem to care why I was with them. They smiled but did not stare at me or check me out in any way, and that was a refreshing change. We drove up the hill for a while until the truck stopped and everyone hopped out to collect firewood. I went with them to lend a hand, and to not be alone. They appreciated my help and showed me where I could find water for drinking, which was a bonus for me. Then it was back in the truck and up the hill to the next gate, which was the official Mount Kenya National Park entrance.

Here there was a proper park warden, an African, who spoke to me in an uncompromising voice. 'You cannot go on,' he said. 'You are travelling alone. You are not allowed into the park.'

That left me standing by the side of the road again, frustration building. The truck and the firewood gatherers continued into the park. I could do nothing but wait.

As I stood there thinking *this is crazy*, the uniformed park warden invited me into his wooden hut and started chatting while making me a cup of tea. He suggested I was going to be there a while, and he saw he had some company now ... *Not again,* I thought. I felt a little scared, but nothing like the terror I had felt in the night.

At that moment two Landrovers came up the track, my knights in shining duco. Both vehicles had big UNEP stickers on the front doors—United Nations Environmental Planning. It was a group of eight people of different nationalities on their way to climb Mount Kenya, with a white African guide named Mark Savage. They were happy for me to join them. The timing and the convenience made it feel like a movie script. I squeezed into one of the vehicles and said, 'See ya later, buddy' to the park warden as we disappeared up the hill.

Up to that point the road had come up through thick forest. By the gate, the landscape opened right out to another vegetation zone of grasses, shrubs and fewer trees, open country and rolling slopes. I could not see Mount Kenya as the day was cloudy most of the time. Nevertheless, I thought it was lovely country.

The trail became steep and rough and I was glad to be with someone who knew what he was doing. At our first camp at the end of the track, Mark took us on a walk of about half an hour through scrubby bush to a rivulet which led to the most beautiful waterfall I have ever seen. I was surrounded by groundsel and lobelias. Above was another double cascade of waterfalls that I imagine few people have ever seen. I felt so privileged.

It was a great experience to be with these people. They were working in Kenya and had taken a week off to visit the country's highest mountain. Most of them had never been camping but they were very excited and took it all in their stride. My excitement came back to me now that my logistical worries were over. I had been inspired to visit Mount Kenya when I read *Upon That Mountain*, a book by Eric Shipton, the famous British explorer and mountaineer who had climbed it in 1929. None of the UNEP group was a mountaineer, which meant Mount Kenya's twin peaks of Nelion and Batian were beyond our reach as these were technical climbs requiring ropes and climbing skills. Instead, our destination was Point Lenana, a sub-peak that could be reached by hiking and which offered good views of the main part of the mountain.

When Mark learned that I had worked at head office of Australian Himalayan Expeditions, he was very keen to talk about his operation and how he ran it. He did not quite grasp that I had left the company. I later found out he was in the process of setting up his own company and was keen to establish some contacts. Meanwhile, he ordered the staff around more than I thought was necessary. Admittedly, they did seem rather lazy, wrecked much of the food, and refused to carry loads of even twenty kilograms; but I think they completely switched off because of the attitude of this bossy expat, even if he was a second or third generation Kenyan. I kept my reservations to myself because I was extremely grateful that Mark had helped me out and allowed me to join the trip for nothing. I had my own food and tent, but it was the knowledge of the route and the safety aspects that were particularly important to me. The camaraderie was wonderful, too.

Our highest camp was a small hut with a door at each end, and Mark tied the doorknobs together from one side of the hut to the other so that the Africans could not get in. As a result they banged on the door all night. It was not my position to ask why he did this. I suffered shocking headaches as we approached 4000 metres, and that night with the Africans banging on the door and me sleeping straight on a wooden floor was the worst. I had not yet learnt how to manage the effects of altitude. I let myself get very dehydrated, I did not eat properly, I pushed myself a bit too hard with a big pack too early, and I failed to wear sunglasses to protect my eyes from the glare. On top of this, for the entire ten days I was away from Nairobi I carried a whole cabbage, a heavy food item useless for most applications. I had very little to offer in gratitude for the help these people had given me, so I thought there might be a place to contribute this or my bread, but it looked rather meagre compared to their tucker. These factors combined made it hard for my body and mind to cope with the strains of altitude.

However, on the day we walked to the top of Point Lenana I felt good. I was so excited to be there, to be looking at the landscape I had read about in *Upon That Mountain*—the curling pond, the big pinnacles of rock known as gendarmes because of the way they stood on the ridge like policemen on guard, and the two majestic towers of Batian and Nelion with their summits shrouded in mist. It was amazing. My enthusiasm pulled me ahead of the others, but when I was about three-quarters of the way up I decided to wait for everyone. I looked down over our route, at the tarns of various colours, the rolling slopes, the scree and the grasses. It was totally wild, with no houses or other signs of habitation anywhere in sight.

As I stood taking in this view, an older Swiss lady from our group suddenly slipped in the snow. Before anyone could help her, she was tumbling down the slope. It was awful to watch and be able to do nothing. I thought she would surely die. She slid down seventy metres before she was stopped by a rock, which she obviously did not hit too hard because she got up, gathered herself and started back up. I was amazed. We reached the top together and she was fine, just sore in places. Mark Savage's eight-year-old son became the youngest person to have climbed Point Lenana. It was a great trip for all of us.

There was no problem with me travelling back to Nairobi with the UNEP group. I had not organised anywhere to stay so I accepted an invitation extended by Liz, an American woman who was part of the UNEP team. She was being billeted at a vast mansion which seemed to be owned by two very wealthy British women. She was not staying in the mansion itself but in one of two granny flats at the back of the huge house; a very nice Dutchman from UNEP, Rudi, was staying in the second. I pitched my tent around the back near the flats, but all of us took our meals in the house. This turned out to be a strange experience, an insight into that class of incredibly rich British people who still lived in Kenya, and no doubt elsewhere in Africa. They were people in a time warp who ignored the reality that the colonial era was long gone. They had cooks and groundskeepers, with buzzers on the floor so they could summon a bevy of servants to perform the most menial of tasks, such as the shutting of a window. They were extremely rude to their servants and made them work six days out of seven while knowing they had large families of their own to look after. I had never seen people so rude, and it made me feel very strongly about the poisonous nature of class structure and racial prejudice, and how these were rooted in arrogance and ignorance. Alcohol seemed to play a large part in the lives of our hosts. One of the women spent most of the time with a drink and *The Times*, which they had delivered daily from London as though they were still there.

The British ladies did not know what to make of me, but they obviously did not like me. When the three of us guests were sitting at the dinner table with them, one of them asked, 'When is she going to go?'

I had never had such openly hostile comments made to me, but they were very intimidating and I was too afraid to speak. I was due to join my African tour shortly, and the UNEP people had made me feel very welcome. Now I was getting the opposite response and it was very awkward. What I should have done was contribute some food or gifts. Alcohol would have gone down well.

I decided I must leave the next morning, which is what I did. I returned to the youth hostel. Liz and Rudi decided they had had enough of this confronting kind of hospitality and left as well.

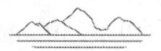

Back now in Nairobi I finally caught up with Clive. Everything had turned out fine for me so I was no longer angry about him not making the rendezvous and otherwise remaining under cover. He had been in Nairobi and environs the whole time, drifting through each day as it unfolded. He was so easygoing that the term 'space cadet' sometimes came to mind, yet he was a very tolerant person who always saw the bright side of things and could tell a funny story. These were good attributes in a travelling companion, and he remained my best buddy for the trip. In fact, over the next three months he turned out to be the only person in our tour group with whom I got along.

On the day of departure the sixteen of us clambered into the back of a covered truck and established that it was a very tight fit. There should have been twelve of us plus the guides, who were also the drivers. However, the group was oversized because the boss of Australian Himalayan Expeditions had expected some cancellations.

As an ex-employee of AHE I received flak from the very beginning. I only worked in reservations, so the overbooking strategy had nothing to do with me. I felt it was a case of shooting the messenger.

Our drivers and guides were two young Frenchmen, Jean-Louis and Michel. Jean-Louis was twenty-two years old and was the son of the owner of the company that AHE had contracted to do the tour. He had been conscripted into the job by his father and did not like being there, which did not make for a happy ambience. He said he did not like exercise, a revelation that did not bode well for a tour of the mountains of East Africa, which was the focus of our trip. None of the mountains had roads leading far beyond their base. I had the idea of finding some work here as a guide, but Jean-Louis could not help me at all, and was not interested in finding out on my behalf. However, he was interested in letting the prettiest girl in the group sit up in the front seat, for a price, and she was happy enough to pay it. I was certainly learning about the basic instincts of men on this trip.

Michel, at twenty-six, was a little more mature, but neither of them appeared to have any enthusiasm for the job. Every suggested variation to the itinerary was either too hard or too far. At the beginning, Michel quietly remarked to me that he was an expert at making porridge—the best porridge, in fact. *This is not good,* I thought, *Three-and-a-half months with guys whose culinary speciality is boiling oatmeal.* So much for French chefs.

Twenty minutes out of Nairobi, at a place called Sultan Ahmet, the axle of the truck broke, which put it out of action. While a new part was flown in from France we had to travel the first stage of the trip by public transport. We caught buses down to the port of Mombassa on the Indian Ocean, then up the coast to Malindi. At Malindi the truck caught up with us again. The axle now worked, but we quickly discovered that the roof leaked when it rained. And it rained a lot. The trip was scheduled to take 105 days, which began to look like a very long time under the conditions we had to endure.

Travelling south again, we crossed the border into Tanzania and headed towards Mount Kilimanjaro. Africa was a world unto itself, which I found fascinating. What was difficult to tolerate was being cooped up in the truck. I hated it. The roads were often very rough, and we frequently bounced around in the back. All the time, it was hard to stay on the inward-facing seats. After one particularly long sector, when we pulled up for a photo stop not far from the lodge where we were going to stay, I rebelled. I told Jean-Louis that I was not going to get back into the truck. Instead I was going to run the last few kilometres down to the lodge. He absolutely forbade me from doing so.

I told him, 'You're a load of crap.'

I knew it would only take me fifteen minutes, and it would allow me to burn off my frustration.

'Not possible,' Jean-Louis insisted. 'There are wild animals here.'

'What a load of crap!' I repeated. 'I'm going. I'm sick of being in the truck.'

Michel spoke up this time. 'No, Sue. We cannot let you do it. It is the rules and the rules are made for good reasons.'

And so I got back into the truck, but I was really annoyed. Less than a minute later, about fifty buffaloes with huge horns crossed the track and blocked the truck. Buffaloes have the reputation of being one of the most aggressive animals in Africa. Everybody just looked at me and laughed. I had to laugh as well.

'Okay,' I said, 'that's one for you.'

The incident made me realise that when you travel you are no longer master of your own universe. At home in Sydney's North Shore suburbs, nothing was going to overrule me because I knew exactly what I could and could not do. I went about my daily life without considering parameters that had become so familiar to me that I no longer noticed their existence. After work I often headed out for a cycle and run to Terrey Hills, which was a fair distance from where I lived, and usually I would not finish until 8.30 at night. Nothing ever happened to me. But here in Africa there were many more forces and influencing factors than I could comprehend because I was in a foreign land, in every sense. The fact that I could have covered the distance to the lodge along the extremely bad road faster than the truck was irrelevant. The rule was that I had to travel inside the vehicle, and I had seen for myself why it was a sensible rule. I could appreciate that there might be other occasions when there would be rules or codes of conduct for which I could see no valid purpose, but I would think twice about breaking them. I had learnt a valuable lesson.

At one camp we had to deal with monkeys who wanted our food, and at another we had an encounter with baboons, which was terrifying. I thought I was going to get killed when a baboon started chasing me when I edged up to take a photo of it. It was so ferocious. There were also hippos that looked across menacingly on at least one occasion when I was out walking, and hyenas that came around at night. We had a terrible encounter with bull ants getting over us and everything in our camp. It was certainly confirmed that wildlife was plentiful, and dangerous, in Africa.

Tanzania's Mount Kilimanjaro, the highest peak in Africa, was close to that country's northern border with Kenya, so it was only a matter of days before we were driving towards the extinct volcano. Consisting of three main peaks, Kibo (5895 metres), Mawenzi (5149 metres) and Shira (4005 metres), the sight of its enormous mass rising from the flatness of the African plains was unforgettable.

We pulled up at the national park entrance and Jean-Louis led us towards the building where we would organise our climb of Kibo.

'Michel and I are not going,' he announced.

'What do you mean, you're not going?' I asked.

'It's too expensive for us to go and we've been before.'

I almost exploded. How could the guides not come with us? What then were their jobs? We were only two weeks into the trip and already it seemed they were sidestepping their obligations. This mutiny or apathy, depending how you looked at it, meant that I became the inadvertent leader of the ascent of Kilimanjaro. I did not seize the role, but as I had trekked in Nepal, had just climbed Mount Kenya's

Point Lenana and was eager to climb Kilimanjaro, my enthusiasm and motivation made me determined to reach the summit despite the absence of our so-called guides. No one questioned my suggestions as to how we should proceed, particularly as I had some experience of dealing with altitude, so I became leader by default. The mechanics of the climb were straightforward, as it was basically a very long walk up a very big hill with a bit of snow and ice on the top. I encouraged the others, spoke with the staff about food and the different huts we stayed in, and led by example.

My only problem with the leadership role was that I was now the one who had to deal with the local guide who was assigned to us. We had porters carrying supplies for us and they were cheerful fellows. But the guide, Winston, was always attempting to manipulate the situation to show off his power or set himself up to make some extra money. The whole time he oozed an aloof but obsequious air, and it was very off-putting. However, I was there to climb the mountain, and I decided straightaway that I was not going to stew in his juice.

The climb was a five-day round trip between wooden huts, where we stayed overnight. On the second day, when we reached the Horombo Hut at 3720 metres, Winston sent one of the porters to fetch me. The Africans were in separate huts about thirty metres from ours, where they took care of cooking and catering. I expect he asked me to come to him to show that he had power, but if this was his motive I was not particularly concerned by it. I dutifully went across to see him.

'Actually, Sue,' he began, 'I understand that you want to go to the top. There is an extra charge to go to the top. Instead of just going to Gilman's Point.' Gilman's Point was the first point on the mountain's crater rim, about a hundred metres lower than the summit, Uhuru Peak.

'Oh,' I said, 'is that right?'

'Yes. And in fact, if you're interested in going to the Reusch Pit, into the crater, that's possible as well. At an extra charge.'

'An extra charge again,' I said. 'Okay. Is there anything else?'

He said, 'I thought it was important to point that out.'

'Thank you,' I replied, then walked away.

I did not argue or commit to anything because none of our group had been up this mountain and I knew we would need Winston with us. I decided to play along with his little schemes. I did not bother to tell the others as some were very money conscious and might make a fuss. It was a beautiful mountain—already we were getting spectacular views out over the plain—and none of us needed a squabble.

At last we reached Kibo Hut, the highest place where we would stay. The scenery was incredible, absolutely fantastic. Almost everyone started getting bad headaches and saying, 'I'm not feeling so good' or 'My headache is terrible.' Also popular was 'I can't eat anything.' These comments told me most of the group were readying for defeat. Meanwhile, I felt remarkably good. I had learnt from my suffering on Mount Kenya by analysing what I had done wrong. This time there was no cabbage in by baggage. I made sure I had plenty to drink and was protected from the elements. I was not going to skimp on food and water because I now realised it was a shortcut to a bad pain in the head. I also think that my foray up Mount Kenya trained me not to move too quickly, so I put this lesson into practice as well.

We left the hut for the summit of Africa very early the next morning so that we could be on top at sunrise. The weather was perfect, but within a couple of hours people began to turn back. It was not particularly cold, but the path was an unenticing zigzag up endless scree. A few people dropped back at various stages, so by the time we got to Gilman's Point on the low side of the crater, there were only three of our group left with me. All of them called it quits, pleased to have reached the crater, even though it was not yet light.

This was good enough for Winston. He turned back to descend with the others, but first he announced, 'I must go down with these people, and you must not go on to Uhuru Peak.'

'Nonsense!' I said. 'I'm going. I've come this far and I'm not stopping now.'

'No, you're not going on, because I'm going down now,' he said.

'Well, I'll go without you,' I said. 'I'll go with one of the staff.'

Apparently this seemed a good solution to Winston—I guess it meant he had not given in. Nor did he have to make the effort to climb the mountain. And so it was that I went on with the cook, whose specialist equipment for the snow on the ground was sneakers and a cheap raincoat.

The two of us went up and around through the deep snow on the exposed slopes. I kicked steps and used a pole I had for balance, while the cook followed in my footsteps in his sneakers. In this fashion we made our way to the top, to the highest point in Africa. As we traversed the rim of the crater, the light came and lit the snow slopes and hanging glaciers inside the crater all shades of gold. I was blown away by the view, which was absolutely extraordinary. Kilimanjaro's summit was the highest I had ever been by a big margin. I thought of the exotica of Africa, the different cultures, the landscapes and the mountains, all beneath us. It was the most glorious day of my life.

As we began to descend, I took the time to look down into the crater. I had never been in such an adventurous situation, staring into the mouth of a once-active volcano. It was an incredible sight. That day was life-changing for me because I had no conception that such places existed. Photos were always inaccessibly surreal, but I was here with the reality — living it, seeing it, hearing the silence and breathing in the cold air.

It was an empowering experience for me in a different way as well. I had been determined to climb Kilimanjaro and had planned how I would achieve it in the narrow context of the truck tour. I brushed aside those people who said I could not do it, and switched off when everyone else was talking themselves out of going to the top. I am sure I could have thought of reasons not to finish the climb as well, but why would I want to do that? Instead I just moved away from the bad energy and got on with the climb. I went to Plan B rather than arguing about Plan A.

I loved being on top of the crater, but I was aware that everyone else had turned back much earlier and that we were a long way behind. I ran most of the way down, easing my pace only when we caught up with everyone else. My only stops were to take photographs.

With gravity on our side, we soon dropped down to an altitude where the greater amount of oxygen in the air made life more comfortable.

I was not looking forward to the inevitable show down with Winston, and his endless extra charges. Sure enough, when we got down to the hotel he began his campaign about tips again. I knew that whatever we gave him, he would not be happy. I needed to know what was fair, so I talked to the hotel manager about the appropriate amounts to give. I was doing this on behalf of the group, so I gave the minimum. I was the only person to make the top, and the others could see no reason to give huge tips. I did the sums quickly and put all the money in envelopes.

Winston was the top dog, so when we called everyone together after breakfast, he gave a long-winded presentation about the climb, about how difficult it was and how hard everyone had worked. I knew that the long speech signalled the expectation of big tips. *You're setting yourself up for a fall here, buddy,* I thought. I was sure he believed he had hoodwinked me because I had not batted an eyelid or queried any of his extra charges. As far as I was concerned, he deserved no more than the others in the crew, and he could forget about the extra charges. They had done all the work while he just gave orders.

When I gave out the envelopes Winston looked like he was going to explode. He left the group and we never saw him again. I said to the others he may not be pleased, but he did not do his job properly and he did not take us to the top. The cook nodded. He was the one who had walked through the snow to the summit in his sneakers.

Meanwhile, Jean-Louis and Michel had returned from the bars and clubs of the Tanzanian capital, Dar es Salaam. In their absence, everyone in the group had gotten along well with each other. It was only when we got back in the truck that we found it hard to cope. The huge distances we now had to drive on bad roads, plus the dust, the mud and the dust again, were enough to wear down anyone's patience.

Our route from Kilimanjaro took us west across Tanzania towards the border with Rwanda. The first stops of interest were Ngorongoro Crater and Olduvai Gorge, both of which were very special places. The border itself was a lake, which we crossed by ferry. We drove through to Kigali, the capital of Rwanda, and spent a night there before driving up to the Parc National des Vulcans, a national reserve where it was possible to visit silverback gorillas in the wild. This was the region that Dian Fossey had made famous with her studies of mountain gorillas—a thick green jungle full of stinging nettle and bamboo, rising up to rugged volcanic cones. We trekked up into the hills to the section of jungle where they were known to be living at the time. It was amazing to me that we could walk up to a family of gorillas without them either attacking or fleeing. Instead, they kept an eye on us while getting on with their lives, foraging and interacting with each other. For me the encounter was extraordinary. I felt an amazing mix of fear and awe at being so close to these huge, magnificent creatures, so close that we were well within their reach. I did not take a single photograph because I wanted to savour every moment of being in their presence. The experience was beyond photography.

Back in Kigali we explored the Belgian district with its colonial houses and cafés amidst the noisy chaos of the Rwandan capital. We stayed at the Hotel des Milles Collines, a remnant of the colonial era that had made the switch to the tourist market. Long days spent sitting in the truck rattling across northern Tanzania had left me feeling chronically deprived of exercise, so I enthusiastically swam dozens of laps in the hotel's sizable swimming pool.

In the morning, when it was time to get back on the truck, the management would not let me leave because they said one of the bath towels had disappeared from my room. I had no idea what had happened to it and felt victimised, and I made no attempt to conceal my anger at the fact. (I discovered later that my roommate had stolen the towel as a keepsake.) Then before leaving the hotel I rang the principal of Australian Himalayan Expeditions back in Sydney because I was considering changing my plans and also wanted to express my concerns about the trip.

'There are too many people on the truck,' I shouted down the scratchy line, but I don't think he could hear me.

'Keep going,' he said encouragingly, 'all will be okay.'

'No, it's not okay,' I said.

The twenty-minute call was a fruitless and costly exercise. Not only was I not sure he could comprehend what was going on, the hotel desk clerk presented me with a bill for US$340.

'How on earth did you work this out?' I said.

'By the clock on the wall,' he replied.

I thought, *This is ridiculous — I'm going to challenge this.* After a defiant verbal dual with the manager, I came away a little happier, settling for US$50.

The hotel incident was not really that big an issue, but it brought things to a head for me. I realised I was on my own and had to solve my own problems. I found travel in the truck particularly hard to tolerate because it took away all freedoms. I had left my world in Sydney to get away from politics and judgment from those with whom I thought I had little in common. After almost seventy days on the road, Clive was the main person whose company I truly enjoyed. I did not think I could last another month to the end of the trip, so with Clive, who was due to finish in Burkina Faso a month or so later, I consolidated a secret plan to leave the truck in Zaire as soon as the Mountains of the Moon hike was finished. We would make our own way from there.

Ahead of us there were still some good destinations. On the Rwanda/Zaire border we stopped at Lake Kivu, which was a beautiful place. Decades before it had been developed as a holiday destination and now was a hideaway paradise for wealthy Belgian businessmen, the kind who preferred not to face up to the normal responsibilities and obligations of the modern world. They were like the wealthy British who had stayed on in Kenya, probably never paying taxes. The Belgians had huge mansions with beautiful gardens down by the lake where they went water skiing. Some of them no doubt made their millions through crooked deals on copper, zinc or gold, never having to answer to anyone. Their demand for mining and their connections with the corrupt government would have directly affected the deforestation of the gorilla habitats. We, mere travellers passing through, enjoyed sampling the fare at the patisseries while taking in the mountainous backdrop.

Our next stop was Niyiragongo Volcano, also adjacent to the Rwanda/Zaire border. Climbing the volcano was a truly enjoyable adventure for me. It was also a warm-up for another highlight, the Ruwenzori Mountains on the border between Uganda and Zaire, also known as the Mountains of the Moon. After reading Shipton's book, I had dreamt of climbing the three great peaks of Africa: Mount Kilimanjaro, Mount Kenya and Mount Margherita, all of them glaciated, all of them over 5000 metres high. With two of these mountains under my belt I was looking forward to seeing what I could achieve on the third. The program did not include a climb of Margherita, but I wanted to get as close as possible to it. The Ruwenzoris had a reputation for bad weather, which unfortunately they lived up to while we were there. Much of the track that we walked along was deep mud—not exactly the kind of challenge I enjoyed, but this time I was just happy to be out of the truck and clambering through the cloud forest. Unfortunately we were not able to reach the glaciers, and the rare glimpses of the mountains through the mists were frustratingly enticing.

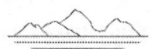

After our brief excursion to the Ruwenzoris it was back on the truck. What lay ahead for the group was many days of struggling northward along boggy roads in Zaire. We had already encountered some ridiculous conditions: clay and water don't mix in a road, and we had frustratingly long waits to get through. Everyone we spoke to who had travelled there told us stories about the roads ahead of us. Northwards beyond Zaire was desert country, and I was not at all enthusiastic about spending weeks and weeks in the desert. By now I felt there was nothing for me in London either, so the time had come for Clive and me to leave the truck. The tour I had booked was 105 days, but others in the group had booked shorter sections. One of the passengers who had only booked from Nairobi to Kigali wanted to stay on the truck, and conveniently he took my place.

The truck was now travelling north along the Zaire–Uganda border, so Clive and I decided that the simplest route for us would be to hitch back through Uganda to Kenya, then fly home to Australia from Nairobi. It was a short detour for Jean-Louis to drop us at a road that led to Uganda. We hopped out of the truck, eagerly grabbed our gear and waved goodbye.

We turned and started walking with all our luggage in the general direction of the Ugandan border. I hoped we might be able to hitch to the border town of Kasindi, walk half a kilometre through no-man's-land to the border on the other side, then get a lift down to Kasese, the first town in Uganda. After an hour or so, a Landcruiser passed us and then pulled up. Out of the passenger's seat stepped a tall black African man with a camera. He took a photo of Clive and me walking up the road with all our gear.

I thought, *What's so novel about us?*, but admittedly we did look a bit weather-beaten.

As we drew nearer to him I saw that he was well dressed, with a gold chain hanging low around his neck, Nike shoes, and cap and sports clothes. Everything was spotless. *Okay,* I thought, *I'm going to take advantage of this.* This was one situation where it was good to be a woman.

I said, 'Hey, mate, could you give us a lift?'

'Sure,' he said, without a second thought. 'Jump in the back.'

Clive and I both hopped in the back of the Landcruiser. We introduced ourselves and he told us his name was Norman. He asked if we would like to visit a coffee plantation, which was where he happened to be going, then he would drop us at the border. We thought that sounded great, and we chatted as his chauffer drove us along. Norman told us he owned several plantations and that all the country around us was dedicated to growing coffee. We drove through the hills on what proved to be a sightseeing tour, stopping for lunch at one of his estates, where he spent some time talking to the manager. He treated us very well. After four or five hours touring he suggested that he drive us to a town where we could complete immigration and walk through to the border on other side, then hitch down to Kasese. We could tell this was out of his way, but he insisted and said that Kasese was the best place to catch a train to Kampala, the capital of Uganda, and he did not mind the diversion at all. We shook hands and said goodbye. He was a wealthy businessman but courteous and helpful, possibly because he was self-made. The interlude was a dramatic change in style and pace. Clive and I left Norman and his chauffer in a good frame of mind to continue our travels.

We caught the rickety local bus to Kasese, a pleasant town and not too busy. We decided to stay there for a day or so, largely because I had to deal with an unusual health issue, something that had been brewing since the Ruwenzoris. During the trek dozens of tiny parasites called 'jiggers' had latched on to me unnoticed, dispersing themselves all over my body, but particularly on my legs and feet. By the time I became aware of them, they had burrowed into my skin and the tiny wounds had become infected. Soon my feet were so sore I could hardly walk. The jiggers were still alive under my skin. My body was trying to repel them by forming pus-filled pimples, but the jiggers were winning the war. They could be killed with some kind of topical poison, which, of course, I did not have. Instead I had to get them out with a needle. It was a painful process, but I could no longer put up with the intense itching. Nor did I like the concept of having a hundred little parasites eating away at me from the inside. I spent hours digging them out, and hours cleaning and dressing the wounds I had made with my excavations. I then dried out the wounds. During this process I stayed put at the hotel and read while Clive pottered around the town.

As the itching of my sores lessened, my itch to get back to Australia grew. We headed down to the railway station to buy some tickets to Kampala. Because we were operating on a tight budget we did not buy First Class tickets. For some reason I expected that the cheaper class would be similar to the equivalent in the Australian rail system, whereas in fact we found ourselves staring into a carriage full of chickens and bananas and with more people than there were seats. We could see this from the outside, and thought we needed to change our plans. It was a twenty-four hour, 300-kilometre journey from Kasese to Kampala, and if we did not find a more comfortable alternative we would be in for quite a trip.

I spotted a train guard, and it was another set of circumstances in which it was good to be a woman. I hurried up to him and asked him, 'How do we get on the train? How do we know where to go?'

'Please, madam,' he said firmly, 'we are shunting!'

'What's shunting?' I asked.

But immediately my question was answered because as I spoke the carriages banged together. Maybe another carriage had been added, maybe all of them were locked in place; in any case, I thought the shunting must be over.

We saw the guard climb on board, so we followed him. I approached him again and said, 'This is terrible. We haven't got a seat! Can we pay money to get better accommodation? Or maybe a cabin? Is there any possibility?'

I was laying it on strongly, but his reply was a gruff, 'Please, madam! Just wait.'

By this stage we were chugging along, slowly picking up speed. The guard vanished, but when he reappeared he led us to a carriage with compartments and installed us in an unoccupied one. He did not charge anything extra or ask for a tip. This was complete luxury compared to our expectations on sighting the over-populated Second Class carriages. There were bench seats which converted to bunks, so we settled in very comfortably. Evening came and we very easily went to sleep.
Then suddenly in the middle of the night the compartment was full of uniformed men with rifles who held kerosene lamps up to our faces. They demanded to see our passports and our luggage. I had to struggle to get my pack out from under the bunk. One of the men kept prodding me in the guts with his gun. I was terrified, particularly because I was unable to see their black faces in the darkness. It was not their blackness that frightened me but the fact that I could not distinguish their features,

and to me this gave them anonymity and a lack of accountability. But as soon as they had checked our bags to their satisfaction they left.

Morning came and the guard reappeared. He maintained his brusque manner but was watching over us like an angel. We were the only white people on the train and he obviously wanted to take care of us.

'We're going to get something to eat,' he said. 'Bring your cup.'

The train pulled to a halt but there was no platform, so along with many other passengers, the guard and I jumped off. Clive decided to stay with our bags. Everyone ran into a small village, obviously well aware of the drill. I had my mug filled with tea, and then there was only time to buy some peanuts and some biscuit-like things before the guard shouted that the train was about to leave.

These experiences aside, the journey was slow but relaxing. Much of our satisfaction was because we had escaped the uncomfortable confines of the truck. Once the guard set us up in a compartment of our own, we relished the dimensional change of travelling by train. Towards the end of the journey he came to inform us that the train would soon be approaching Kampala station. His kindness towards us was heart-warming, with his gruff manner telling me that he felt no need to ingratiate himself. He was a man proud of his job, and of doing it properly. We thanked him, hoisted our bags onto our backs and headed for a cheap hotel.

I did not like Kampala at all, but we did get off to a bad start by choosing the wrong hotel. There were voices and banging all night, and I lay there wondering, *Why aren't they asleep? What are they doing?* Clive worked it out early on in the night. In the morning he told me we had checked into a brothel.

That day we went to Entebbe, which was very close to Kampala. I wanted to go there because I had seen the movie *Raid on Entebbe*. It was an amazing place, with the feel of an abandoned city. Despite its nice gardens and beautiful setting on the shores of Lake Victoria, so many of its buildings, including the airport where the raid took place, had fallen into major disrepair. We looked for somewhere to stay and checked into what seemed like a pleasant hotel. As evening turned to night, however, we realised we had made the same mistake: we were in another brothel. Probably the quality of service was better than the one in Kampala because it was a better hotel, but our sleep was equally disrupted. We chose the hotels from our supposedly reputable guidebook, not by random guesses, which made me wonder about the predilection of the author. I wondered if sex was Uganda's biggest industry. I was not interested enough in the question to spend any more time in the country than was necessary. By now I was just thinking about getting home.

In the morning we caught the bus back to Kampala, then boarded another one for the 500-kilometre ride to Nairobi. It was an awful journey that took thirty hours. There were over two dozen police and army checkpoints and the bus had to stop at every one of them. Sometimes it was searched. The bus also stopped because it broke down. The culprit was dirty fuel, which meant a long halt at a petrol station where some fiddling was done with the engine. Before the vehicle was refuelled, every litre was filtered through a stocking that one of the passengers had with them. It was an interminable process, so I lay down on the concrete to rest and fell asleep there. At least time passed quickly that way. Clive did not enjoy the bus trip, but he did not let it get to him, either. He had a good threshold for discomfort, and he seemed to be able to disengage himself from what was going on and watch the world go by.

As the bus trip went on, I became stricken with terrible diarrhoea for the first time in my life. I had always thought this was something other people suffered when they travelled. I had no medicine for diarrhoea; in fact, I did not even know it could be treated with drugs. The only treatment I could give this introductory bout was simply to sit it out. It was very disconcerting not to have control over one's bowels on a long bus trip, and I had a couple of very close calls.

As if this was not enough, at a military checkpoint in the middle of the night everyone got off the bus and we stood beside it in the dark and the dust and the noise. Without me realising it, the bus reversed and the open door slammed into my back and knocked me to the ground. Others had seen it coming and had stepped out of the way, not uttering a word, not worried about anything other than their own safety. And no one took much notice of me lying on the ground, winded. That was it for me. I just wanted to go home.

At last we arrived in Nairobi. By this stage I had had enough of Africa, and I had had enough of travelling. If that's what travel is, I thought, it's not real flash. It was a significant contrast to my treks in Nepal, where I did not get sick and was not exploited or made to feel like a sexual object. The treks had been much more wholesome experiences, with the added value of providing lots of exercise, which I loved. I did not feel negative about my African experiences; I was simply glad they were almost over.

I had very little money because I had intended to find work at the end of the trip, so it was a challenge for me to organise a ticket home from Nairobi. My only contact in Africa now was Iain Allen of Tropical Ice, an adventure company Australian Himalayan Expeditions worked with. He allowed me to ring AHE in Sydney. I spoke to the reservations supervisor, whom I had trained and who had been promoted above me, to ask for an agent's discount ticket, which I knew they would be able to provide through Air India because the two companies had done so much business with each other during the years I worked with them. It was true that I was no longer employed by them, but they knew how hard I had worked during the years I was there, and I felt they owed me one.

At first they said no, but I rang back and pleaded. 'Look, you have to help me. It is my only way. I will pay you when I get home immediately. Please ask again and advise.'

Eventually they agreed, and I was forwarded a one line telex of my booking. I could fly in a week's time. I had to be grateful. I found ways to pass the time in Nairobi, such as joining a group that Iain had organised to take rock climbing on a cliff along the road to Mombassa.

The only catch with my ticket was that it included a stopover of five days in Bombay. I was really exhausted when I arrived. After nearly three months of travelling, enduring the long immigration queue and the forty-degree heat of May, I was almost asleep on my feet. I went to the YWCA but it was very busy. When I finally got to the counter, the lady on reception told me they were fully booked for several months, and that there was little chance of a cancellation. I was so tired that I checked into the first hotel I could find using my guidebook. I should not have been surprised, but I discovered after I had checked in that it was another brothel. If Greater Forces were giving me a sign that I should make a career change, they had another think coming. My room had no windows, gaudy red wallpaper and 'decorative' curtains. I had a shared bathroom, and when I wanted to use it I had to lock the neighbouring room's entry door. There was a horrible fat Indian man in the next room who kept coming in through the bathroom entry to ask if he could use it.

The place was awful, and expensive. I checked out as fast as I could in the morning and went to the YWCA ready to plead, figuring there would be no ambiguity of purpose there.

'We're full for two months,' the lady at the reception desk repeated.

'No!' I said. 'Please, don't say that. You've got to help me! I've got nowhere to stay! The place I stayed is awful and I am alone.'

I could not summon the energy to go out into the chaotic streets of Bombay with my luggage again, so I sat in a lounge chair in the lobby and unwittingly fell asleep. The lady must have felt sorry for me because sometime later she woke me up. 'We've found a room for you,' she said.

It was fantastic. I almost cried. The lady arranged for me to be brought tea and breakfast and it was all beautiful. The window overlooked a park-like area, with big fig trees growing in the grounds of a grand old museum dating from the days of the Raj. It was comfortable and cost around ten dollars a night, so it was perfect for me. I filled my time with excursions to Juhu Beach and Elephanta Caves, making the best of things until I could fly home. At the airport, there was drama and chaos again, this time during the check-in queue. Everyone was pushing in front of me and I had to say something. I stopped a big man in a turban who was sliding himself and his mates in with their ten pieces of baggage.

'Excuse me,' I said 'I know you are a gentleman, but I think you are pushing in front of me.'

He said he was very sorry, and backed off while I waited for the next queue jumpers to make their move. The check-in fellow must have been watching because he waved me to his desk and checked me in straightaway. As I boarded the plane I found he had allocated me business class seats all the way home — Bombay to Singapore, Singapore to Sydney. I had an agent's ticket, so he may have thought he could take the liberty of upgrading a little camper like me who was not demanding anything much but was obviously worn out. Once again it was all beautiful. I felt like I was going to live happily ever after.

Africa was a mixed bag for me. On the human side, it was the first time I was confronted by many things: the evil side of sex, where lust overpowered all other values; manipulative people whose friendly faces hid self-serving agendas; lazy people who shirked serious responsibilities. Over the years I was to encounter these types of people again and again in all sorts of situations, but I was better able to deal with them because of the lessons I learnt in Africa. The North Shore suburbs of Sydney where I grew up were in many ways a sheltered environment. I played a lot of sports where rules and attitude were important, and so I respected both. I had not been exposed to people with a total lack of ethics. Promiscuity had never intruded into my life; I had no direct experience of marriages breaking up because of mistresses or lovers. I knew these things occurred, but they were not in my orbit. To quote the phrase, I knew shit happened. In Africa I realised how much stronger the impact is when it happens to you.

Out of everything I did during those three months, most vivid in my mind was Kilimanjaro. There was an immense, empowering feeling when I stood on the highest point in Africa. It was not a feeling of conquest at all, but one of privilege at being in such a special place. There was also the achievement of having engineered my own way to the summit. I had implemented the lessons I had learnt on Mount Kenya, so on Kilimanjaro bad headaches and altitude sickness had not been an issue for me. This gave me a great feeling of excitement because it indicated there was a likelihood that, with proper planning and management, I could climb to higher altitudes as well. The views from Kilimanjaro's summit were extraordinary, and the weather was perfect, which only helped to imprint the quality of the experience in my mind.

That amazing feeling on the summit filled a gap that I had sensed in my life but had been unable to define. I believed I could find this feeling on other mountaintops. At last I could see the path ahead.

2

FINDING THE PATH

Perhaps it all began with the 'tinny', the boat that launched their first adventures. Or even before that, with the Purple Hat Club. The origins of the name are long forgotten, but as young children Sue Fear and her brothers Grahame and John were members of the club. All the kids in the cul-de-sac called Kerriwa Avenue, which was around the corner from where the Fear family lived, were members too.

They were never short of activities, whether it was racing matchboxes down the miniature rivers in the unformed dirt gutters when it rained, or riding to the creek on their pushbikes. Sometimes they would take over the yard of a particular set of neighbours who had a huge open area. Here they would play touch footie and cricket, or climb the liquidambar trees to catch cicadas. They went camping as well, usually in the Fear's backyard because it was big and bushy and felt like the outback. They were allowed small fires, which they sat around while cooking potatoes in the coals or toasting bread on forked sticks. There was a night game of stealth called 'Spotto', the object of which was to creep up through bushes and gardens unnoticed to someone with a Dolphin torch at the lamppost at the end of the street.

Best of all was heading out in the tinny. For many years, Ron Fear's favourite pastime had been fishing, but as a father of three he somehow had to involve the kids. His solution was the four-metre tinny, a basic metal dinghy powered by a small outboard. The kids would squash into the car and Ron would drive to Bobbin Head or Bayview and head out into the many rivulets and bays of Cowan Creek, Broken Bay and Pittwater. Once the boat was in the water, Sue, Grahame and John would clamber aboard with a few other kids from the Purple Hat Club, and Ron would motor across to a shallow bay or a beach where the kids could fish from the boat or patrol the shore for crabs. Everything that the kids caught, or even saw, was greeted with great enthusiasm by Ron. In the 1960s and early '70s there was very little suburban development along the bushy shores of Pittwater, a vast, sheltered inlet on the western side of Sydney's Palm Beach peninsula. There were dozens of deserted coves and small beaches accessible only by boat, a paradise for the kids to explore.

Of course, there was life outside the Purple Hat Club. The beach figured large in their lives, particularly Mona Vale beach, where their friends the Armstrongs had a holiday house. Apart from their home in St Ives, the Fears spent more time there than at any other place. The beach was the focus of their holidays. It was in the surf that Sue learnt about respecting the forces of nature. She owned a surfboard, although her mother, Joan Fear, did not approve. Joan would get extremely anxious if any of the kids were swimming 'out the back' beyond the breaking waves. Joan had grown up in Wales, had never been a swimmer and was not comfortable around water. The rest of the family knew she only worried because she cared about them, and in an endearing way they called her a 'panic merchant'.

On the home front it was a different matter. Joan was very good at running the family household and she kept everyone organised. The Fears were a regular family where the sharing of chores instilled a basis of self-reliance. This particularly applied to Sue, who learnt to do 'boys' chores' as well as domestic ones. She was expected to chop firewood as well as cook and iron. Joan Fear took pride in whatever she did, whether it was cooking, sewing, painting, helping with homework or playing tennis. Her daughter could not help but develop the same tendencies, if not the same interests. It was not unusual for Joan to turn up on a new neighbour's doorstep with some biscuits for a 'welcome to the neighbourhood' chat.

As a young girl Sue learnt to play hard ball with her brothers. Under the daunting nickname of Fearie, her elder brother Grahame often commanded the local pack of kids. Although Sue was younger than most of the gang—and a girl to boot—she was never the last one chosen when sides were being picked for rough-and-tumble team games. Sue learnt at an early age to hit the ground running and not be intimidated. Against these bigger and older boys, she learnt that success came when she believed she could achieve. With this confident approach to sport, and a degree of natural athleticism, it was not surprising that Sue was school captain at St Ives North Primary, and in high school at Abbotsleigh was captain of the softball team. Here she discovered a passion for photography which her father encouraged. At Barker College, where she moved for her senior high school years, she was a prefect and captain of the school's hockey and cricket teams, as well as one of the first female competitive swimmers—and she swam against boys. She was also a recipient of a Gold Duke of Edinburgh Award. And this was only what happened at school.

During those high school years the Fears still headed to Pittwater on the weekends, but now with the purpose of sailing. Fishing no longer held anyone's interest, except Ron's. He realised it was a static pastime for the kids as he could not take the kids rock or surf fishing which he did quite regularly because of the dangers. But sailing was participatory and unpredictable. It was also quite a social activity. It started with Ron buying a do-it-yourself kit for a Mirror dinghy, which he built and they raced. He went on to build other boats as well. They joined a club with the Armstrong family, who also sailed. Alan Armstrong was Ron's best fishing mate, and their daughter Fiona was a good friend of Sue's. Sue took to racing a one-person craft, buying herself a Moth and then a Laser with money she earned working at the St Ives supermarket.

While Sue was still at Barker College she joined the Ocean Youth Club to investigate sailing at sea. The adventurous potential of ocean voyages excited her, an extension of exploring Pittwater in the tinny and little sailboats, so she wanted to experience the reality. On one occasion she crewed on the twenty-metre Buccaneer, a classic wooden boat that had competed in the Sydney-to-Hobart yacht race. Her trip from Sydney to Jervis Bay and back was a personal disaster as she was seasick for the entire voyage. She felt humiliated because she was not able to help sail the boat or do jobs below deck. It seemed that all she could manage without vomiting was to lie horizontal in her bunk. However, her perspective changed on the return leg. At sunrise one of the old sailors encouraged her to take the huge wheel and showed her how to work with the wheel and the swell to maintain course. She could feel the power of the wind and the sea, and it felt fantastic.

She began to read her way through her father's collection of sailing books—David Lewis, Sir Francis Chichester, Kay Cottee and Naomi James. Sue guessed that he dreamed of sailing the world, but Ron Fear was of a generation of Australians whose values were shaped by the Second World War, a war that shattered the peace of childhood and darkened teenage years with visions of a world destroying itself. Adulthood began when the war was over, when hard work gave a man the power to provide security for his family and, gradually, to make the world feel whole again. This was the social expectation of the time, and it was a rewarding path to follow. Dreams beyond that blossomed, but almost inevitably they remained dreams.

Sue was of a different generation. Like her father, her imagination had sparked at the idea of sailing across the seas in search of adventure. The difference was that she felt she was in a position to pursue that course. But on a longer voyage, from Gladstone in Queensland to Great Keppel Island and back, she spent the large proportion of the time being seasick. This made her give up ocean sailing. She loved the concept, but the reality was too painful.

She remained in love with the idea of adventure, however. Even if she had taken to sailing, there was not a career in it as far as she could see. An alternative with a physical component was sport. When she was sixteen and still at school she went out with a boy from the year above who was a great swimmer, almost of Olympic standard. It occurred to her then that she might be able to find a profession in sport. She was one of the sport stars at school, and after she left she continued to play hockey at both club and representative level. She trained hard and loved it, but when she proposed to her club captain that she miss a game because she wanted to join some friends on a ski trip, she was regarded like a creature from another planet. Sue realised then that as a professional, sponsored athlete—if she could make the grade—she would need to be totally obsessed with her chosen discipline, and she wanted more from life than a hockey field or a black line along the bottom of a swimming pool.

Recreation of some kind seemed to be an industry with lots of potential, so with no other firm ideas Sue enrolled in an Associate Diploma in Recreation Studies at Kuringai College. Although she found some of the units of interest, much of the vocational subject matter was of no relevance to her, so she left after a year without completing the course.

She was still working out what to do with her life, and she thought that an Outward Bound course might help her decide. In February 1982, she travelled to Canberra to participate in the twenty-eight day program. The venue was the Brindabellas, the dramatic mountain range that forms Canberra's western skyline. Self-conquest through conquering of the natural world was the ethos of the program, which involved rockclimbing, caving and several days spent completely alone in the heart of the wilderness. Sue loved the experience, but she could not relate to the ethos because she did not see the bush as a hostile place against which she had to battle. Conquest of any kind did not come into it from Sue's point of view. Yet she enjoyed the course immensely because it taught her some basic skills, and, more significantly, because it revealed to her the limitless recreational potential of the outdoors. It was a whole new arena, quite different from the traditional sports at which she excelled.

For the time being Sue was still directionless, but she was not a person to sit still. She decided that some general career preparation would be useful, so she enrolled in Business College to learn typing and other skills that she could utilise across a range of professions.

Through a friend of her father's, Sue landed her first regular job with a big travel agency. It was called World Travel. She was twenty years old. It was very much a desk job, but she kept fit with her newly discovered interest in triathlons, which were just beginning to boom in Australia at that time. She wondered whether this would become her discipline, given that triathlons linked her love of the outdoors with her competitive spirit. She trained hard and achieved fourth place in her first race, which gave her great satisfaction. She enjoyed these multi-discipline races, but the very high level and volume of training needed to race competitively began to block out everything else in her life. She was playing soccer too with a crew from work and loved that as much. Again she faced a choice.

While she considered her options, a brochure from exotically named Australian Himalayan Expeditions landed on her desk at World Travel. It immediately caught her eye. She followed up by attending a slide show about Kashmir given by Garry Weare, one of the partners of AHE. She was hooked but too shy to ask questions. This was what she wanted to be involved with somehow, some way, some day. Her immediate response was to take a few days leave and participate in one of AHE's local programs, a cross-country ski tour in Kosciuszko National Park.

She was now aware that adventure travel offered a whole new world of possibilities, and she wanted some of them. In June 1983, aged twenty-one, she joined a trek to Kashmir. It was a travel agents' familiarisation, which she joined because Meg Cooney, an associate at work, pencilled in Sue's name instead of her own. Sue loved the trip, a five-day trek to Kolahoi Glacier and a stay on a houseboat. On the advice of the office girls at World Travel, she took a box of Weetbix plus Ryvita and Vegemite in order to survive India. She never opened them.

Sue next talked her younger brother John into joining her the following December on a trek to the Annapurna Sanctuary in Nepal, organised by AHE. Both of them loved it, even if they were somewhat culture shocked. Sue could not believe how people were so resourceful and resilient as they lived their lives among such big mountains. In the sanctuary, surrounded by peaks, she and John took a long day-hike on their own. It was an amazing day for them both, unlike anything else they had experienced in their lives.

Sue's knowledge of these out of the way places helped her secure a job with AHE in 1984, working in reservations. Her approach at that time was never to say no to any offer, which was how she found herself on a tour to Papua New Guinea with Lewie Gonzales, one of the AHE managers. Afterwards, she took extra time to hike part of the Kokoda Trail.

She decided to broaden the scope of her travel industry résumé by adding some qualifications and experience. In 1985 she enrolled in an intensive five-day wilderness first aid course, and went through training programs to become a certified cross-country ski instructor and rafting guide. She followed this with a Technical Mountaineering Course in New Zealand in February 1986. Sue had mentioned to her 'panic merchant' mother that she was simply going 'travelling' in New Zealand because she knew that her mother would not approve. The following April, again as a group member not a leader, she tackled the spectacular trek to the Base Camp of Makalu, the world's fifth highest peak, set in remote and rugged country twenty-five kilometres east of Mount Everest.

With her career path still uncertain, Sue began to consolidate her life in other ways. Her father encouraged her to buy a two-bedroom unit at Gladesville for $60,000 as an investment. She was reluctant at first but saw that it made sense, particularly as she only had to borrow half of the money. She had been saving since she began work, and had inherited money from her aunt and her grandmother. She found tenants to cover the mortgage payments. These first steps towards financial security were enough for the moment. A few months later she decided that she needed to stop working in travel so that she could do some travel of her own. Rather than representing a company, or travelling with a group of other travel agents, she wanted to explore the world. She booked a one-way ticket to Africa.

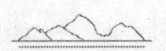

There were several reasons why Sue returned home early after three torrid and eventful months exploring the African continent. She left the tour prematurely because she discovered it was not her kind of trip. She had not foreseen the claustrophobic atmosphere in the back of the truck, the huge amount of time that would be spent there, and the tiresome social dynamic. It made sense to abandon the tour. Sue did not continue on to London because she had no real reason to go there and she was homesick. Most importantly, her mother was very ill. Eight months earlier Joan had been diagnosed with breast cancer, but she had been treated and it had gone into remission. Now the cancer was back.

When Sue arrived home and went to the house at St Ives, her mother answered the door. Sue was shocked to see the transformation caused by the spread of the cancer. Joan Fear looked like the flame of life was about to be blown out. The outcome was inevitable but the timescale uncertain. The initial therapy that followed the diagnosis had been very difficult to go through, and this time Joan was letting nature run its course. Ron found it very hard to deal with his wife's illness, even when she stabilised in her weakened state. In these circumstances Sue could not cope with taking another travel industry job where she would be in an office constantly talking to people. Instead she lined up to spend the ski season at Adaminaby in the Snowy Mountains, working full-time as a guide for AHE, and then to go to Nepal to lead a trek or two afterwards. Between times she worked in her father's factory at Rydalmere. His business was the screen-printing of designs on cosmetic bottles.

Down in the Snowy Mountains, Sue did not find as much use for her cross-country ski instructor credentials as she had hoped. Supposedly she was working as a guide, but she found herself assigned mostly to the jobs that were chores—serving in the gear shop in town, cleaning the lodge, chopping firewood. There was a lot of driving, mainly pick-ups at the beginning of a tour and drop offs at the end. She managed to go on some tours as a snowcraft assistant ('snow slave') as well as being a regular day guide on weekends. However, as the least experienced guide and one with little flair in style, she felt this was what she had to do. She was prepared to work hard too, but it seemed to her that some of the guides exploited her willingness to do any job to earn her stripes. Many of the instructors greeted the clients, led the cross-country ski trips and did little else. Eventually Sue saw that the situation she found herself in was of her own doing, and that things would have been different if she had spoken up.

With the winter over, Sue found it difficult to accept the international guiding work she was offered because her mother was so sick. But her mother encouraged her to pursue her career or the opportunity would slip by. Sue's first trip as a bona fide tour leader, involving two treks in Nepal followed by a Thailand adventure, was challenging because of staff problems and difficult group dynamics. At the beginning of the second trek her kitbag was stolen from the bus, making life very awkward, particularly as she wanted to appear to be the organised and well-prepared guide. Sue enjoyed the work, but she could not see a secure future for herself as a guide. For one thing, she was paid nothing as she saw the experience as an apprenticeship to getting paid work.

Back in Sydney Sue was very aware of the need to keep paying the bills, so she bit the bullet and took another desk job in travel, this time with Adventure World in North Sydney. Despite the name, Adventure World was a mainstream travel company. One week after starting the job, Sue found herself flying to South America on a trip to familiarise herself with different destinations so that she could market them to clients. With fifteen flights in two weeks and a different hotel every night, it was no holiday, but it was not intended to be. South America's farewell gesture came when someone approached her at Buenos Aires airport, effusing warmth and friendliness and asking for advice. At the end of the brief conversation Sue turned to find that all of her luggage had disappeared.

Two weeks after Sue returned from South America, Joan Fear died. She had been in hospital for several weeks on high doses of morphine, and the tension and uncertainty were unbearable, especially for Ron. Joan's death was a release for her, but for the family there was the shock of a redefined reality—she could no longer be with them, there could be no further contact. It was May 1988, fourteen months after the cancer was first diagnosed. Although the writing had been on the wall in big letters, Sue, John and Grahame were stunned by the fact that their mother was dead at only fifty-six. Their sense of loss was enormous because they realised there were parts of their mother's life and character about which they knew little.

Eventually, at different times, John and Grahame left Australia to live in Europe, each following his own path, each wanting to leave his North Shore roots and experience life fully after seeing his mother's life cut tragically short. Sue responded differently. Still working for Adventure World, she moved to St Ives to be with her father. The ramifications of Joan's passing began to manifest over the next few months. Sue was now twenty-five, and her mother's death forced upon her a degree of emotional independence, especially as she was an only daughter. Less immediate was the strengthening of her already strong bonds with her father and two brothers. As the years passed, she would find herself in the position of being the person in the family who best understood the perspectives of the other members.

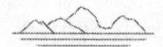

One day late in 1988 fate played Sue a favourable hand when Steve Coleman and Tim Macartney-Snape walked into Adventure World, offering their company, Wilderness Expeditions, for sale. After some hard bargaining, Adventure World broadened its portfolio by buying the adventure company. Sue was immediately given a managerial role in the new division because she was the only genuine adventurer on staff.

The acquisition brought Tim into her orbit. He was Australia's most accomplished high altitude mountaineer at the time, and he was to prove a great friend and mentor over the years. Wilderness Expeditions guides Sue Ashe and the indomitable Milton Sams also became two of Sue's closest friends.

Sue now decided it was time to find herself a home that would fulfil her needs for the next decade or more. This time it was her idea, not her father's. She sold her Gladesville unit for a good return, which allowed her to buy in her preferred area, the lower North Shore. Her new unit overlooked a bush-filled gully, had a huge balcony that was the roof of the unit below, and was close to North Sydney pool, as well as being much nearer to the beach, the city, the airport and her father. She took in a tenant to help deal with the mortgage.

Sue seized every opportunity she could to travel during her years at Adventure World. Her initial trip to South America was followed by travels in Turkey and Greece, skiing in Japan, exploring Micronesia and climbing her first Himalayan mountain, Mera Peak, in 1991. Although a straightforward mountain in terms of the climbing techniques involved, the high altitude of Mera made it challenging. The panoramic view from the 6400-metre summit is one of the best in the Everest region. There had been a time-lapse, but Sue was reminded of how much she loved this feeling, the feeling of being on a spectacular mountaintop after earning the privilege by hard physical effort and focus on every step taken. The next on her list were peaks in Peru's Cordillera Blanca—Nevado Pisco, Vallunaraju and Chopicalqui. These she climbed in 1992.

In 1993 the next unexpected twist in Sue's circumstances came along. While she had been working at Adventure World, Australian Himalayan Expeditions had changed its name to World Expeditions and been bought by Nick Kostos, a Melbourne businessman. In April 1993, Adventure World management announced that they had agreed to sell Wilderness Expeditions to World Expeditions. Tim and Sue were stunned that they had not been consulted. Tim had originally left AHE some years before to start the international arm of Steve Coleman's Wilderness Expeditions, so now he was finding himself back at square one, and so was Sue. (Steve had by now moved on to start a new business.) However, Nick Kostos allowed Wilderness Expeditions to retain some autonomy within World Expeditions, which proved a workable solution.

Once Sue heard that Wilderness Expeditions had been sold to World Expeditions, she booked a holiday in the changeover. She had always wanted to visit Mount Cook, the highest peak of New Zealand. Unfortunately, her attempt to climb it was foiled by new ill-fitting boots, which became cripplingly uncomfortable. It was a simple error but one with huge ramifications, a lesson about vital equipment that she took to heart.

Sue had always felt that guiding was not viable as a full-time profession, largely because the downtime between trips amounted to a considerable period of unemployment. However, by this stage she had all but paid off her unit, and without that financial burden she felt comfortable about focusing on guiding for a couple of years.

With this decision began an exciting period of Sue's life. As a guide she was able to spend extended periods in the mountains, with the opportunity between working trips to climb the peaks she wanted to climb. One trek led to the next, whether in Nepal, Chile, Argentina, Bolivia, Ecuador or the Karakoram Range of Pakistan. Her travels were peppered with climbs. Most were guided ascents, with Sue as the chief guide, but some were private adventures for her own satisfaction. The lifestyle kept her very fit and enabled her to double or triple her climbing experience in a short time. By guiding others on easy mountains, her mountaineering skills consolidated to the point of becoming second nature.

After a few sets of those 'couple of years as a guide' Sue had grown to like the guiding lifestyle. She was supplementing her income with two permanent but flexible part-time jobs when she was back in Sydney: slide presentations and research for World Expeditions and as a sales assistant in the city store of Mountain Designs. It had been a long search for the road, but at last Sue had found the path she wanted to tread, a path to high passes and mountaintops and to the remotest corners of the world.

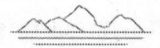

During the 1996–97 trekking season, as Sue guided clients in Nepal up Mera Peak and across glaciated, high altitude passes, she contemplated tackling a giant Himalayan peak. It would have to be an attractive mountain with an appealing and safe climbing route that would provide good adventure, rather than just a climb to the summit. She dreamed of climbing Cho Oyu, the world's sixth highest mountain, but she did not want to bite off more than she could chew. She needed a stepping stone between 8000 metres and 6400 metres, the height of Mera Peak's summit which she had scaled three times. The mountain she chose was 7680 metre-high Makalu 2, a distinct subpeak of Makalu, the world's fifth highest peak at 8463 metres. She had first seen the mountain when she trekked into Makalu Base Camp in 1986. Makalu was a strikingly beautiful peak which would provide a magnificent backdrop to their climb.

Sue gathered a team of three other climbers. John Maraz was an old friend from rafting guide days who had a solid outdoors background. Matt Gregory was a Tasmanian whom Sue had met in the Mount Cook pub in New Zealand in 1996. They enjoyed climbing together, with a degree of success, and Matt was interested in taking his climbing to the next level. Sue would not normally invite someone on such a major trip in the Himalaya for their first visit, but there was a good connection on both the climbing and friendship levels so it made sense to give things a try. The fourth member of the team, a Canadian named Jim Gilding, was referred to Sue by Ringi Sherpa, organiser of World Expeditions mountaineering trips. Jim had an impressive mountaineering resume on lower peaks and now wanted to climb a big mountain.

When they arrived in Kathmandu in August 1997, Sue was very excited. This was a very big trip for her, not only because of the size of Makulu 2 and the fact that they would be in the hills for forty or fifty days, but also because this could be a major turning point. Either her mountaineering would continue because she was able to cope with the numerous challenges involved in climbing such a high mountain, or it would plateau and lead to other things. This was the expedition which would really test her capabilities.

After only a few days in Kathmandu, Sue was feeling overwhelmed by her role as expedition leader. All the responsibilities for the expedition came to rest on her shoulders. She delegated tasks, but everyone, including the local crew, was new to this level of logistical planning.

John had spent some time in Nepal, but it was an entirely new experience for Matt. By way of contrast, Nepal was Sue's second home. Jim was a member of the team, but not in the capacity of someone involved in managing the trip. In fact, at the last minute he asked Sue to buy him water bottles for the trip, as if he were joining a fully serviced trekking holiday. The expedition almost had a financial meltdown when Sue outlaid more money in advance than was wise. They also made some errors of judgment about the best and most economical stoves to use. Sue decided not to buy walkie-talkies, which they later regretted. Neither Matt nor John complained about such hiccups as they were also learning as they went along.

A mountaineering expedition is very different from a trek, or the climb of a trekking peak like Mera. The duration of an expedition lifts it to another dimension logistically, as does the fact that Base Camp is generally at or above 5000 metres, the high point of most treks. Along with the permit—which Sue gained after exhaustive paperwork at the Ministry of Tourism's Mountaineering Section—comes a Liaison Officer whose job is to make sure the expedition runs smoothly. Often they are incapable or unwilling to perform this task as it can involve some serious troubleshooting. At least Sue was lucky to be assigned a good LO named Surya Bandari, a pleasant and helpful man from the lowlands whose physique was closer to that of a beach ball than an athlete. Having spent so much time in Nepal in a trekking capacity, Sue was easily able to bridge the cultural gap, and Surya became an important member of the team, especially when it had crises with the porters. The merchants selling food and kerosene, especially at the last big village of Tashigaon, were also tough customers for Sue, but the authority of Surya's reprimands and compromises were begrudgingly accepted.

The other essential person on the team was Nima Tamang, a good friend with whom Sue had shared many summits and crossed many a high-glaciated pass. Raju the cook was on his first expedition, and while he cooked very well, he did not quite grasp the logistical requirements of a seven-week expedition into the mountains. The team managed nevertheless.

Tumlingtar airstrip, east of Everest, was their starting point. The trek to Base Camp was spectacular but difficult. Access to the Makalu massif was blocked by an impassable gorge which forced the team to climb up and over a high and rugged ridge. The people here were equally rugged, and the local porters drove a hard bargain and were partial to helping themselves to the food they were meant to be carrying. An icebreaker moment occurred when Sue fronted the whole team in Tashigaon to give some words of encouragement and direction for the pass crossing ahead. She had a big bloodstained dot on the centre of her forehead, as though she had obtained a local *tikka* blessing for the journey ahead. There were fits of laughter when she explained that it was not a *tikka* but the legacy of a leech that had fed on her all night. The tone for the trip was now set. There were no more issues of mistrust or lack of respect, and all the loads eventually arrived safely at Base Camp.

Sue's capabilities and the respect she was shown by locals made an impression on Matt. His compliments and good looks led to recognition of a mutual attraction. *Maybe this is going to be a really good trip in unexpected ways,* Sue thought.

The challenge was now for the climbers facing the mountain. They walked for several difficult days and then entered the Barun Valley at 3600 metres, still two days' trek short of Base Camp. As they climbed up the valley, Jim became seriously ill with altitude sickness. He exhibited symptoms such as incoherency, headaches and eyes rolling back in his head—indications of potentially deadly cerebral oedema. Sue immediately took charge. She dispatched a runner back over the pass and down the mountain to Tashigaon to request that a helicopter be called via radio. He covered the distance in just seventeen hours. Meanwhile, Sue felt the expedition should keep on schedule and encouraged the others to continue. Matt and John went ahead with Nima and the porters, while she helped Jim back down the valley, with the support of Raju and Yuddha Rai, the kitchen boy. It was important to lose altitude as this could well save Jim's life.

With several days to wait for the helicopter, Sue kept a close watch on Jim. He had lucid periods when they talked at length. She learnt that for the last decade or so he had had a bumpy home and work life, including a drinking problem and divorce. He was now fifty-eight and hoped the expedition would provide him with a fresh start. Significantly, he had done no trekking or climbing for many years. Sue was astounded at this bundle of information, and that he had expected to be capable of making the climb. She was no longer surprised that he had hiked so slowly. To her immense relief, the chopper arrived and Jim was swept away to safety.

Being now thoroughly acclimatised, Sue, Raju and Yuddha Rai walked non-stop up the Barun Valley to Base Camp. The next morning Sue readied to push up the mountain with Nima to find a site for Camp One. Matt took exception to this—when he had arrived at Base Camp some days before he had been exhausted, and now he felt that Sue should allow herself to acclimatise for twenty-four hours before moving higher. Sue felt strong and confident, and she knew very well how she coped with these altitudes. She was surprised by the vehemence of Matt's reaction. She wondered whether Matt, as a man, did not want to acknowledge that she, as a woman, was physically performing better than he was. The refusal to accept this reality may have been heightened by the electricity that had begun to spark between them.

Matt was accustomed to carrying enormously heavy packs in New Zealand and Tasmania, yet here he was finding the altitude harder than everyone else, apart from the now-evacuated Jim. Sue wondered if he was responding this way because he was worried that she would exhaust herself. She thought it more likely that he was a climber who acclimatised slowly, and who would in good time come to full strength.

The next day when the four of them set off up the glacier to establish Camp One there were signs that Sue had guessed right. Nima and Sue made good time. They pitched the tents and were on their way back down before Matt and John arrived. When they passed Matt he was angry, and was obviously finding it hard to cope with the altitude. Sue thought he should show some maturity and slow down, that he should accept his current limitations and go with the flow. After all, this was his first time at high altitude. At the same time she also greatly respected his climbing ability and the flexibility he had shown with her when climbing in New Zealand several years earlier. She valued the potential of what might happen between them, but she was very clear that she had come to climb the mountain. She did not want to exacerbate Matt's problems, whatever they were.

A much more significant drama unfolded at Camp One while Sue's team was back at Base Camp. A Danish team had also set up their tents at Camp One, but during the night a thirty-two year old Dane with bronchitis died of pulmonary oedema. The Danes appeared to need help, so Sue offered to organise an evacuation. This was much more difficult than getting Jim out because the helicopter would have to come right to Base Camp, and most pilots would not fly into the upper Barun Valley because there were several high passes to cross where the weather often closed in. But Sue knew that Ringi Sherpa's brother was an excellent helicopter pilot in the army and would honour a request made by his brother. Again the runner made the long run back to Tashigaon, not stopping to sleep. In due course a chopper arrived for the body. The Dane had been fit, enthusiastic and very strong in appearance. It was a chilling illustration of how easily life could be taken away on the world's highest peaks.

The Australians pushed on up the mountain, setting up Camp Two at 6800 metres and fixing a section of rope above. Sue was flattered when an American expedition waved her and Nima ahead and let them fix the first 200 metres of the steep slope leading up to Makalu La, the low point in the ridge between Makalu 2 and Makalu, its mother peak. Out of gratitude for Sue's help, the Danes offered them the use of the two tents they had pitched at Makalu La as they were not yet ready to make a summit bid themselves. Sue most gratefully accepted; they did not have the person power themselves to carry two tents up the 700 metres of fixed rope and mixed climbing to the campsite on the La. Without the generosity of the Danes they would have had little chance of mounting a proper summit bid. That generosity was typical of the spirit of many people Sue had met in the mountains, a spirit she shared.

By this stage, Sue had a severely frostbitten finger, which meant she could not work a stove or pack anything. Matt did it all, always in good spirits. Unfortunately, Nima and Sue were stricken with food poisoning at Camp Two in the middle of the night of their planned summit push. They both had severe diarrhoea. Nevertheless, they set off with Matt and John in the early hours of the morning. Sue had to keep stopping and quickly realised she was too weak to climb. She turned back, enormously disappointed, scarcely able to believe she had missed out on the most important day of the climb and perhaps of her life to date. Several hours later she heard the crunch-crunch-crunch of footsteps in the snow. Nima, Matt and John had returned as well. They had also run out of steam. Sue suspected that Nima may have steered them into turning back because he knew how important the summit was to her.

They descended to Base Camp to recover, and over the next three days, issues from earlier in the trip began to build tensions again. Sue smoothed the troubled waters by encouraging everyone to put aside their differences, whatever they were, so that they could climb the mountain as a team. With this pact came a surge of energy. They headed back up the mountain, climbing smoothly from camp to camp, and on 10 October 1997, a day of perfect weather, all four of them made it to the summit. It was a huge triumph for Sue, an indicator that she could climb safely at a greater altitude, and a green light for future challenges.

But there would be no further climbs if they did not make it down from the summit safely, so Sue turned everyone's attention to the descent. On their return to Base Camp, others congratulated them on their success. There was no end of big, strong mountain hands being extended to Sue as expedition leader, but because her frostbitten finger was on her right hand, she took to extending her left hand turned over when someone wanted to shake her hand, and keeping her right hand behind her back. As an extra precaution she wore a black fleece glove to remind her not to do anything else with that hand.

The summit had taken a huge toll on John, whose severe, undiagnosed illness outlasted the expedition. In the early days of the walk out from Base Camp, he was able to catch a ride in a helicopter with another team, which saved him from even more suffering. Sue was not so fortunate. As the team left Base Camp, she tore a muscle at the back of her knee and could barely walk because of the pain. This made her very slow on the downhill sections which comprised most of the trek out. Matt stayed with her, never getting in front, always at her side, saying nothing except words of encouragement. It was a long hard walk for Sue, down the Barun Valley, over the high pass to Tashigaon, and then the long descent to the lowlands and the airstrip. Matt was with her every step of the way, never succumbing to impatience. Perhaps it was his way of showing respect to the values of teamsmanship and of doing the right thing by people, as Tassie folk tend to do, regardless of other considerations. Perhaps it was the calming release that came with success on a dangerous venture. Sue could feel that release as well, mixed up with the euphoria of knowing she had made the grade.

On her return to Kathmandu, she received the unexpected good news that they had made the first Australian ascent of the mountain.

3

TO HEAVEN AND HELL

Before I left Australia for Makalu 2, I had scheduled my return so I could attend Megan Hammond's wedding the day after I got back. Megan was one of my closest friends. She had been born one day before me, which we felt created a bond between us. Our friendship went back to our early days at World Expeditions. She was a resilient kind of person, always positive, always pleasant.

The wedding was a particularly special occasion for the two of us because at work we had talked a lot about marriage, or at least about finding a man for starters. The conversation usually finished with us agreeing that we were too picky or we had left our run too late, depending on the mood we were in. Making those kinds of choices was more difficult for me, perhaps, because of my lifestyle. If I found the right man, it was conceivable that I would change my priorities and get married. A couple of relationships had shown the potential of being good enough to lead to marriage, but the fact that I had not let them interrupt my guiding and climbing was probably proof that essential parts of the equation had been missing. The relationships I had with other guides were doomed from the start because they were 'GI' (geographically impossible). One or the other of us would be away leading a trip, but we were never away on the same trip together, so it was impossible for us to build a solid foundation of understanding and trust.

The marriage issue was obviously not a huge one for me or I would have been making some compromises to achieve it. However, Megan really wanted to have a family. She was not just looking for a husband; she wanted children in the package as well. In the end she was the beneficiary of a matchmaking ploy: a special barbeque dinner. Of the eight people there, only Megan and Michael did not know the true purpose of the get-together, which perhaps is why it worked out for them. These and a few other such stories made this more than just another wedding for me.

Luckily we were able to fly out of Tumlingtar to Kathmandu on time and there were no problems with my flight back to Sydney. After a long sleep in my own bed—which was a delight—I bustled through my preparations. It was a perfect morning for a wedding, and I was very excited. I dressed in a suit with a short, tight skirt, stockings, and shoes with heels. It was a strange feeling after two months in the Himalaya living in baggy mountaineering clothing that scarcely got washed. The ceremony was at the stone chapel at Riverview School, one of Sydney's oldest and best-known private schools. I set off in my car and arrived in plenty of time. One hundred-and-twenty people filled the building. Megan looked positively radiant. Michael looked shy. It was a lovely ceremony. Megan was delighted that I had made it back on time, so that pleased me.

The reception was at Harbord, about forty minutes drive away, but I decided to make a diversion back home because I had forgotten my belt. I had lost weight from being at high altitude even though I did not have any to lose, and I did not want to spend the afternoon focused on stopping my skirt from falling down. By the time I arrived at the reception I was running late and could not find anywhere to park. When I finally found a spot, I locked both the present and the keys in the car, with the keys in full view. Since the car was not insured, I was worried about leaving it. Two separate people thought they knew how to break in but they were wrong, so I spent the first third of the reception trying to get my keys out of the car. This was the only time

I have ever locked my keys in a car. At last the NRMA arrived and solved the problem in an instant.

I missed half of the speeches and all of the special canapés. These may not seem like events of equal importance, but after the expedition my metabolism was running on overdrive and I was continually hungry. I had been looking forward to the wedding so much. What upset me most was that I arrived just as Sue Badyari finished her speech. Sue, Megan and I were a trio at World Expeditions and had been in adventure travel together for so long. But I reminded myself I had just survived a huge mountain, and if these were my only problems on Megan's most important day, then I had no problems. I could not expect to climb my mountain and have my canapés too.

Everyone asked about the frostbitten finger on my right hand, after they had shaken my left hand, extended upside down. Tashi Tenzing, a friend who had climbed Everest twice, demanded to see it and would not take no for an answer, so I revealed the big, black and very tender scab down the side of my finger. Then everyone wanted to hear the story, which actually was just one of neglect. A small cut below the quick of my fingernail had become infected and swollen and thus susceptible to cold damage. After days of fixing rope with my hand constantly in the snow, I was horrified to discover that my finger was frostbitten. The Danish doctor at Base Camp said I might have to have the tip amputated. At that stage I was so motivated about getting to the summit that I did not care, and I felt that I certainly would not miss the tip. Contrary to the doctor's advice, I just wrapped a bandage around it, shoved it in my glove and pretended it did not exist until the climb was over. Amputation proved unnecessary, but it was a dramatic sight, for the time being at least.

After the luncheon we went to a nearby pub, and I was able to relax and kick my shoes off. I was really annoyed with myself for making silly mistakes because they had spoiled the day for me. A few forgetful incidents made me realise that I needed to pay conscious attention to putting my life back into Sydney mode.

I arrived home early in the evening, drunk and hungry. In the morning I pondered the events of the previous day. No one except Tashi had understood how hammered I felt after the expedition. How could they? I did not even know myself that it would be a dimension beyond what I'd done before—and I had done some hard times in the mountains. On my return I had allowed myself no time to make the adjustment from rough expedition life to frenetic city mode. Makalu 2 was my first fully-fledged mountaineering expedition, and I had not appreciated how much my mental processes had adapted to the demands of the mountain. It was life or death stuff, so there was a fair incentive to think differently.

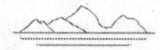

Makalu 2 had been a difficult expedition because of people and logistics issues rather than the climbing. The climbing was just a matter of a keen awareness of what was happening around me, and the hard physical work of dragging my body up through the thin air to the summit.

My next expedition the following year went more smoothly. My goal was Cho Oyu (8201 metres), which I had seen several times with Nima Tamang as we had trekked up the valley towards it when approaching the Everest area from the west. There are fourteen peaks in the world that rise above 8000 metres and Cho Oyu is one of them, coming in at sixth tallest. Our approach to the mountain in September 1998 was through Tibet, where logistics are much less complex. Our small expedition drove up into Tibet from Kathmandu, along a spectacular road zigzagging its way up through a gorge. The Tibetan plateau reminded me of Bolivia's Altiplano, barren and set at a similar height. The big difference, of course, was that in Tibet the biggest of the Tibetan mountains, the Himalaya, soared an extra two kilometres up into the sky. Cho Oyu was one of these mountains, and we had many views of it as we drove towards Base Camp—we would catch a glimpse, then the road would cut behind a spur or drop into a valley and we would lose sight of it until we reached another high point. The final hours involved driving directly towards the mountain with nothing obscuring the view for most of the way. It was a huge mass with a dome-shaped summit, and as far as I could tell from a distance it seemed very climbable, from the point of view of its features. However, snow conditions could make straightforward slopes too dangerous to tackle because of avalanche danger, and there was the personal unknown of coping with the thin air above 8000 metres, so I certainly was not counting my chickens.

On this expedition I reduced the probability of human problems by reducing the number of humans. My sole climbing companion was Nima, with whom I had climbed so well on Makalu 2. However, I had several other people on my permit as a cost-sharing measure. They were a Finnish woman called Tuula, her girlfriend and their two climbing Sherpas, plus Constantin, a Romanian climber. At Base Camp we had a skeleton crew of a cook and a kitchen boy who looked after us all. On the mountain we looked after ourselves.

Ours was the smallest expedition on Cho Oyu. During the ascent we witnessed every variation on the high altitude climbing theme, with an equally diverse mix of nationalities. It might seem strange that the sixth highest peak in the world is so popular, but there are good reasons. Cho Oyu is one of the easiest 8000-ers from a technical point of view and is a common training peak for climbers planning to tackle Everest.

After Jim's evacuation and the Danish climber's death on Makalu 2, here on Cho Oyu I followed a careful plan of acclimatisation. I paced myself carefully, adopting the proven strategy of climbing at least twice to above 6800 metres before returning to Base Camp to recover. At the next window of good weather on 21 September, Nima and I made our push for the summit. We overtook several larger parties and felt grateful to them for opening the last stages of the route for us. They were commercial groups with some clients using oxygen. Although I had climbed to 7700 metres without oxygen equipment on Makalu 2, I could not be sure that I would be able to make the extra 500 vertical metres to Cho Oyu's summit. However, I had performed well to this point and saw no reason why I would not be able to keep climbing until there was no more mountain to climb. It was not rash of me to attempt Cho Oyu without oxygen because this is the approach taken by the majority of climbers. Of those who failed to reach the summit without oxygen, many would also have failed to reach it with oxygen. There is a high fall-out rate on these mountains as climbers become discouraged by the cold, the commitment required or some physical limitation.

The lack of oxygen did mean that I was pushing myself towards exhaustion as I climbed, so I had forced myself to stay aware of the need to keep something in reserve. Too many people had died on these mountains because they had given their all to reach the top and had nothing left for the descent. I was thrilled to reach the summit in control, without any altitude problems, and well within the time frame we had set ourselves. Compared with Makalu 2, there were very few problems, and I felt a huge sense of achievement. There was a good view of Everest from the summit, and I looked at it carefully.

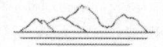

It was with a heightened level of confidence that I returned to the Andes in the middle of 1999. I should have remembered the saying that pride goes before a fall. I had a Summits of Bolivia trip to guide in July, but before that I went to Peru to reconnoitre a mountain called Ausangate (6375 metres). World Expeditions were looking for a guidable 6000-metre peak that would provide a more challenging experience for clients who had completed the challenging treks in the Andes, or who had climbed mountains of similar difficulty in Nepal and were looking for a change of scene and culture. Ausangate was the peak selected by Andreas Holland, World Expeditions' Peru specialist. He organised a guide for me, a slight young man called Jorge Pezo. Andreas was a trekker, not a mountaineer, but Jorge was an accredited guide keen to take on the job.

I was eager to research the trip because I would then get the opportunity to lead it every year. First I had to establish its viability. To lessen costs I found a couple of people who were interested in doing some exploring. One was Phil Caithness, a keen mountain-biker from Melbourne who was happy to leave his bike at home and climb as far up the mountain as he could with his minimal experience. The other was a past client called Colin Chaplin, a salt-of-the-earth vegie farmer from Tasmania, who had already been climbing in Peru with me and my friend Milton Sams.

From Cuzco it was a ten-hour bus trip to Tinqui. The pre-trip organisation was frustrating because Jorge was not around to help us, but by the time we were underway I was confident we had everything we needed. Also with us was Mario Huaman, our cook, and two helpers, Genarao and Cayetano. Mario turned out to be a fabulous cook, as did Genarao. Cayetano was our mule skinner and roustabout whose job was to tend the animals that carried our gear and to help out around camp.

The bus trip was not much fun as we rattled across the dusty switchback roads of the Altiplano hour after hour, but eventually we arrived. Jorge sorted our gear and we got ready to start walking. Then he headed off into the distance. None of us could keep up with him, and it was a very bad sign about his attitude as a guide. The terrain was as open as could be—not one tree to be found anywhere—and I got my period. I felt nauseous and uncomfortable, then I thought, *Urgghh! I don't think I've got any tampons anywhere.* I kept stopping and searching my pockets. Colin was a real gentleman and Phil followed suit. I stayed behind but they kept an eye on me, and when they saw me go off behind a rock, they waited a bit further up. They didn't take off and leave me, which was good, but it was a miserable start to the trip.

We reached camp on dark and the place was disorganised. Mario, the cook, was late, but the food he eventually produced was fantastic. Jorge certainly was not running a tight ship, and he did very little for us except walk ahead in the distance. However, the scenery was lovely, making it all worthwhile. Our route had us starting from the east and then heading around the north of Ausangate in an anticlockwise direction as we climbed. We would then make our final ascent of the mountain from the south-east, almost at the end of the circuit. This allowed us to acclimatise and left the toughest pass on the trek until the end.

It was the middle of winter, which is the climbing season in Peru and Bolivia, but the nights became even colder as we gained altitude. When we got to the Base Camp, Jorge set himself up in a tent alone and made the staff wait on him as if he were a client. It was quite strange. He always got served first, and got a bowl of washing water and tea in bed like we did. His English was good, but he had a knack of not seeing where there was work to do or problems to be solved. I thought it was incredibly disrespectful to make the other staff treat him this way. But Mario and his crew, who were regular staff employed and trained by Andreas, had a very good work ethic, and they took everything in their stride.

I anticipated that Jorge prided himself on his climbing and expected to be lauded for it. Shortly we would see. Studying the mountain now that we were up close I could tell it was not suitable for Phil. He was quite happy to hang out at Base Camp for a couple of days while we went up because he had been struggling with the altitude.

The next day we headed up to the high camp on the mountain, leaving Genarao, the second cook, with Phil to guard the camp and do the few other daily chores that were necessary. The route was diabolical from the very beginning. A climb up very loose scree, where it was three steps up and two steps sliding back down, eventually brought us below some cliffs. In his usual style Jorge had charged ahead, and from above he called out, 'Watch out for the rock fall!' I could see the rocks tumbling down across to the right. Jorge had already passed through the danger zone. Immediately I thought, *This is not a commercial trip. It's far too dangerous a place to bring clients.*

Rocks bounced down as we made our way past the cliff. Rock fall is one of the many dangers of mountaineering. Rock faces are constantly being weathered by the freezing of water in cracks in the rocks, causing them to split, and when the ice thaws the rocks fall apart. The idea is to avoid such places when climbing, but today we had no choice. Not too many rocks fell, but I climbed in fear of a cavalcade. Luckily we passed through the danger zone without incident.

We set up camp and Jorge outlined the program for our summit climb the next day. 'Right, the program tomorrow, it is pretty easy. We don't need to leave too early. We can leave at six o'clock and we'll be back for lunch. We should be down at Base Camp around lunchtime.'

'So you've been there?' I asked.

'Yes, yes, yes.'

I clarified what I thought we should take. 'Space blanket, a torch, waterproofs, some lunch ...'

'No, don't worry about that,' he said. 'We'll be back before lunchtime. Don't worry about food; the cook will have it here for when we get back.'

He was so confident in the way he said this that I did not even pack a torch.

We left about 6 am just as it was getting light. Cayetano came with us, so we were four: Jorge, Cayetano, Colin and me. We could see clearly, so we could weave our way through some quite big crevasses. Finally we negotiated a single narrow gap, and with that accomplished we started getting on to the slope. It was quite steep and sustained, with more than ten 50-metre rope-lengths of hard snow. A fall here would have been messy so we had to rope ourselves up one at a time, with either Jorge or me controlling the rope. This took a considerable amount of time. From the top of the slope the vista was incredible, an unobstructed view out across the mountains and the barren red and yellow plains. It was a crisp clear day.

A small snow basin now lay before us, and it was to cross this basin that Jorge had insisted we bring snowshoes. He quickly put his on and set off, leaving the rest of us, who had never worn snowshoes, to work out how to use them. They got us across the basin, but then the deep soft snow steepened and the shoes were no longer any use. Jorge was waiting for us, having trouble with the slope like the rest of us.

The summit was not far above us but I did not like the situation we found ourselves in. I sensed danger in the deep snow. The stretch we were on concealed deep crevasses, while that above us could avalanche.

'Let's pack it in,' I said. As a woman I had no issues about turning around here. Men often do not like defeat. They prefer someone else to be the one who calls the climb off. I did not see this as a retreat. My aim had been to assess Ausangate's suitability for commercially guided ascents, and to my mind it was not suitable at all. Having climbed most of the mountain, I would have liked to have reached the summit, but safety was my priority. We turned around and began to descend.

At the top of the big steep slope, Jorge gestured toward one side and said, 'Let's go down this way. It's an easier way.' It was a big snowy spur with rocks on the edges. Lower down the rock would offer secure anchors for our ropes. This meant we would be able to abseil, which would be quicker and safer.

I did not question him, and we ploughed through the deep snow to the edge. There was a metal anchor already screwed into the ice, which showed that others had taken this route before us. Jorge clipped into the anchor and said, 'Okay, you lead.'

I was nervous about dropping over the edge without knowing what lay below, but as the lightest member of the team it made sense for me to test out the rope and the terrain. In theory, Jorge was the guide and should have gone first so that he could set up a safe anchor below for our next abseil.

With one end of the rope attached to Jorge and to the anchor, I threw the rest of it over the edge and then abseiled down. It was straightforward enough and I was able to secure my end of the rope amongst the rocks where I now stood. Cayetano began to come down next, and I moved off to the side in case he dislodged loose rocks. He was struggling, and suddenly I realised he had never abseiled before, and Jorge had not briefed him in any way.

'Necesita …' I shouted, fumbling for appropriate Spanish words to guide him as his knowledge of English was restricted to greetings and food.

He was strong and plucky and quickly picked up the technique of controlling his rate of descent. The others came down, and Jorge again wanted me to go first. I felt even less enthusiastic because there were no signs of anyone else having been this way before. We were now on rock cliffs. Below me it looked very steep and the snow was embedded with rocks that had obviously fallen from above. This was another danger. But we had to keep moving, so I abseiled and everyone else followed. Jorge said he had found another piton and quickly set up the rope for the next abseil. Because we were on a narrow ledge, side-by-side, I could not see the anchor fully, but I had seen that he had good technique with his climbing and with the rope. Again he said, 'You go.'

I looked down carefully. Two short rock walls came together to form a corner that ended three or four metres below, then a narrow, sloping snow tongue disappeared over the edge. After that was nothingness; my guess was that beyond the snow tongue was a vertical drop. I was wearing my big plastic mountaineering boots and carrying a sizable pack, so I did not relish the idea of dangling on a vertical cliff, my pack pulling me backwards, while I tried to find a ledge that offered a safe anchor point and room for all four of us. I decided to go down to the snow ledge and assess the situation from there.

I rigged the rope ready to abseil, positioned myself at the lip of the drop, and glanced across to Jorge. For about the third time I asked, 'Are you right to go?'

'Yes,' he said for the third time.

I leant back so that the rope would take my weight as I began to abseil, but instead the rope was completely loose and I fell. I slammed onto the rocks in the corner on my left side, and then slid down the snow tongue. Unless I could stop myself on the snow I was going to die.

Thoughts flashed through my mind: something is going to block me. There is going to be a huge bang against a rock, or I'll go off the cliff and splat on to the glacier hundreds of metres below. Time was distorted but the words were in my head, *I'll go splat! And then I'll be dead. I wonder what it's like to be dead ...*

Then I vanished over the lip of the cliff.

I know now that Colin grabbed the rope, burning his palms very badly as he tried to stop it rushing through his hands. Jorge may have helped him when he realised that things had gone badly wrong, but it was Colin who checked my fall. He saved my life. All I knew at that stage was that I had stopped and that I was dangling in midair like a piece of meat on a string.

I could not breathe because my harness was pulled up under my diaphragm, so I could not speak to say, 'Let me down.' Just below me I could see a little ledge where I would be able to stand and breath if I could reach it. They could not see me, and there was no move to pull up the rope. Nor did they want to let me fall another inch. I thought, *My God! I'm going to suffocate. I'm not going to make it.*

The cliff was overhanging, but by swinging and kicking frantically, I was able to hook my left crampon on a ledge and wedge it there. I was able to take just enough weight off the rope to take a couple of breaths. Then I noticed that my abseiling device, a stitch plate, had jammed on the rope and I realised that this had saved my life. Colin stopped the rope above, but if my stitch plate had not jammed, the rope would have slipped through it as I fell and I would have dropped off the end and fallen to my death. From where I was dangling I could see that the cliff ended at a snow slope about seventy metres below, more than enough of a drop to kill me. I quickly tied my rope immediately below my stitch plate to eliminate the possibility of falling those seventy metres.

I remembered the legendary story of a man who died dangling on a rope on the North Face of the Eiger only a few metres out of reach of his companions. The thought powered me with adrenalin. I managed to shout loud enough for them to hear me and they lowered me twenty centimetres on to a narrow ledge. I took only a moment to take a couple of deep breaths then managed to climb the few metres up to the snow tongue. They could see me from there.

'Is there a way down?' Jorge called. 'Can you see a way down?'

Had I been up there with him I would have knocked him off the mountain. He had no idea of what he had just done. I did not even waste the breath of answering because there was no time for anything but action, appropriate action. There was no way we could continue our descent from where we were.

'What do you think we should do?' he asked.

He had gotten us into this mess, almost killed me, and now he was handing over the responsibility.

I looked across to both sides for some alternate route down. Nothing looked safe.

I said, 'We should go down the way we came because we know that will work.'

We climbed back up the two rope lengths we had abseiled and traversed across to the route we had ascended hours earlier. The severe pain across my chest from the fall made me suspect I had broken a rib, but I just had to ignore it. I knew that climbing down would take hours, and there was a chance we would be caught out on the mountain in the dark.

Jorge could also see the urgency of our situation. He set up an anchor at the top of the steep slope and lowered us down one at time. His skills were good, which was more than I could say for his decision-making. He then down-climbed to where we all waited and repeated the process. The sun was sinking low in the sky. At last we reached the bottom of the slope with darkness almost upon us. Colin dropped a mitten and as a consequence suffered bad frostnip, but he never complained.

We came to another steeper section and Jorge set up to lower me again—always me as the guinea pig. It was almost dark by now, but I could see the shadowy slashes of crevasses across the slope below.

This doesn't look good, I thought, and I shouted, 'Stop! Stop!'

But he kept lowering me and I went straight over a lip into a huge crevasse. Loose snow slid down over me like a heavy-duty cold shower, pouring down the neck of my Gore-Tex jacket. Again I was dangling in space.

'Pull me out!' I shouted, 'On the count of three!'

The rope tightened, and as they called out the word 'three', I lunged up with all my might. The rope took enough of my weight for me to wriggle on to the snow-covered edge of the crevasse without it collapsing. I instantly shifted away from the lip to firmer snow.

I was sore and tired, and now I was cold as well from snow getting all through my clothing. We continued on as it was almost completely dark. The slope of frozen snow steepened so Jorge began lowering me again, once again too quickly. I could just see outlines of the crevasse and I knew we had to traverse across a little and zigzag through. If I had not made the foolish error of listening to Jorge's advice about leaving my headtorch at camp, I would have been able to see our crampon tracks and follow them. As it was, I took a few more steps and the next moment I was dangling in another crevasse.

I thought, *That's it. I'm not going a step further until I can see what I'm doing.* I was sick of Jorge using me like a plumb bob. I asked them to lower me another metre, and that put me on the lower lip of the crevasse. I decided that this was where I was going to spend the night. I kicked a ledge in the snow.

Colin was the next to 'drop in'. I said to him, 'I'd rather freeze to death than fall into a crevasse to my death.' He immediately decided to stay with me. Jorge thought we were crazy, and he and Cayetano continued off into the darkness.

I had plenty of time to contemplate how I had got into this mess. I was really annoyed with myself. I was an experienced guide; if only I had listened to my instinct, not to Jorge, I would have had a torch, warm clothes and food. Jorge's timing was way off the mark, and for him to suggest that we did not need food or a headlamp was grossly negligent.

It was a very cold night. Colin and I were hugging each other the whole night to stay warm. I got the better benefit, of course, because Colin was much bigger. Every hour or so we would swap sides so that we would not get too cold on one side and would not go to sleep. Jorge had taken the rope, and we were concerned that if we fell asleep we might over balance and topple into the depths of the crevasse, never to be seen again.

At about 3.30 am we saw two lights coming towards us. It was Jorge and Cayetano with our down jackets and a drink bottle full of hot tea.

These revived us enormously. They also brought a spare torch, but it did not work very well and we decided it was safer to stay put.

When it grew light, Colin and I followed their footsteps through the maze of crevasses. It was only ten minutes to the high camp. As soon as we arrived Jorge said, 'Right, we'll go down now. We'll get out of here.'

I could not believe it. First he dropped me off a cliff, which injured me. Then he lowered me into two crevasses under a cascade of snow. As a result I was totally exhausted. He had no idea how much the fall and getting myself back up had taken out of me. I could barely put my pack on because I hurt my back in the fall, but Jorge just threw his pack on and took off. Colin was the only one who waited for me.

This was how it was for the next four days. I walked very slowly, was always the last into camp and was too exhausted to have more than a mouthful or two of food. When we finally arrived back in Cuzco, I wondered how on earth I was going to be able to lead the Summits of Bolivia program in five days' time.

When I crashed into bed that night, I felt like I could sleep for three weeks. But I had to vacate the room at 6 am due to another group arriving. I also had to move to another hotel. It was an awful experience. I spent three days in my hotel room, sleeping and resting, only going out to get something to eat or do laundry. After that I began to feel almost normal—sore, and black and yellow from bruises, but able to function.

The Ausangate debacle was not the ultimate indignity; that was yet to come. From Cuzco I flew to La Paz where I met with World Expeditions' Summits of Bolivia program. This was one of my favourite trips, as I had researched it two years earlier and had led all the departures to date. I loved working with Carlos Escobar and his Bolivian crew, and we had become very good mates.

The night before our departure for the mountains, I left some of the group after dinner and headed towards a coffee shop where I had arranged to meet three of the other group members. It was 8.30 at night as I walked up a deserted cobbled street. Suddenly from behind someone grabbed me and started strangling me, pulling my head back so far I thought it was going to come off. They just kept pulling. I did everything I could to get free. There were three or four of them, and they were probably surprised at how much fight there was in a slight woman like me. They tried to push me up against the wall, but I got my feet up the wall and pushed back. Then I passed out.

I came to my senses lying in the gutter looking up at the stars. I had no idea of the time. I thought, *That's nice—stars. Where am I? Why am I here?* Then I looked down and saw that I was lying in a gutter at the side of the street. The first thing I did was check my trousers to see if anything had happened to me. They were still done up, with a special cute little knot that I always tied, and I thought, *Well, things could be worse.* I looked for blood or cuts to my body, but there were none. Some of my papers were on the ground and I knew I had been robbed. My wallet was gone. I had wet and soiled myself, obviously having gone into major shock. I began to panic, suddenly desperate to get away from that place. Witness to all this was a *cholita*—a woman dressed in the traditional Bolivian costume of a bowler hat and long, heavy dress. She was standing by her stall in the shadows, and called out something to me in Spanish which I couldn't understand. I knew that she had seen what had happened but was too afraid to act.

I rushed off, heading to the café where I was to meet Jade and Gay, two members of the Bolivia trip, and Phil, the mountain biker from Ausangate. Gay was an anaesthetist and she helped me to the toilet where I cleaned myself up. Back in the café I tried to look at my watch but it was gone—only the strap was there. I burst into tears and was shivering from shock. A glass of wine calmed me down enough for me to walk back to the hotel. The girls walked beside me and Phil was right behind. Gay offered to sleep in my room with me, but I was okay by then. In the morning I woke up and I could not swallow, which meant I could not eat either. My throat was black and I could barely speak.

Apart from the people who had been with me the previous night, the other group members could not comprehend what had happened to me. They knew I had been mugged, but they did not grasp what an incredible violation it had been of the universal boundaries of respect and trust that are such a part of everyday life. It deeply affected my psyche. I was able to cope with the trip by taking one day at a time. Teaching the clients how to climb mountains grounded me again, and I began to feel comfortable with myself and my relationship to the world.

Even the mugging was not the final indignity. I flew from South America to Auckland to give some promotional slide shows for World Expeditions. I stayed in a motel on the second floor but woke in the middle of the night to see a huge man wearing dark clothes and a beanie going through my things.

'Can I help you?' I asked him, my sleepy mind a little slow in telling me that I was being visited by a burglar.

He did not reply or turn around. He casually picked up my daypack with the two carousels full of my best slides from around the world, then walked out on to the balcony and climbed over the railing. He landed in the camellias. He lay there for a few moments and I guessed that he had hurt himself—not surprising given that I was on the second floor. Then he hopped up and ran limping down the road and out of sight.

By this stage I was already screaming, 'Burglar! Somebody help! There's a burglar!' No one appeared at first, but the message got through somehow. After some minutes a policeman arrived with a German shepherd.

Again I felt shattered. All of my best slides were gone and I had been oblivious to my vulnerability. I lay awake for a long time, then realised I should cancel my credit card, which gave me the chance to talk to someone at 4.30 in the morning. Even though she was in Bangalore, I felt that she was with me and very supportive, which was a great help. Of course she knew nothing of the events in Peru and Bolivia. How could I begin to explain? At first light I put on my running gear and ran for an hour and a half run to clear my head. After that I felt much better.

Numerous phone discussions with the police led nowhere, and I realised that the burglar was not going to be found and my slides were gone. Kirsty from World Expeditions Auckland drove me to the airport that morning. Now there could be no slide show, I just wanted to get home where I could feel safe and secure and surrounded by friends.

As we drove Kirsty's mobile rang. The bag with my slides in it had been found flung under a car in someone's drive near the motel. The kind people who found them had seen the World Expeditions sticker and had rung the office. We made a u-turn and drove directly to collect the slides. The bag also included my plane ticket, which I had not even realised was missing! How lucky was I? All's well that ends well, and I was certainly at the end of my tether.

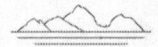

I took everything very easily for the next few months, but my schedule had me travelling again to Tajikistan and Uzbekistan, and bike riding into the new millennium in China. The year 2000 was looking good for me, with an expedition to Shishapangma in Tibet in April and May. Colin from Ausangate was one of the team members, and it was good to have him along. I followed the model I had used on Cho Oyu, but this time we did not get the breaks. I was forced to abandon the climb at around 7400 metres when Nawang, the Sherpa climbing with us, contracted pulmonary oedema. In the end it was an achievement to get him off the mountain alive. It was exhausting in the bad conditions. I was disappointed, of course, but I learnt a lot, and I struck up a special friendship with Cherie Silvera, a documentary producer from Aspen in Colorado, who summitted the mountain as part of a team filming a ski descent of the peak.

In February 2001, two weeks short of heading off to Shishapangma again, I cut all my plans short by breaking a bone in my foot when skipping in the lounge room of my apartment. I was so angry with myself because I felt it may be the end of my career as a guide and mountaineer. Feet are important tools to a climber, and I was now up to my knee in plaster for two months. Yet by July I was back in Bolivia, with modified behaviour to minimise a repeat performance from the muggers. Other travels followed, but my mind was occupied with the idea of another attempt on Shishapangma.

I decided to tackle it in the spring season of 2002. I had organised my Cho Oyu climb through Kathmandu-based Asian Trek, which provided basic services including Nepalese cooks and Sherpa guides, the number depending on the expedition's budget. Through my contacts there I was able to join a Belgian team as an addition to their permit. I would be self-contained but we would share various costs. I would be climbing independently with my friend Nima Tamang. This time I was totally focused on getting to the summit, so I chose to climb with someone I knew very well. The last thing I wanted was to be dealing with other people's problems, and as much as possible I stayed out of the Belgians' business. They took a risk having me, and I benefited from the great price they had secured as a group. They were always courteous to me, and overall I enjoyed this trip a lot more than my previous visit.

As well as our team there were also several European expeditions at Base Camp—Austrians, Germans, Dutch and Russians—as well as a Singaporean team. The Austrians in particular were very gung-ho, declaring that they would climb the mountain without Sherpa support.

The Belgians seemed a disparate bunch of people in terms of appearance, from the guitar playing Michel, who must have weighed 120 kilograms, to George, who was as skinny as a rake. Johan was their leader. Chocolates and beer are the main products of Belgium, and these were the main topics of conversation. They were real gourmets and had brought all sorts of amazing foods with them—they were not fond of the local fare. They appeared to hate vegies, and I liked vegies. Admittedly our cook, Kasi, was not good and I can well understand how they turned to chocolates. Often a couple of them would have just chocolates for dinner. Breakfast was their meal of the day, and there would be great discussion about the kind of eggs or pancakes to be made.

On one occasion I said, 'You can't climb a mountain on chocolates.'

'On pralines, my dear,' was the reply. I laughed. A least they knew how to enjoy themselves.

Initially the Belgians had an unfortunate relationship with the Tibetan yak herders and the Nepalese staff. Their climbing guide was a very accomplished mountaineer named Pasang Sherpa. He was in overall charge of the Nepalese contingent, but essentially he was a climbing guide. Johan kept ordering Pasang to do things, but I think this was because he didn't understand the structure of how an expedition crew works—that the guides don't do menial tasks or solve camp problems. Pasang was working very hard to be all things to all people. He was a very proud character, mature and very handsome, and he wanted to show that he could do a good job.

I was keeping my distance from the organisational activities of the Belgians, so I was amazed to learn one morning that Pasang had just up and left the trip. Johan told me that he had gone home.

'What do you mean?' I said, astonished.

I learnt that it was all about Coca Cola (not usually a major issue on mountaineering expeditions). A slab of Coke had mysteriously gone missing in Nylaam, which made the drink a sensitive subject. Now, at Base Camp, some of the Belgians stormed into the tent and accused Nima and Pasang of stealing more of the precious elixir. It seems the Belgians had put it in the kitchen tent, but Nima and Pasang had handed it out to visitors. The Belgians did not realise that this is how things work on expeditions; if you don't want food or drink shared around, you don't put it in the kitchen tent. It was just a stupid misunderstanding.

Up to this stage I felt that the Belgians had not thought too much about me. I was an appendage sharing their permit, and they were happy to include me in that capacity. I had not wanted to get involved with their debacles, but this meant too much to me. Pasang had gone, so I went to Nima's tent to ask for his version of events. I found him crying, and I had never seen him cry before. Sure enough, it was because they had been accused of stealing the Coca Cola.

I went back to Johan and said, 'You can't say that to them. Just think about it.'

'What's wrong? What's the big problem?' he asked.

'You're in trouble because Pasang has left you. You accuse them of stealing, but you left the carton open in the kitchen. You should expect people to have some. Now Pasang doesn't want to work with you. Who cares if a slab of Coke goes missing? You're here to climb the mountain.'

'That's a good point, Sue,' Johan conceded, and I knew I had made my point.

I told Johan I would go and look for Pasang because I did not think he would have gone far. I walked down towards the other camps and found him at camp Singapore, sitting in the kitchen tent with some Sherpa mates. He was quite teary.

He said, 'I'm never going to work for those people. I hate them, and I'm going.'

'Pasang, I don't think it's that bad,' I said. 'The best thing is to look at it like this—what is winning for you? Winning is for you to climb the mountain with them, nobody having an accident, and you getting paid and going home. After that you'll never see them again. Think about that.

'If you leave now, there'll be problems, questions and explanations. What's a few more weeks? Don't you want to show that you lead successful trips? The trick is for you not to go into their mess tent and have discussions. Don't take orders from them. Johan should report to the cook about the food, and you are the climbing guide.'

Pasang took this on board, as did Nima, so I went back and talked to Johan. Already he was contrite.

'He's a guide, not a servant,' I explained. 'So look at it like that.'

The Belgians had been very hospitable to me from the time I joined the trip, but now I felt they viewed me differently, as someone who might know what was going on. Nevertheless, I was determined to paddle my own canoe. I explained to Nima that I was happy to carry loads up the mountain to Camp One by myself, but that we would be together for the serious climbing.

The climb to Camp One took eight hours, the first half a slog through scree and an ice fall, but it was important for acclimatising. When I wasn't load-carrying, I relaxed in my tent with a few books and spent time in the kitchen tent with the Sherpas. The Belgians invariably stayed in the mess tent, being happiest in their own company, and I certainly did not add to things by not being able to speak more than school-level French. An advantage of being a woman was that I was invariably welcome at the other camps, and I sometimes visited them.

I certainly wasn't antisocial, but I did enjoy heading up to Camp One on my own. However, one day I found myself seriously underdressed halfway to Camp One. The sun disappeared, the wind picked up and suddenly it became bitterly cold. I had warm clothes up at Camp One and warm clothes down at Base Camp, but nothing with me. My pack was full of climbing gear. I cursed my stupidity because I knew very well that I should always carry survival gear. There was no one else around so I forced myself to climb more quickly despite the shortage of oxygen. I was shivering furiously by the time Camp One came in sight. The danger sign was if I stopped shivering. I reached my tent in a mini blizzard and had to dig it out as best I could, bag some snow for melting, get inside and get the stove fired up so I could get some hot liquid into me. It was a close call.

Another time I was descending in a white out, but I was dressed appropriately. I caught up with a bunch of people from different expeditions, including some of the Belgians and some of the big macho Austrians. There was a maze of seracs where you could be lost for hours if you got it wrong.

One of them said, 'We don't know where to go.'

I knew they had been in the same spot for more than forty-five minutes as I had been watching them from the time I left Camp One and never expected to catch them.

'We can't stay here,' I said. ' We've got to get a move on.'

Another said, 'Well, you lead, Sue. You're the most experienced.'

We made a start since I had a rough idea of the route having been through quite a few times now, and I was always mindful of natural markers. After a while we came across a bamboo marker pole, which meant we were on route. I led the way until the deep snow exhausted me, then I asked someone else to take the lead. With the ice field behind us, we were well on the way home and I started to run out of gas in what had become quite a blizzard. I became disoriented and slipped into a hole between some snow-covered rocks. I was tired now, and Marc and Koen from the Belgian team had kindly been keeping an eye on me and came to help me out. It was a good feeling to work together. I was hypothermic by the time I reached the mess tent as I hadn't anticipated the storm, nor that it would take me such a long time to get back. I had doubts about my ability to go back up again, but I appreciate how the mind works and knew I just had to tell myself that tomorrow was another day.

Our first summit push was on 7 May and it looked as though we might make it. Then the weather turned bad and we had no choice but to turn back.

We returned to Base Camp to rest and recover, heading back up when the weather started to look good. Nima became quite sick at Camp Two, coughing and spluttering, and we agreed it was best for him to go back down. Unfortunately, I ate food that had spoilt in the sun, and suddenly had several bouts of violent diarrhoea in close succession. I must have looked a wreck because Pasang asked me if I was okay.

'I'm a bit sick,' I said. 'I'll probably stay here for the day. What are you guys up to?'

'We will go up,' he said.

I thought, *Uh-oh. The train's going and I'm not on it.* I decided I had to go with them, as this could be my only chance for the summit.

I said, 'Would you have the patience to wait for another half hour while I get ready? I'd like to come, if you'll have me along.'

'We can do that,' Pasang said.

'Sure we can,' Johan agreed.

Fantastic, I thought. I dashed to my tent, put on my all-weather gear and threw the essential items into my pack — sleeping bag, headlamp, mitts, fluid, goggles and so on — along with a couple of Musashi bars, my standard food when climbing. I made the load as light as possible because I felt weak. I zipped up the tent, plucked my ice axe out of the snow and was ready to go.

I felt very ordinary as I set off behind Pasang and Johan, but the exercise seemed to burn off the toxins in my system. Rehydration with some Tang in my drink helped me along as well. The mountain face was a mix of rock and snow, which made for more interesting climbing. After a couple of hours I was feeling quite strong, and I began to gain on Johan. Soon I overtook both him and the Singapore climbers, who seemed to be struggling. The weather looked changeable, and I wanted to reach Camp Three at 7400 metres before it turned bad. I came over the crest of the slope and Pasang was tending to the stove and sorting a few things. Johan was the slow but steady type and arrived half an hour later. We rested, slept and woke up early. The weather was perfect. Pasang and I were ready to leave at 2.30 am, but Johan took almost another hour to get ready.

The final day's climbing turned out to be more technical than I expected. I needed to be careful where I stepped. The day before, the Austrians had turned back because they were unable to find a route around a rock buttress now ahead of us.

'There is a way through the rocks in the middle,' said Pasang. 'They said they don't need Sherpa support, so no success for them.' He seemed quite satisfied with this.

When we reached the buttress Pasang led us up some cracks, which were the key to the difficult section. No one had yet summitted that season. The other teams were waiting for Pasang or another Sherpa who knew the way to set the route. The Sherpa who opens the route is usually taking the biggest risks, then there is a surge as others follow along behind. Pasang knew what he was about. He had climbed Everest and other major peaks and took everything in his stride. We waited for Johan to catch us, and I shouted some encouragement. He enthusiastically waved and shouted back instead of saving his breath, a sign of how passionate he was about the climb. Then we kept moving up because I could see the clouds were beginning to gather and I did not want to miss the view from the top. But sure enough, for the last hundred metres to the top we were climbing through the clouds.

The final ascent to the summit with Johan was really enjoyable. He was slow and steady like a snail, never quitting, while wearing his heart on his sleeve. When he arrived at the top there was no room for the three of us, so Pasang stepped down. I pulled out my camcorder and passed it to him. I had turned it on but Pasang had turned it off, thinking he was doing the right thing, so I got no footage of the summit. It was not that important as the view was limited to a few glimpses of Tibet through the swirling clouds.

It was time to head down. Pasang wanted to get off the mountain as quickly as possible, which is a common response for Sherpas, but Johan and I were content to stop at Camp Three. On the next day's descent my foot was very painful where I had broken it in my apartment, so I bailed up at Camp One while Johan continued to Base Camp. I radioed to say that Johan was on his way but I was staying, which was fine by Nima and Pasang. To my great surprise, Nima appeared at Camp One at seven o'clock in the morning. He must have left Base Camp at about 3 am. He was really proud of me and excited by my success. We rolled up the tent together and packed the rubbish. Nima carried almost everything, which made the long slog down the loose lumpy moraine to Base Camp much more bearable.

At Base, I gave my own down jacket to Pasang, which he loved. I had given one to Nima at the beginning. He said proudly that it fitted perfectly even though it was clearly too short in the arms.

To celebrate, young Kasi, the cook, made a cake, which was a huge effort for him as his cooking skills were basic. I was very enthusiastic, mainly about the fact that he had made the effort. The cake was served with French champagne which the Belgians produced out of nowhere. They also had pâté, canapés they had made, and of course pralines. Best of all was that they had waited for me to come off the mountain. There had been no other arguments after the Coca Cola incident, and I felt proud that I had helped smooth the way and that the expedition had such a happy ending for everyone.

'You are right, Sue,' Pasang said. 'We all had success. We are all happy. And now we can go home.'

4

FOR WHOM THE BELL TOLLS

The day Sue came back from Shishapangma in June 2002 she caught a taxi from the airport to her flat in Wollstonecraft. She heaved her eight bags of climbing gear out of the taxi—they had filled the boot and back seat—and paid the driver. There was one more chore to be tended to before she could sit outside with a beer in her hand, reacquainting herself with the dozens of pot plants of all sizes that created a virtual forest on her huge balcony. She had to lug the heavy bags up the stairs to the entrance of her first floor flat. She managed to squeeze them through the front door and pile them in the hall. On checking the number of bags she realised there was one more to come, but as she was thinking this she stepped back and tripped over the missing bag. She fell down the stairs onto the landing.

She lay there, hurting in many places at once. Gingerly she moved her arms and then her legs, and was immensely relieved that nothing was broken. But when she tried to stand up she realised that her tailbone must be broken; she recognised the pain from when she had injured it years ago at school. Despite the agony, she managed to drag herself up slowly and pull the bag inside.

Sue opened a few windows and then rang her dad, as she always did if he had not met her at the airport when she returned from a trip. He knew about her success because she had called him briefly from Kathmandu. This was more of a call to see how he was doing and, given what had just happened, to tell him that she was not feeling the best herself! They talked for a short while, then she threw her most dangerously dirty clothes in the washer and relaxed on the couch with a pile of mail untouched beside her. She already had a pain in the butt without opening bills and junk mail.

The next day Ron Fear appeared at the door.

'How are you doing?' he asked.

'Actually, it hurts a hell of a lot.'

'I thought it might, so I brought you this.'

He produced a strange cushion from a plastic bag he was holding. He had made a special trip to a mate's place to collect the cushion in the hope it would ease Sue's discomfort. There was a circular hole in the middle of it so that the central part of one's backside did not bear any weight. She tested it, and it was a definite improvement.

'That's great,' he said. 'Glad it wasn't a bum steer.' He chuckled at his own joke.

'Yeah, Dad,' Sue grinned. 'Would you like a drink?'

'No, thanks,' he said. 'I've got other things I have to do, so I'll just go.'

Sue nodded. If he did not want to elaborate, she was not going to ask. That was the way they worked things. They agreed to spend an afternoon together, either that weekend or the next, beginning with lunch, then said goodbye. It was the last time Sue saw her father alive.

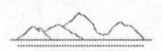

Sue cursed herself for being so careless as to fall down the stairs, and had no choice but to take everything at a gentle pace. As the pain began to lessen over the next few days, she started getting out and doing things around town. She needed to let Mountain Designs know she was available for part-time work again, and she wanted to confirm some guiding arrangements with World Expeditions for the coming year. There were various other people that she had to see, and with one thing and another, she did not manage to visit her father that weekend.

Mum and I admiring Dad's catch

Mum, me, John and Grahame before heading off to watch Grahame play footy

My first mountain climb, in New Zealand 1986. Every piece of gear was borrowed!

Here I am (in the red jacket) with the UN group on Point Lenana, Mount Kenya, in January 1987. Mount Kenya was my first mountain top in Africa.

Mount Kilimanjaro was my first high mountain experience. The sun came up to greet me as I reached the summit.

At the summit of Mount Kilimanjaro with the reluctant cook who accompanied me to the top after the group and guide had turned back

The beautiful view from Mera Summit across to Makalu and Makalu 2, the satellite peak to the left of Makalu's main peak

Mount Ausangate in the Vilcanota, Peru, where I fell after being accidentally dropped over a ledge by a climbing partner

Cho Oyu, the climb ahead

I summitted Cho Oyu mid-morning, 24 September 1998

The team at Mount Everest Base Camp. At the back from left: Zeddy, Herman, Matt, Chung and me. In the front from left: Trynt, Gernot and Tony.

Me climbing an ice cliff up the North Col on Mount Everest at approximately 6700 metres

A storm about to descend on ABC, Mount Everest

At the North Col on Mount Everest our tents were flattened by storms three times

Courtesy Ted Mahon

Our tiny cluster of tents perched on Everest at the North Col camp

Courtesy Ted Ma

However, she made definite plans with her brother John that they would meet the following weekend at their father's St Ives home.

One day during her first full week back in Australia, Sue was busy in the city. In the afternoon she dropped by the World Expeditions office in York Street, where she was immediately told she had just missed an urgent phone call from her brother Grahame. Sue had never had an urgent phone call from him in her life, and her initial thought was that someone had had a car accident. She called back and Grahame told her, 'Dad's had a heart attack and he's in Mona Vale hospital.'

Sue was stunned. 'What do you mean?'

'Well ... it's not good.'

'What does "not good" mean? You have to tell me straight away. You have to tell me exactly.'

Grahame explained that he did not know because he had only just arrived at the hospital.

'Well, ring me the second you know.'

A few minutes later Grahame rang back and said, 'He's dead. You should come.'

Sue could not believe what she had just heard, but death was a conclusive diagnosis. She knew from the experience of her mother dying that she had to be there. She had to put everything else aside and be with her brothers. Part of it was saying goodbye to the body of her father (she saw that was all it was now). Another part of it was being there as a family together to comprehend the enormity of the event. Steph Hammond, a friend and workmate at World Expeditions, drove Sue to the hospital as she was obviously in no state to drive herself. When they arrived, she met the two policemen who had been on shift when the emergency call was made. For them it was just another incident, another day at work. Sue rushed through to John, Grahame, his wife Anna and the friend of her father's who had been there when he died. The events of the day were outlined.

That morning Ron Fear had been planning to head up the Hawkesbury River in his sail boat, a comfortable ten-metre Arends with a little cabin and a galley. In his retirement he spent one or two days a week, sometimes more, living on the boat, exploring the Hawkesbury's bays and inlets and fishing when the tide was right. Then he would bring the boat home to its mooring in Pittwater and slip back into suburban living until the next week. Over the last month he had not been feeling well, and so on that day a friend had gone with him. Ron spent an hour struggling with the engine before he managed to get it started. With the motor in neutral he moved to the front of the boat and sat there to pull up the anchor. It was halfway up when suddenly he stopped, sat back and died on the spot.

For Sue, it was the suddenness of his death that made it so terrible. He had been so active and full of plans and schemes that none of them had seen the end in sight. He was seventy-two when he died. Sue had just returned from summitting Shishapangma and had not had the chance to share a debrief of the expedition with her dad—something she had been looking forward to doing. Normally after a major mountaineering trip, her dad would meet her at the airport and they would go to a nice café, where Sue would talk about the good and the bad and what she thought about it all. Ron would just listen, asking a question if he didn't get the picture, being there for her, enjoying his daughter's success and the deep satisfaction that mountaineering had brought to her life. Sue was surprised now by how sad she felt because this time she had not been able to perform this ritual. It was just the first of many specific and, on the face of it, unimportant routines which from that day onwards would be discontinued.

Grahame had kept in very regular contact with his father because his job as a sales rep gave him the opportunity to drop by every time he went past St Ives, which was often. However, John was distraught because he had not been seeing his father regularly, largely through not owning a car, and there were many face-to-face conversations he would have liked to have. Sue felt an enormous sense of loss, but took some solace in the fact that between her and her dad there were no vital issues or opinions that had been left unsaid. She had lived at home with him when her brothers had been living overseas, and there had always been much to talk about—values, human strengths and failings, and their own beliefs. They had shared so many common interests and understood each other's points of view. Not surprisingly, she missed him dreadfully from the very day of his death.

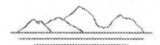

As soon as Sue recovered sufficiently from her injury, she took to exercise with a vengeance. Long swims and runs provided something positive to focus on in the weeks and months that followed. Fitness was the conscious purpose and meaning for each run, but the engagement of her mind with her physical performance helped keep her emotions on track.

The months which followed Ron Fear's death were difficult times. A lifetime's worth of belongings had to be dealt with in the family home at St Ives, and there were seemingly endless bureaucratic aspects. These chores were not the issue; it was the pervasive sadness of his absence and the loss of the warmth and emotional backup that their father could no longer give them.

When Sue began travelling again she found that transplanting herself to foreign countries did not take him out of her mind. When her mother had died, it had been a protracted, heartbreaking decline. That she would die was obvious. That Joan was aware of her fate made her death more comprehensible, if not acceptable. Sue and her dad grew closer during that sad process, and the relationship only deepened when their mother and wife was no longer with them. Sue had never really considered life without her father. They had not said goodbye, and without that signing off it was natural that he kept appearing in her mind. She could see very clearly how much a part of her life her father had been. Even on her longest trips away he had always been there with her. She would wonder what he would think about the fishing methods used in Vietnam, or how he would regard the people who had befriended her in Buenos Aires and then stolen all her luggage. Ron and Sue had been best buddies. They had reached the point where between them the important things no longer needed to be said, such as the fact that they would be there for each other, come what may. But only a week after she returned triumphant from Shishapangma, 'what may' had come with a vengeance. From this point onwards she could not be there for him, nor him for her.

Two weeks after the event Sue flew to Bolivia to guide a World Expeditions group of novice climbers to the summits of several glaciated peaks. She found herself still thinking of what her father would say about things, only to find these thoughts suddenly followed by feelings of emptiness. However, she loved the Bolivian Andes and the *bolivianos* with whom she worked, and the climbing lifted her spirits because it demanded her total concentration. The climbs themselves were not difficult, but she always paid the utmost care when mountaineering with clients. The simplest mistake could lead to disaster, and it was her job to foresee and forestall those fatal potentialities.

In August 2002 Sue spent three weeks trekking with clients on the Kamchatka Peninsula in far eastern Russia. Then in October she found herself in Nepal again, climbing Mera Peak for the sixth time with a group of ten clients, eight of whom reached the 6400 metre-high summit.

The weather was perfect, and from the top Sue had a clear view of Mount Everest, forty kilometres to the north, towering above the giant peaks which surrounded it. Sue's success on Shishapangma meant she now had two 8000-metre summits under her belt, both achieved without supplementary oxygen, plus the experience of four self-managed expeditions, and this had made her feel that Everest might be within her reach. She had planned to share the idea of an Everest expedition with her father. She had daydreamed about the climb, and part of the daydreaming had been thinking about how proud he would be of her success. Now, of course, he would never know.

A few weeks later, when Sue was back in Australia, it occurred to her that the way to bring her father into the equation was to dedicate to him the greatest possible feat of life triumphing in the face of death — the climbing of the world's tallest mountain. Death was no stranger on the summit of Everest, and if Sue were to climb to the peak—to steal a few moments of glory from that inhospitable place—it would be the perfect closure for the untimely death of a man who had been fully engaged with life. It would be a symbol, and symbols were timeless. Sue would climb Everest for her dad. Ron Fear never quoted the dictum that actions spoke louder than words. He went one better—he lived it. He would not have wanted her to stay still in her life.

With this private plan she realised she had found an appropriate eulogy. What she needed to do now was get the show on the road.

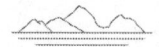

The next few months were ridiculously busy. Her first challenge was to work out how she was going to climb Everest. It was not an obsession, not something she had to do at all costs. She also wondered whether she should climb another big mountain first to consolidate her skills. She was very aware of not letting herself be ruled by her emotions. An expert opinion could be useful, so she decided to contact Russell Brice, who was arguably the most successful organiser of commercial Everest expeditions through his company Himalayan Experience. While this statistic was relevant to Sue, more important was her memory of him from their encounters on Cho Oyu in 1998, where she had found him to be a down-to-earth Kiwi who called a spade a spade. She had other strong and positive memories of Russell from Cho Oyu, and now she was leaning towards joining his Himalayan Experience expedition.

Sue emailed him at his home in Chamonix, the epicentre of mountaineering in the European Alps. Four years had passed since the Cho Oyu expedition, but when she contacted Russell she realised that she had earned his respect without setting out to do so. She had put together the Cho Oyu climb on the smallest of budgets, and unlike most other small teams on the mountain that season, she had done her part in opening up the route. She had been minimalist in her presence and had climbed the mountain without supplementary oxygen. At first Russell did not realise she was enquiring about a place on his March

2003 Everest climb because she asked him what he had been doing and what his plans were. Somehow she felt it was audacious for her, Sue Fear, to ask about going to Everest. When she was finally more up front about it he immediately responded positively. He obviously felt she was up to the task, and Sue was delighted.

Her major requirement was that the expedition be organised and operated by someone else so that she could focus on her climbing. As far as she could see, Himalayan Experience offered the best opportunities. Russell was someone to whom she could speak her mind, knowing that he would reciprocate, and this openness was very important to her. Himalayan Experience had a great track record in terms of both safety and a high percentage of summit successes achieved by their clients. The organisation's infrastructure had proven itself again and again over many years, and the reputation of Russell's Sherpa team was beyond equal.

Another vital factor for choosing Himalayan Experience was that Russell always tackled Everest from the Tibetan side of the mountain. Sue wanted to climb the North Ridge because this ascent route was less crowded than the more popular South-east Ridge route in Nepal. She also believed it was safer and offered more interesting climbing. Her own expeditions in Tibet had been much more straightforward logistically than her climb of Makalu 2 in Nepal, yet another reason for choosing the north side. She was also fascinated by the history of the early British attempts to climb Everest via Tibet during the 1920s and '30s. With basic equipment, several climbers had come to within 500 metres of the top, and the disappearance of George Mallory and Andrew Irvine in 1924 after they were sighted high on the North Ridge posed one of adventure's great unsolved questions. Did they reach the summit thirty years before Edmund Hillary and Tenzing Norgay? Sue did not expect to find the answer, but she looked forward to following in their footsteps and climbing beyond their known highpoint.

March was only a few months away, which did not leave her much time to gather the specialist equipment that only Everest required. World Expeditions and Mountain Designs helped her with some sponsorship, as did the Australian Geographic Society, Oakley, Icebreaker clothing and Musashi, the sports nutrition company. Despite the short notice, all supported her with little hesitation. Otherwise, she funded the expedition herself, partly because of the shortage of time but also because corporately sponsored expeditions had never been her style. Physical training was not a huge issue for her because she had spent much of the year trekking and climbing on three continents. When not trekking or climbing, she adhered rigorously to the daily training schedules which for years had been as much a part of her life as breakfast, lunch and dinner. Psychologically she was primed and ready to go.

She saw that the next step was to prepare for the challenges of two months at and above the high and dusty Base Camp in Tibet by taking some time out to finetune her attitude and her fitness. She left Australia early so that she could trek into the Everest region of Nepal. The trekking trails on the Nepalese side of the mountain were much more user-friendly than those in Tibet, and the environment was far less bleak.

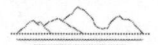

Sue's fortieth birthday was 18 March 2003, the day she planned to arrive in Kathmandu. Mount Everest was her present to herself. Three days before she left Sydney, she threw a big party, which was also a thank you to all the people who had helped her through her tumultuous thirty-ninth year.

During the party Sue hoped to avoid serious conversations about the issues of safety and risk-taking on Everest, but it was a futile wish. These became one-way conversations, because Sue was not going to buy into the dangers debate. Her decision to tackle the world's highest mountain was not made lightly, and assessing her ability to handle the perils had been part of that process. She had learnt that time spent worrying about what might happen was worse than time wasted. She had seen how obsessive worry and fear undermined climbers' resolve. Many a safe passage to a summit had been left untrodden because of fear, worry and lack of self-confidence. On the flip side, many a return from a summit had been left uncompleted as well, when climbers had pushed themselves beyond their limits to reach their goal and had nothing left for the long descent. It was clear in Sue's mind that she would avoid both misjudgments. There was nothing more to be said.

Nevertheless, her party was the last chance for her friends to voice their reservations, and her heart was warmed by their genuine concern. Sue Badyari, speaking not as general manager of World Expeditions but as a close friend, took Sue aside. She spoke very quietly, almost hesitatingly, because she knew that Sue believed women climbers were often disempowered by lectures from 'well-wishers' about the dangers of mountaineering.

'It doesn't matter if you come back empty-handed,' Sue Badyari said, then pointedly added, 'We'll still love you whether you make the summit or not.'

Sue hugged her friend. 'Thanks,' she said, 'I know.'

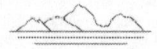

The seventeenth of March was a Monday, and everyone was tied up at work except for one of Sue's long-time friends, Marnie. She drove Sue to the airport because she had not been able to make it to the party, and it was her opportunity to say goodbye. Sue was happy that it was a low-key departure. She felt like relaxing, and she did not need any more of 'those conversations' about risk-taking.

It was a relief for Sue to flop into her seat on the Thai Airways 747 flight to Bangkok. As with every expedition, there had been many last minute odds and ends that had kept her frantically busy, and organising her party had not lessened the load. The final headache had been her 129 kilograms of luggage. But once she was on board the aircraft nothing further could be done, and it was a great feeling.

On the morning of 18 March 2003 she boarded her flight to Kathmandu. The flatlands of India fell behind as the aircraft approached the mighty Himalayan range, which stretched west-north-west along the entire northern border of Nepal. Sue peered eagerly out of the window, waiting for the world's highest mountains to come into view. Although she had seen the aerial panorama of these peaks many times, she never tired of the sight—first Kanchenjunga, the easternmost of the 8000-metre peaks, then Makalu, Lhotse, Everest and Cho Oyu.

As they approached Kathmandu the aircraft dropped down through the clouds. It was the end of the winter, the dry season, and the Kathmandu Valley was murky with dust and smoke. Sometimes, when rain had taken the dust out of the air, the white snow on the peaks north of the city could be seen from the tarmac of the runway, but today was dry, and smog hung over the valley. Inside the terminal building, the unhurried stamping of passports was an immediate reminder that life, and time itself, marched to a different drum in Nepal.

Outside, porters clambered for her bags, but she was met by Bhupendra of Highland Excursions, the Kathmandu end of World Expeditions' operations. Bhupendra was a lovely, reliable fellow, just like all the staff Sue worked with in Nepal. For them, her visit was no different to any other. They always looked after Sue and her needs whether at work or play—not that Everest was much of a game. She chatted with Bhupendra as she gazed out at familiar landmarks and listened to the incessant honking of horns—nothing aggressive in the cacophony, just the noisy way that traffic ebbed and flowed. Sue welcomed the feeling of subconsciously easing herself back into Nepal.

The Radisson Hotel had offered her six nights' accommodation free of charge by way of supporting her attempt on Everest. A member of the famous international hotel chain, the Radisson nevertheless had a distinctly Nepalese style. Sue had stayed there dozens of times over the last decade with different World Expeditions trekking and climbing groups. Lhakpa Sherpa, who manned the World Expeditions desk in the hotel, welcomed her warmly.

When she checked into her room she was stunned to see a magnificent birthday cake waiting for her on the desk. Chocolate-coated strawberries circled the 'Happy 40th Birthday' lettering. White rose petals rimmed the cake's perimeter, a delightful surprise organised by Lhakpa. She wanted to share the birthday and the warm welcome with all her friends at Highland Excursions, so she put the cake back in its box and walked for half an hour to the Highland office. It was a great start to her trip. Although she did not know it at the time, Meraj Din, the director, had sponsored her climb by providing her Everest flight tickets free of charge. On this birthday afternoon, the icing on the cake was indeed the icing on the cake.

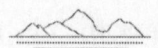

The fifty-minute Twin Otter flight to Lukla, the airstrip in the foothills below Everest, was familiar airspace. Sue had made many trips to the Everest region over the years, her most common destination being Mera Peak in the valley immediately to the east of Lukla. At 2800 metres above sea level, Lukla was a good height to begin acclimatising. Sue grabbed a quick cup of tea from her friends at the Sherpa Coffee House, then swung her pack on to her shoulders and headed out of town along Lukla's main street, a few hundred metres of flag-stoned path never more than a few metres wide. The only traffic jams were caused by an occasional yak standing contemplatively.

The track led her across the hillside into the deep, V-shaped Dudh Kosi Valley, carved by the glacial melt from the Himalayan giants of Mount Everest, Gyachung Kang, and Cho Oyu. Forests of tall conifers led from the boulders flanking the Dudh Kosi River up the slopes to the steep rock walls of the gorge. The trail often traversed high above the river, until a rock buttress forced the track down to the water's edge to bypass the obstacle. Wherever a bend in the river had trapped enough alluvial silt, there were a few small ploughed fields, or a lodge had been built to accommodate some of the thousands of trekkers who headed up the valley towards Everest every year.

Sue spent her first night at Monjo, where a side stream cutting into the main gorge had created enough space for a small village. She sat out on the verandah and enjoyed a San Miguel beer, feeling welcome in Nepal and happy to be on holidays with a big adventure ahead. The trails were not busy because the trekking season was over and the mountaineering season about to begin.

In the morning she followed the track upstream to Sagarmatha National Park, just past the village of Jorsale. A narrow gap between two huge boulders formed a natural gateway into the park, which extended northwards all the way to the top of Mount Everest and the border with Tibet. The trail soon left the pebble flats by the river and headed up into the forest. A swing bridge spanned the vertical-walled gorge of the Imja Khola, the river that came direct from Everest. On the far side of the prayer flag-strewn bridge, the trail zigzagged up the steep spur between the two rivers, a 700-metre climb up to Namche Bazaar. At two points on the spur, where the trail U-turned at the top of rocky bluffs, it was possible to see over the forest to the distant summit of Everest. Only the final summit pyramid was visible as the rest of the great mountain was hidden behind the 7500 metre-high summit ridge of Nuptse, Everest's southern rampart. Sue's heart quickened at the sight. The next three months would be devoted to reaching the top of that distant peak.

At Namche she stayed in Thawa Lodge, one of the oldest lodges in town, operated by a long-time friend of Ringi Sherpa, the man who organised World Expeditions' climbing trips in Nepal. Namche nestles in a sheltered, shallow bowl-shaped valley on a steep hillside. It is a market village situated at the junctions of the paths from the rice fields at Lukla, the trade route from Tibet's Nangpa La pass near Cho Oyu, and the yak pastures below Everest. Today it is also a thriving trekking town, with lodges, restaurants and shops, having quadrupled its size in twenty years.

From Namche the trail skirted the western flank of the valley, 500 metres above the impassable Imja Kola gorge. The magnificent backdrop of the jagged peaks of Thamserku, Kantega and Ama Dablam made for a spectacular morning's walk. At the head of the valley, Sue could see the summit of Everest, but the bulk of the mountain lay hidden behind the vast mountain wall of the Lhotse–Nuptse ridge.

Bad weather brewed as Sue hiked up the valley. Her thoughts turned to the climbing of the mountain. She reflected on the many situations she would encounter that might make her want to quit—intense cold, gale force winds, the possibility of AMS (acute mountain sickness) and lesser illnesses which nevertheless could be crippling in the unavoidable extreme conditions. In the face of constant hardship, it was inevitable that her mind would push her towards quitting and heading home. Only a small percentage of the climbers who attempted Everest reached the summit, and Sue wanted to be among that small per cent. She knew she would need the patience to persist when the mountain rebuffed them all and others were packing up and going home. Sue told herself that she must not be governed by other climbers turning back around her; their reasons for quitting would be theirs, not hers.

Sue knew she could make those all-important decisions herself. She was the only person who knew her capabilities, so it was ludicrous to be governed by the thoughts and actions of others. Of course, she would listen to the expert advice of climbers she respected, particularly when faced with scenarios she had never faced before, such as the use of supplementary oxygen. But when it came to her capabilities, no one else was going to tell her what she could do. As a woman in the macho sport of mountaineering, she had become accustomed to men thinking she was out of her depth. They may not say anything—usually they did not—but she could sense this assessment in their behaviour towards her. The only justification they had for this point of view was Sue's slight build and the fact that she was a woman, neither of which was valid. She had learnt that if she let herself be governed by the expectations of men, then she would never get above Base Camp. With the expeditions she had led to Makalu 2, Shishapangma and Cho Oyu, she had earned her stripes for Everest, so she hoped that the other members of her team would see her as having equal footing with them. But if they didn't she would not let this undermine her spirit. In fact, she knew from experience this would only make her strive harder to succeed. It was an unhappy kind of motivator to have, but she knew that if others thought she would fail, she had to believe in herself even more strongly. There could be no success without belief.

With these thoughts passing through her head, the morning passed quickly. The trail dropped down to cross the river at a tiny village of Punki Tenka. One feature of the place was a series of prayer wheels that had been built over a rivulet so that water power could keep them spinning incessantly. Sue took her lunch in one of the small restaurants and began the steep and continuous climb up the hillside above. The pine trees gave way to rhododendron forests, the lower trees already blooming with red, white and pink flowers. The 200-metre height gain to Tengboche monastery took only an hour, even with the obstacles of yaks plodding slowly up the hill. The yaks had loads of kitbags and sacks of food strapped to each flank, so along the narrow parts of the trail it was impossible to overtake them. Sue took advantage of the steep short cuts that by-passed the zigzags to put herself ahead of the yak trains.

The Tengboche Ridge was a spur protruding from a ridge that ran down from Ama Dablam. The spur jutted into the valley, rising to a knoll where the famous Buddhist monastery had been built. Sue never tired of the view from here, one of the best mountain panoramas anywhere that was accessible by walking trail, but today the clouds obscured the biggest mountains. Sue visited the monastery and pondered the huge celebration that would be held here at the end of May, when seven different World Expeditions treks were scheduled to celebrate the fiftieth anniversary of the first ascent. A huge tent had been purpose-built for the occasion. As she looked across the grassy meadow in front of the monastery, she found it hard to visualise the event.

In the morning Sue followed the trail down the northern slopes of the knoll through beautiful rhododendron forest. A short narrow gorge provided the perfect place for a swing bridge, giving access to the less steep western bank of the Imja Khola. Shortly after the village of Pangboche, the altitude and exposure to the elements had forced the trees to give way to scraggy conifers and then grassy slopes, with low heath growing in sheltered gullies.

The next village up the valley was Pheriche. During Sue's second expedition to Shishapangma, Pasang had told her that he and his wife ran a lodge here, so Sue decided this was where she would stay. When she arrived she had trouble finding the place. There were many lodges in Pheriche and she could not remember its name. Eventually a passing Sherpa was able to direct her to the Mountain Guides Lodge. When Sue located it and identified herself as Pasang's climbing companion, she was welcomed very warmly by his wife, Ang Yangzen. Pasang was away making arrangements for an upcoming expedition, but Ang Yangzen insisted that Sue must stay. In fact, she was so excited that she invited her neighbours to join them for dinner, introducing Sue as 'the *didi* who climbed Shishapangma with Pasang'. (*Didi* is the Nepali word for 'elder sister'; it is common and respectful to address women in this way.) Sue was treated like family. Ang Yangzen would leap up to serve other customers, leaving Sue to entertain her two young children, then would return to sit with her by the fire.

Pheriche was at the edge of the broad glacial valley below Nuptse, which meant that Everest was not visible at all. Sue wanted to spend some time pondering the mountain, even though she would be climbing it from the other side, so the next day she made a day trip up the valley. Ang Yangzen prepared a packed lunch for her and she left Pheriche in bright sunshine. She walked though the tiny settlement of Duglha and passed the popular camping site at Lobuche, at 4900 metres. After three hours she branched up a side valley just beyond Lobuche then headed up the steep grassy slopes to get a good view of Everest. At first it was completely obscured by the mass of Nuptse, and then by the time she had climbed to an altitude from where Everest would have been visible, clouds had closed in around the mountains. Everest was totally obscured. Sue would spend much of the next three months looking at Everest so she was not too concerned. Besides, she was already at altitudes that were higher than the tops of most mountains in other parts of the world, and that was one reason why she had come. She aimed to have at least an hour at her high point, so she sat down to eat her lunch, watching the clouds darken above.

Even though she could not see Everest, there was plenty to think about. The ascent to the peak of the highest mountain on Earth embodied the struggle of the human will against the rationally impossible. The cold, the storms and the oxygenless air at the summit created an environment beyond the limits of human existence. Medical science indicated that there was not enough oxygen at the top of Everest to sustain life, and yet some people were able to bend the graphs of the possible by climbing the mountain without breathing apparatus. Sue was not planning to attempt this most extreme feat. Even with oxygen, the climb involved an almost superhuman effort. Frostbite was common, and there were deaths from exhaustion almost every year. Those who returned alive often appeared ten years older, so huge were the demands placed on their metabolism and their psyche.

Sue was well aware of these facts. She had tasted the harsh realities on Shishapangma and Cho Oyu. Her priority was to be as self-reliant as she could, and this was more achievable with the use of oxygen. Everest would provide a full menu of challenges and discomforts, but she was quietly ready to tuck into the meal. She knew that if her father were alive he would be proud of her should she reach the summit, but he would be equally proud if she stopped short after giving it her best shot.

Her introspection was interrupted by the worsening of the weather. The clouds darkened and sank lower down the mountainsides, and it began to snow heavily. She huddled in her Mountain Designs Gore-Tex jacket and watched the storm, then began to make her way down. She stopped at a teahouse for a cup of hot lemon tea. Outside again, there was enough snow for Sue to glissade, a mountaineering technique which was like skiing, but using boots as skis, and in this way she rapidly descended to the valley floor. She wondered whether Everest's summit was above the cloud level. The storm was now so powerful that it seemed inconceivable that anything could rise above it. It was almost dark by the time she returned to Mountain Guides Lodge, invigorated by the storm. Ang Yangzen gave her a warm welcome, and in the morning refused to take any payment for food or lodging. Sue thanked her for the gift of her hospitality.

As she headed back down the valley, Sue encountered an expedition of disabled people being filmed by National Geographic heading up to

Base Camp. Among them were people attempting to negotiate the trail in wheelchairs, with a couple of Sherpas in attendance to lift them over boulders. Further down the trail were an Indian Army team and a French expedition. Now that she was about to become an Everest climber herself, she was interested to observe other expeditions. What she saw gave her confidence. The climbers did not look superhuman or special in anyway, and that was how Sue saw herself. Mountaineering was just the path she had chosen to follow.

As she headed down from the mountains she was pleased she had made time for the trek. The exposure to altitude would certainly help her, and the extra ten days in the region would hopefully strengthen her resistance to diarrhoea and respiratory illness. The trek was also time out, a technique she had habitually employed before a big game when she had competed in other sporting realms. The time to 'zone', as it was called in sports jargon, was a time to clear her head of clutter so she could make clear-minded decisions when the pressure was on. She knew from her years of competitive sport that athletes performed badly if they did not prepare themselves properly, even if they were very talented. If nothing else, the trek would be a comfortable transition to the bleak heights of Lhasa on the high Tibetan plateau. And Sue had enjoyed being in Sherpa country without guiding a team of trekkers or climbers.

One of the features of the Buddhist highlands is the rows of *mani* walls, which are built with rocks carved with the most common of all Tibetan Buddhist prayers, *Om Mani Padme Hum*. There may be several hundred engraved rocks of different sizes in one *mani* wall. Their function is purely religious. When people walk past a *mani* wall they keep the prayers on their right, as they do with all Tibetan Buddhist structures. This means that a *mani* wall on a mountain trail is always set in the middle of the path, with prayers carved on both sides, so that whichever direction a person is walking they can keep the prayers on their right. Trekkers generally follow this one-way traffic custom out of respect.

On the day that Sue left Pheriche on her way back down to Tengboche, she passed a *mani* wall near Pangboche monastery. There were two Sherpas walking up valley on the other side of the waist-high wall. One of them looked vaguely familiar, and he seemed to be thinking the same about Sue. Suddenly Sue realised that it was Pasang, whose wife she had farewelled an hour earlier.

'Sue *Didi*!' he exclaimed at the exact moment she called out his name.

He looked just as he had when she had seen him at the end of their Shishapangma expedition two years earlier, except a little less weather-beaten and with a big gold earring. Pasang was thrilled that Sue had thought to stay with his wife at their lodge. When she told him she was heading back to Kathmandu so she could fly to Lhasa to tackle Everest from the north, he was again delighted.

Both of them had places where they needed to be. Sue had to be at Lukla within two days, and Pasang and his friend were required up at Base Camp to stake out a good site for a Canadian Everest expedition that was walking up from Lukla.

'It's a pity we can't be on Everest together,' Sue said. 'But you never know, maybe we'll meet on top.'

Pasang smiled his big Sherpa smile. 'Next time, Sue *Didi*. Next time we can climb another mountain together.'

They shook hands, hugged each other quickly and headed off to their different Everests. For Sue the brief meeting confirmed that their bond was still strong, that she was not just another climber with whom Pasang had climbed a mountain.

5

LEARNING MY ABCs

My flight from Lukla touched down in Kathmandu early in the morning of 28 March, giving me almost four full days before I flew out with the expedition team to Lhasa. I was very happy with the time I had spent in the hills. I love Nepal. I love the long days of walking and interacting with the locals. As I had hoped, the trek had been a great way to de-stress. I took the time to consider my motivations and thus strengthened my resolve, and of course I kick-started my acclimatisation; all of this was only going to help me. I also hoped that my resistance to disease would be elevated. This is a difficult thing to judge, but I had found that if I was going to fall sick when I was away, whether I was in Nepal, Tibet or Bolivia, then it generally hit me at the beginning of my journey. Here, I had begun my journey and I was in good health. I had every reason to be optimistic.

I returned to the Radisson, my regular haunt in Kathmandu, even though the Hotel Tibet was where the Himalayan Experience Everest Expedition (Himex) would be based. The Radisson had been kind enough to provide me with some free accommodation to help lessen the financial burden of my Everest climb, but I also liked being there. It was my Kathmandu home-away-from-home. I had two days before the official start of the expedition, then another day before we left for Tibet. I figured I had plenty of time to get myself organised before beginning to mix with the other members of the Himex Everest team. I valued having time to myself before slotting into the dynamic of all expedition members living in each other's pockets, which I knew would be the reality of the next ten weeks.

Any thoughts of a quiet time by myself vanished when I discovered that the Australian publicity machine had worked out I was back in Kathmandu. In a sense this was my own doing—Steph Hammond, my friend Megan's sister who also worked for World Expeditions, had organised some publicity for my sponsors, and had also sent out the first email newsletter about my climb. The plan was that she would put this together with information from my emails to her as well as from the regular news dispatches from Himex. The upshot was that much of my hoped-for free time was consumed by conversations with the press and radio stations. In these last busy weeks before I left Australia, I had been surprised by how much enthusiasm my prospective climb had generated. Mine would not be the first Australian female ascent of Mount Everest—that honour belonged to my friend Brigitte Muir—but it seemed that being the second woman was quite a big deal as well. Kathmandu was a long way from Sydney in more than the geographical sense, so I was delighted that my climb was not a case of 'out of sight, out of mind' as far as the media back home were concerned.

On 30 March 2003, before leaving the Radisson and heading off to my first meeting with the other Himex members, I sat in my room and looked through the paperwork I had accumulated about the expedition. I had been too busy to sort through it before leaving Sydney, and much of it could now go in the bin. On paper there seemed to be a reasonable amount of experience amongst the other climbers, with three of them having attempted Everest in the past. I was not sure if this was entirely a good thing. Everest could become a fixation, and throughout the mountain's history there had been many examples of people who had turned back from the peak once and then refused to heed the warnings when they returned for their second attempt. Some of these people had died, and others survived only because they were rescued, often putting their rescuers' lives at risk or crippling themselves with frostbite in the process. This is the worst end of the spectrum, of course; but although I was not about to make quick judgments about our team after flicking through a few paragraphs in an email printout, I was determined not to get entangled in anyone else's disaster. I had learnt in Peru and elsewhere that this is always a possibility when climbing with someone you don't know. It may sound melodramatic, given that we were still in comfortable Kathmandu and I had not even met the team, but one of my big concerns was getting caught out high on the mountain with a group of people—or even just one person—who could no longer take care of themselves.

This was not an idle worry of mine. Everyone who had signed up for this trip would have been aware that the worst disaster in Everest's history had occurred when two commercial expeditions and other climbers were trapped by a storm on the highest reaches of the peak. I expected that every member of our expedition would have read the famous account of those tragic events in John Krakauer's book *Into Thin Air*. Krakauer was one of the climbers who survived the storm that struck the mountain on the afternoon of 10 May 1996. Eleven people died. Eight of the dead had climbed up the Nepalese side of Everest, including the head guides from both commercial expeditions. The other three climbers perished on the Tibetan side of the mountain, on the route that we would be following.

Krakauer had been sent to Everest by *Outside* magazine, a US hiking and adventure publication which sells half a million copies per month. His brief was to write a major feature article about the phenomenon of guided climbs of Mount Everest. So dramatic were the events of 10 and 11 May 1996, and so much publicity did they gain, that market demand led *Outside* to run huge reprints of the issue containing Krakauer's story. Because he was an accomplished climber himself, one who had never participated in a guided climb, he was well able to appreciate the differences between expert mountaineers and ones who required the services of guides. In the pages of *Into Thin Air*, he used his knowledge of the mountains and his insight as a climber to explain the realities of commercial Everest expeditions. He did not have to theorise about how commercial expeditions might handle the 'what ifs' because the worst possible scenario materialised before his eyes, much to his horror.

His book portrays the mechanics of guided expeditions not only because this was the story he was originally commissioned to write, but also because when disaster struck he was right there with guides and their clients. His book was so widely read that the *Into Thin Air*-style of expedition was soon thought to be the norm, and because of this the popular misconception spread that anyone with fitness, determination and a modicum of mountaineering knowledge could climb Everest. The publicity seemed to increase the popularity of guided ascents of Everest despite the fact that the book was the story of a tragedy.

There is another side to the Himalayan climbing coin, the side where expert climbers explore a mountain, work out a route, set up their own camps and find their own way to the summit. These climbers make their own decisions and have no guides. This was what I did on Makalu 2. I find it a challenging and very demanding form of climbing, not the least because I have to stake my life on the judgments I make. I regard myself as a serious climber, meaning that my motivation is the act of climbing. The summit is the goal, the elusive prize that makes me deliver my best. I do not see myself as an elite mountaineer but I can certainly look after myself in the mountains. I like finding my own route up a peak and working out where to pitch my camps. It is difficult to take such a freewheeling approach when tackling the standard routes on popular mountains such as Cho Oyo and Shishapangma, because the regular line of ascent soon becomes well-trodden by the multiple teams attempting the climb. But even on these much frequented peaks, where there are invariably other people around, I like to be in control.

High on the big Himalayan mountains the safe path is a very tenuous one. Sometimes there is no safe path, so you have to know how to deal with the dangers, whether to stay put or run the gauntlet, and the wrong decision can mean death. On a guided climb the participants are shielded from making such decisions, as it is the guides' responsibility to lead them safely past the dangers. The system falls down when the dangers manifest suddenly and unrelentingly, when even the guides find themselves battling for their lives. At such times the participants have to make life or death decisions for themselves without guidance, without experience. This is exactly what happened on Everest in May 1996.

Despite the downsides which became obvious in 1996, there are definite advantages to commercial expeditions. This was obvious to me, otherwise I wouldn't have joined Russell Brice's Himex expedition. The expedition offered everything possible to maximise the odds of making a safe climb to the summit and back. Every service you could possibly want was available with Himex, from calls home by satellite phone and hot showers at Base Camp, to high-tech satellite weather reports and a team of highly skilled and experienced Sherpas. For the vital parts of the ascent, the Sherpas partner with the climbers one-on-one. Some people think that if they sign up with a commercial team, then such a system will take them to the summit. But this attitude is akin to the mentality used when you catch an elevator—once you begin the ascent you take no responsibility for what goes on in between. Of course, to complete a climb of Everest, everybody has to take every one of those many thousands of steps that lie between Base Camp and the summit. This great physical effort is acknowledged and prepared for by rigorous fitness training. What some people lack is not only any real understanding of the possibility of disaster but also the ability to deal with its eventuality. On guided expeditions the participants do not expect to be fighting for their lives. They undergo no psychological training on how to cope with pushing beyond their limits, how to maintain the will to continue against seemingly insurmountable odds, how to fight off the demon of despair. These strengths may be needed on the climb of any major mountain, yet I had heard from high altitude guides some amazing stories of unpreparedness, such as clients who arrive at Base Camp not knowing how to put their crampons on or how to light a stove.

Understandably, this was the sort of climbing partner I wanted to avoid. I intended to stay as self-sufficient as I could when I was on the mountain. I knew that Everest was no pushover for anyone, regardless of how fit and motivated that person happened to be. And I was very clear about my reasons for joining Russell's team. One was that Russell had a great safety record, and safety on Everest is not something that depends on luck. Logistics was another issue. During the expeditions I organised myself, I expended a lot of energy and stress on the mechanics of keeping the show on its rocky mountain road. With Himalayan Experience the entire structure of the expedition was thoroughly organised. I didn't have to worry about logistics, or porters' strikes, or whether there was enough food or fixed rope. Everything was in place, and Russell's systems had been finetuned by a dozen successful seasons on Everest's north side. All I had to do was show up and climb, which was exactly the position I wanted to be in.

I shoved my Himex file into my daypack and headed down to the Red Onion Bar, conveniently between Hotel Tibet and the Radisson. I saw Russell as soon as I entered. He greeted me with a big smile. His confidence and good spirits made me realise it was time for me to relax and enjoy what was going on. Chairs had been arranged in a huge circle, so we sat down amidst the noise and introduced ourselves by name. Then we listened as Russell explained how the expedition would be conducted. No doubt all of us had read through the information that had been sent to us and had poured repeatedly over the Everest pages on the Himex website, so we already knew much of what Russell said. Nevertheless, it was good to hear it in person. The spoken word suddenly made the expedition real. Russell introduced us to Purba, the *sirdar* (manager) of the Sherpas, and his team. He was a very strong looking man who stood quietly to one side drinking orange juice.

The first of the climbers who had attempted Everest before was Tony Kelly, an affable Englishman in his mid-forties who had been with Russell on the North Ridge in 2000. Also with Himex again from that same expedition was Kin Man Chung, a businessman from Hong Kong, who owned three outdoor equipment shops and who had already climbed six of the Seven Summits. It was his dream to climb Mount Everest, and this was his third attempt. The Seven Summits are the highest peaks on the Seven Continents, and the climbing of them has become a major quest (although among hard-core climbers they are almost irrelevant because several, such as Mount Kosciuszko, are little more than a long walk).

The last of the three who had already attempted Everest arrived half an hour late. His hair was dyed white, a startling effect against his dark Arab features. His name was Zaid Al-Refa'i, but he introduced himself with a big friendly smile as 'Zeddy'. He was a wealthy Kuwaiti businessman living in Geneva who wanted to be the first Arab to climb not only Everest but also the Seven Summits, and with only Everest and Kosciuszko remaining he was well on his way to achieving those goals. He may have achieved much, but I felt this was no excuse for being late for what was a very important meeting. However, Russell didn't bat an eyelid at Zeddy's tardiness, which made me suspect that Zeddy was very wealthy, with idiosyncrasies that Russell was prepared to tolerate. It was soon apparent that he had a very cheery disposition, which I saw could be a handy attribute for the long cold days and nights of waiting—inevitable parts of any expedition.

The other expedition members were similarly diverse. Matt Comotto, an America based in Angola who worked in the shipping industry, was open and upfront in the way that Americans often are, even on first meeting. He had climbed Cho Oyu and Kilimanjaro, so we had some common ground with these mountains. My first impression of Matt was that he was someone I could get along with, someone who might make a suitable climbing partner.

At the other end of the scale, in terms of the mood he projected, was Gernot Overbeck, an intense and serious German. He was a physicist and entrepreneur, obviously intelligent but not attempting to make this impression. Also German was the guide whom Russell had employed, Hermann Berie, a professional alpine guide with very impressive credentials. Russell explained how grateful he was that Hermann had been able to join the expedition at short notice, after Russell's original choice of head guide had to pull out.

I was delighted that the last of the seven clients was another woman, an American called Tryntje Young. Trynt, as she liked to be called, was a forty-one year old professional firefighter and paramedic. The path that had led her to the expedition was extraordinary. Russell had already informed us that our expedition would be run in tandem with a second Himex expedition, a team called 'Global Extremes', and these very fit looking Americans were with us for the briefing. They were certainly a team with a difference, unlike any that had been on Everest before. In 2002, from January to June, Global Extremes athletes had participated in competitive adventures all over the world. The events were televised as a series, a kind of adventure racers' *Survivor*. The five winners had won $50,000 each and a place on the Global Extremes Everest Expedition. Trynt had been a Global Extremes member but she not made the grade for Everest, having been voted out of the group in the final stages. However, she was so strongly motivated to tackle the mountain that she had joined our expedition so she could still achieve her goal.

This was an amazing scenario. I was unclear about the implications of her decision to join us. With Russell in charge of both expeditions, it seemed inevitable that we would be closely involved with the Global Extremes team for the duration of our stay in Tibet and that tensions might develop. However, I was sure I would find out more of the finer details since it was fairly obvious that, as the only women on the team, the two of us would be sharing hotel rooms in our travels across Tibet.

As a trekking guide I had given dozens of pre-trip briefings where I outlined the route, the daily routine, my role and the responsibilities of the participants, our staff and myself. Russell's briefing was along the same lines, except of course that our Everest expedition was a much more serious trip than any I had guided. He raised a range of issues that I had never needed to deal with on a trek. It was an informative meeting, only ten minutes long, open and friendly. Afterwards there was an undertone of everyone trying to get a feeling for how they would get on with everyone else. An exception here was Zeddy, who seemed to assume that we would all get swept up in his easy-going cheeriness, regardless of his indiscriminate cigar smoking.

Over the next few days I was quite busy with my own activities, so I did little socialising with the rest of the team. Each of us had to assemble our climbing gear and other things that we would not need before we got to Base Camp. My gear was already reasonably organised, so this did not take me long. The kitbags and big plastic barrels were then stacked in the back of two trucks, which would head directly to Base Camp in Tibet by road.

This beginning to our expedition was quite different to the scenario enacted on the Nepalese side of Everest. Some expeditions flew helicopters into the Nepalese Base Camp. The risks of this procedure became obvious to me the previous week when I was trekking up past Lobuche and a chopper had crashed, killing several people. Helicopters at high altitude are not only dangerous but also expensive, so most of the Nepal-based Everest expeditions flew their equipment into Lukla in fixed-wing aircraft. At the small mountain airstrip the loads were strapped to wooden cargo saddles on the backs of yaks. A five-day trek led to the Base Camp on the Khumbu Glacier. The climbers followed the same route as the yaks, but allowed themselves more time to acclimatise, much as I had done a week earlier.

On the Tibetan side of the mountain a road led directly to Base Camp, and had done so since 1960. Because the Tibetan side of the Himalayan range was in the rain shadow of the world's tallest mountains, the roads were in most cases less subject to landslides. Nevertheless, the Base Camp road was a huge engineering feat that involved the crossing of a 5000 metre-high pass and major rivers. Such a project might seem hard to justify given that the road did not lead onwards to any constructive destination, such as a town or a border crossing. But in those days, when it came to glory for the Motherland, no effort was too great and nothing could be more glorious than the first Chinese ascent of Everest, achieved by a huge expedition in 1960. The Chinese called the mountain *Chomolungma*, the name used for many centuries by the Tibetans. The Chinese saw absolutely no point in using the imperialist British name recognised by the rest of the world.

Our expedition would eventually be travelling to the mountain along that road, but first we had to fly to Lhasa to begin our acclimatisation. In Kathmandu the busyness of our packing and our group get-togethers, plus my media schedule, saw the morning of our departure arrive all too quickly. Almost before I knew it, I was eating my last breakfast at the Radisson for at least two months.

As soon as we began travelling I realised that I had certainly guessed right about the close involvement of our team with the Global Extremes group. We followed the same itinerary, flew to Lhasa on the same plane and travelled across Tibet together. Their six person climbing team—five athletes and their American mountain guide—was more than doubled in size by the addition of their film crew. With the raison d'être of the expedition being to entertain a television audience in the grand tradition of the Global Extremes expedition series, this was not surprising.

I found that the ease of mind which I had readily slipped into during my trek was now slipping away from me, perhaps because the show was turning out to be bigger than *Ben Hur*. Already I was wondering if I would be able to control my position on the expedition. I was not concerned about being high in the hierarchy; I just wanted to be able to make my own decisions. Everest is a very serious mountain, and now that we were finally getting underway, doubts began to make themselves felt. My confidence was strong, but I wondered whether this season would give us good or bad conditions, and whether the good weather would occur when we were in a position to capitalise on it and make a push for the summit.

The flight eastwards across the Himalaya from Kathmandu to Lhasa was spectacular, with quite a few clouds around but a good view of the highest mountains. We flew directly past Makalu and the sub-peak Makalu 2, my first high altitude summit. Makalu 2 rose high into the sky but was still dwarfed by the mother mountain's dramatic main peak. This didn't lessen my sense of achievement, but just emphasised the scale of these mountains at the heart of the Himalaya. That climb was six years ago, and my capabilities as well as my ambitions had risen with the years. West of Makalu was Everest and the dramatic ridges of Lhotse and Nuptse. Looking down to the mountain and the severe wind blowing across the top, I felt very nervous but ready for the challenge.

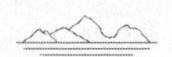

When we touched down in Lhasa it was noticeably colder than Kathmandu. The airport Arrivals terminal was a big, chaotic hall made of concrete. It was so cold inside that it felt like I was in the cool room of a bottle shop, but with piles of huge kitbags and backpacks everywhere rather than slabs of beer and cases of white wine. Already I had a dry throat from a few nights of air-conditioning in the hotel, with the dryness converting itself into soreness. Foolishly, I had not packed a warm jacket in the daypack which was my hand luggage, and I kicked myself for not taking this simple and obvious precaution against catching a chill. Physical condition is such an important part of success on these big mountains. We had barely arrived and already I had played my cards wrongly.

Fortunately, Trynt was able to lend me a fleece jacket, but it soon appeared that the damage had been done. The altitude of 3500 metres did not worry me, but that initial chill, the dry dusty air, my already-sore throat, and probably the build-up of stress quickly bought me down with laryngitis and flu. So much for having boosted my immune system with my short trek.

Luckily, I got on well with Trynt. She was very courteous to me, almost deferential, which made me think that Russell or someone else must have told her about the big mountains I had climbed. I was no Edmund Hillary or Alison Hargreaves, but Trynt respected my climbs for what they were. She saw that high mountains were the domain of men and gave me credit for making headway in that world. This warmed me to her, not because she was boosting my ego but because she was not pulling the 'I'm a film star and therefore more important' gig.

Trynt may have been voted off the Global Extremes team but she was definitely still a star, at least as far as the men around us were concerned. She also fell sick—I don't think it was out of a feeling of sisterhood—and men began appearing out of the woodwork to wish her well. Admittedly she was more melodramatic than I was, vomiting her heart out into the toilet for most of the night, moaning that she was about to die. She was also flirtatious (although not while vomiting), whereas I tended just to stare at men who attempted to be cute—

unless I found them cute as well. But even then, my heart was set on climbing a mountain, and I would not be distracted by anyone, however attractive. I was very clear about that. The first guys who appeared to see Trynt were from the Global Extremes team, which was an encouraging sign that the dynamic between our two groups might prove to be healthy after all. Also knocking at our door were some of the guys from an International Mountain Guides Everest team, also Americans, who were travelling on an itinerary almost parallel to ours.

We had a few days in Lhasa but, rather than rushing around doing the sights, Trynt and I spent most of the time laying low in our room—through necessity, not choice. We made the most of the opportunity to rest up while we could, and we took it in turns to buy drinks and sweets and other comforting items from the shop across the road from the hotel.

Nonetheless, we did manage to get out and see some of Lhasa. One day we went on our own little tour, taking in the Potala Palace and the Jokhang, the main Buddhist cathedral. The Potala Palace was an amazing building, a huge fort-like structure with whitewashed walls. Set as it was on a hilltop, it loomed over downtown Lhasa. I had expected Lhasa to have a very Chinese feel because I had heard there were more Chinese than Tibetans. But there were still plenty of Tibetans, and I was pleased to see that the Tibetan style of architecture was commonplace around the Jokhang. The buildings were made of stone and concrete, but the block-like shapes of the flat-roofed buildings harboured colourful wooden window frames and followed Tibetan design principles, if not construction methods. The authorities were at least being sensitive to this aspect of Tibetan culture, perhaps because of the value it added to the growing tourism industry. It also appeared that the Tibetans had a substantial degree of autonomy when it came to running businesses, although it was obvious that the Chinese were ultimately in charge.

Lhasa was hundreds of kilometres east of the parts of Tibet I had visited by road from Kathmandu on my previous expeditions. I found it very interesting to get a feel for life in the capital, but I was not in the best frame of mind for enjoying it. I had been so determined to do well on this expedition, yet here I was with the flu and a fever, barely able to speak because of the severity of the infection. At least the others did not expect me to contribute because I was obviously very much under the weather. Zeddy's big Cuban cigars, which he insisted on smoking in restaurants, did not help me at all.

Trynt and I were still sick when we left Lhasa. Ahead of us was a three-day drive by Landcruiser to Everest Base Camp. From Lhasa we backtracked along the road we had taken from the airport until we crossed the bridge over the Tsangpo River. Here we turned right and headed upstream away from the airport and east towards the mightiest part of the Himalaya. Further downstream the Tsangpo was renamed the Brahmaputra, but even here in central Tibet it was a mighty river. At first we drove through a landscape of grassy hills which in places were dotted with grazing yaks. After we entered the rain shadow of the Himalaya towards the end of the first day, the grass gave way to endless stony hills and the occasional snow-capped peak. The roads were very dusty. Only in the alluvial flats of the valleys was there greenery—groves of trees, fields of potatoes and other vegetables. Where the valleys were broad enough there were vast fields of wheat. The Tibetans had once grown barley as their sole grain, but the Chinese had forced them to replace it with wheat for export even though it was less suited to the dry, high-altitude climate. For most of the drive the landscape was barren and deserted, yet magnificent in its immensity.

Our first night out of Lhasa was spent in Xigatse, the only other town in Tibet that could be called a city. It took a long day of driving to get there, but on arrival we still had time to walk through the Tashilhunpo monastery, one of the largest in Tibet. It was good to stretch our legs and climb a hillside to the highest part of the monastery, although I was very slow. From here we could look out over Xigatse, which was big and noisy. Unfortunately, the appearance of our hotel was much better than the service provided by it. The showers were not hot—which is an important issue when your next encounter with plumbing is not scheduled for two months—and the food was rather ordinary. A major part of the breakfast was fried peanuts and greasy eggs. The rooms were air-conditioned to fixed Arctic temperatures and the windows were sealed

I do not have the best memories of Xigatse because Trynt and I were still sick. My respiratory ailments were aggravated by the dust of the drive, and Trynt's stomach was still upset. Laura, a trekker travelling with us, brought some drinks and food up to our room, which was very considerate but not of much help to Trynt. Neither of us went to dinner.

Next morning we were on the road again. The two Himex groups formed quite a convoy. As well as our climbing team of seven plus Hermann, and the Global Extremes team of five plus their American climbing guide and seven-person film crew, there were three trekkers who were coming to Base Camp in the hope of trekking to Advance Base Camp, despite its considerable altitude of 6400 metres.

Although there was no particular reason why each of us should sit in the same Landcruiser every day of the drive, this is what eventuated. It was almost as though we had bought assigned seats. I was in a vehicle with Chris Warner, the climbing leader for the Global Extremes team, and Mark Whetu, an accomplished climber and guide who on this trip was working as a high-altitude cameraman.

I had first talked to Chris one-on-one during the drive from the airport to downtown Lhasa. This took well over an hour, much of it travelling upstream beside the Tsangpo River, crossing it on a bridge, then heading back downstream on the northern bank. Chris certainly brought some good credentials to the trip. He had made difficult first ascents across the Himalaya covering mountains in Nepal, India and Tibet as well as in Pakistan's Karakoram. Back in America he ran a business called Earthtreks, which included several indoor climbing gyms, a climbing school with choices of lessons indoors and outdoors, and an international operation which organised guided ascents of mountains all over the world. Chris had been involved with some of the Global Extremes team's activities in the lead-up to their Everest attempt.

When I first met Mark in Kathmandu something about his easy-going Kiwi attitude made me feel we shared a common outlook on life. During the drive across Tibet, Mark revealed his enthusiasm about the film project ahead of him. As well as shooting the Global Extremes team as they climbed, his brief included filming the Toyota 4Runner SUVs, the vehicles that were meant to be carrying the athletes across Tibet to Everest. However, the SUVs had been impounded in China while clearances were arranged, so Mark had to be content with visualising shots as he hung out the window. Nothing missed his eye, and he loved the potential of one particular set of switchbacks, even though we would be well established at Base Camp before the SUVs arrived.

During the three-day drive I learnt more about the Global Extremes project. It was nothing short of remarkable, the inevitable evolution of televised adventure racing. The extravaganza was the brainchild of Outdoor Life Network (OLN), an American cable television network. Global Extremes started out with fifty athletes and adventurers from all over the USA competing in events in Utah and Colorado. This initial stage was the first elimination round when the number of participants was cut down to twelve. The second elimination round was more protracted, taking the chosen twelve to the furthest corners of the earth where they were put through a range of challenges, with an equally wide range of viewing experiences for OLN television audiences.

Trynt had been eliminated at the end of this selection process, leaving five people whom she had grown to know well heading off on a free trip to Everest while she demonstrated her commitment by paying her own way. Of course, the dynamic among the five athletes was different now that they were no longer competing for the prize money and a place on the final team; nonetheless, even though I was fresh on the scene, I could sense some uneasiness among them. I was glad there were a couple more women in the Global Extremes team—not that I was desperate for female company, but I welcomed the change from being the only woman on an expedition. I was also curious to see how they managed themselves, wondering what strategies they had that enabled them to be so highly capable. Endurance athletes are people I respect.

The women were Petit Pinson from California and Colleen Ihnken from Colorado. Along with Colleen, two of the male team members were also from Colorado: Jesse Rickert and Ted Mahon. Colorado is a real focus for mountain sports enthusiasts so the emphasis was not all that surprising. The final member, Troy Henkels, lived in Alaska, which is even more famous for its mountains.

I didn't know what to make of the Global Extremes team. Each of them had certainly proved themselves as athletes. Petit had competed in the 800-mile (1290-kilometre) ELF Authentic Adventure event across Brazil in 2000. Colleen had sailed around the world then taken up adventure racing, with one of her recent events being the ten-day, 400-kilometre Primal Quest race. Perhaps she felt sailing was a bit sedentary. I had once dreamt of circumnavigating the globe so I certainly respected her achievements.

It was easy to discover what Jesse had done because he liked talking. He had climbed all fifty-four of Colorado's 14,000-footers (Americans measure their mountains in feet; the 14,000-footers are peaks over 4267 metres high); he had also climbed Denali and Aconcagua, the highest peaks in North and South America. Ted was a bit quieter, but with a similar track record in the mountains; he too had climbed all of the 14,000-footers and Denali. He worked as a mountain bike guide in the summer and a ski instructor in the winter. Based in Aspen, Colorado, he had the advantage of long-term acclimatisation to the 3000-metre altitude of the ski resort. Troy was certainly the team's expert in cold climates, with eight climbing expeditions in the Alaska Range under his belt, and sixteen months in Antarctica as a member of a search and rescue team. He had climbed in South America as well, but compared to Alaska these experiences would have seemed tropical.

By the time we were on the final drive to Base Camp, I knew more about the Global Extremes team members than I did about the members of my own team. This was fine as I expected that our teams would separate into distinct expeditions once we arrived at Base Camp, and then I would have plenty of time to get to know everyone. In any case, I hadn't joined the expedition for the social experience but because I felt it was the best way for me to get to the top of Mount Everest.

However, it was good to have discovered at least one kindred spirit in Mark Whetu, the Kiwi cameraman. I immediately felt we were on the same wavelength, partly because New Zealanders and Australians share a similar outlook. Mark was a close friend of Russell's, a good climber and an experienced cameraman. I already knew that Mark had been involved in a particularly tragic episode of Everest's history. In 1994 he worked as a cameraman for an expedition led by Eric Simonson, an experienced Everest guide who ran International Mountain Guides. One of the members of this expedition was Michael Rheinberger, an Australian climber from Melbourne, who at age fifty-three was on his seventh expedition to Everest. Mike had declared that this was to be his last expedition to Everest and that he would give it everything he had. Mark climbed with and filmed Mike on his push for the summit.

At their top camp, strong winds pushed back their planned departure time of 1 am to 3.30 am. They headed up in the darkness, with Mike climbing at a very slow pace. Mark found this frustrating because he knew that at this rate their chances of reaching the summit were slim. Dawn arrived but Mike did not speed up. At 12.30 pm other climbers passed them on their way down and they chatted briefly. Mark had set a turn-around time of 1 pm, so he took the example of the other climbers descending to suggest to Mike that they turn back since they had at least four hours of climbing ahead of them to the summit, probably six hours at Mike's slow place. It was obvious to Mark that they would be putting their lives at risk if they continued to the top of the peak because they would have to face the long descent in the dark. Mike refused to turn back. If Mark had tried to drag him down the mountain, in their struggle both of them would have tumbled to their deaths. Mark had no alternative but to stick with Mike. He felt this was his duty as a friend and as a guide, but it was with great foreboding that he continued upwards.

The Australian and the New Zealander reached the summit at 6 pm as the shadows replaced the sun on the summits of the lower peaks surrounding them. The sun then left the summit of Everest as well, and while Mike was too exhausted to feel any euphoria, he suddenly appreciated what Mark had been telling him all afternoon — that they must descend as fast as they could. Unfortunately, Mike had spent all his resources. Mark was only able to force Mike to descend a short distance below the summit before he was overwhelmed by exhaustion. The climbers spent the night out in the open. Mark felt his toes were literally freezing but there was nothing he could do about it. He focused on keeping himself and Mike on the right side of consciousness. At these oxygenless heights, it would be so easy to slip into a sleep from which they would never awake. At first light Mark struggled to get Mike mobile again. He had to push and pull Mike with every step he made. In this fashion they were able to descend, but only to a point 150 metres below the summit. Here Mike collapsed again and Mark wasn't able to get him to move. He radioed Base Camp, where the rest of the team had feared that both climbers had already died.

Close to the summit of Everest, Mark's focus was on saving Mike, but at Base Camp Eric Simonson had a different priority. He believed that if Mike was unable to move then there was no hope for his survival, because he knew Mark would not be strong enough to carry Mike down, even if he had not just spent a night in the open at the top of Mount Everest. As expedition leader, he told Mark to descend to the expedition's cache of oxygen bottles because survival depended on oxygen. He did not mention that the survival he was talking about was Mark's alone. Mark followed the directive and descended the long summit ridge to where the oxygen bottles were stashed. He had counted on there being someone to help him bring the oxygen back up to Mike, but Eric knew that even if Mark was able to re-ascend the ridge in his exhausted state, he would arrive to find Mike already dead. Eric explained this to Mark then ordered him to descend; he was to take an oxygen cylinder for himself and head down the mountain. At first Mark refused, but Eric and the other guides at Base Camp all insisted over the radio that all Mark could do now was try to save himself. He had been above 8300 metres for much too long for his own safety. At last Mark agreed. He shouldered an oxygen bottle and began the long descent to Base Camp.

He reached the glacier at the bottom of the mountain crippled by the frostbite damage to his feet. In the cold light of day, breathing air that was relatively oxygen-rich, Mark accepted that retreat without Mike had been the only sensible option. At a logical level he understood that if he had returned to Mike both of them would have died. At an emotional level it was a different story. Back in New Zealand all of his toes were amputated, and it seemed like he would never climb again. And his position was made worse by the attitude of people who passed judgment while knowing nothing about extreme high altitude, nothing about the intensity of the cold and the desperate challenge of performing any task at those heights, and nothing about how much Mark gave to saving Mike before he was convinced by other teammates that he had to save himself.

Mark had required extraordinary will to survive his ordeal, and even more strength to deal with the aftermath. However, he did go back to climbing mountains and working as a guide, a profession that he loved. *The Fatal Game*, the documentary he helped to film, portrayed some of the hopeless reality that led to Mike Rheinberger's demise. Mike proved himself to be an extraordinarily determined man. In the end, he was a man whose mind was stronger than his body.

These events happened nine years before our expedition to Everest. Meanwhile, Mark had become one of the world's most experienced high altitude cameramen. As well as Mountain Works, the guiding company he operated in New Zealand, he had a great professional relationship with Russell and frequently worked on his expeditions as a guide or cameraman.

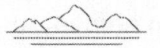

When our travel was interrupted by meal stops, and at other times when we were hanging out together loosely as a group, I was able to learn more about the Global Extremes athletes' ways of doing things just by listening. Exercise and training were their major topics of discussion. This was to be expected given that over the last year they had devoted much of their time to performing at their personal best. It wasn't until Tingri, our final stop before cutting south towards Everest, that Jesse Rickert got around to asking me about myself. My illness had kept me quiet and in the background until Russell ordered Cokes and Sprites for us during a briefing and I drew attention to myself by swapping my Coke for a beer. Not that having a beer is a world-shattering eccentricity, just that it made the Americans realise I had a mind of my own. Trynt had already worked that out.

Tingri was a classic Tibetan roadside stop: houses, shops and a few restaurants lining the main street, which was also the highway from Lhasa to Kathmandu. Grasslands spread towards Cho Oyu in the south, so we spent most of our time looking in that direction. Behind us more grasslands stretched northwards to some lower ranges. From certain places, the peak of Everest could be seen poking up from behind a ridge in the middle distance, closer than we had yet seen it.

The accommodation at Tingri was much more basic than anything we had enjoyed to date. The toilet was a roof top with a view, open to the skies. The rooms where we slept were very small, fitting nothing more than two beds with a narrow space between them. Outside the rooms was a dusty courtyard, and the wall opposite housed the toilet block, the hotelier's quarters and the restaurant. The courtyard design gave some protection from the winds that regularly lashed the floodplain where the village was situated. It was comfortable enough, the basic nature useful as a psychological transition between the hotels we had been staying in and the deprivations of Base Camp. Russell and the Sherpas had travelled ahead a few days earlier to set up Base Camp, and while I knew there would be all sorts of luxuries that I had never experienced on an expedition before—the most obvious a being heated mess tent and reputedly hot showers—I also knew that nothing could be done to lessen the unpleasantness of the altitude, the bitter cold and the ravages of the strong, dusty wind.

We spent two days at Tingri, adding to our acclimatisation, and the time there was fun. We had good views of Everest, where a gale was blowing from the top. I spent one day on my own, acclimatising high up on a hill, and looking in wonder at Everest and Cho Oyu. I valued the opportunity to do this as it cleared my head and clarified my resolve about what I was here to achieve.

The next day was the final leg of the drive to Base Camp. Our convoy of vehicles made the slow zigzag up to the Pang La Pass. Awaiting us was a stunning panorama of the world's highest mountains—Cho Oyu, Gyachung Kang, Makalu—with Everest as the centrepiece. The sky was clear but clouds streamed from the summits of the peaks. From this viewpoint, Everest presented a dramatic silhouette and set off ripples of excitement amongst us. At the same time it was a sobering experience, because prominent in our minds were the dangers of climbing this magnificent mountain. We bundled back into our vehicles with some more real issues to think about.

It was a long descent to the alluvial flats below the pass, and the final drive up the valley seemed interminable. At last we had our first close-up view of the north side of Everest. For most of us, it was the first close-up view of the mountain from any direction. We pulled to a halt at Rongbuk monastery for some photos. This Tibetan Buddhist monastery had been almost totally destroyed during the Chinese Cultural Revolution, but over the last two decades it had been restored and expanded. Beyond it rose the huge North Face of Everest, and we watched the wind blowing snow off the long North Ridge, although still more than twenty kilometres away.

On every mountain they climb, the Sherpas always seek a blessing through a special ceremony given by a Tibetan Buddhist monk. If no monks are available, then the most devout of the Sherpas will officiate. Our *sirdar*, Purba, had already obtained blessings in advance from the Rinpoche (Abbot) of Rongbuk monastery, who lives in Kathmandu where there are greater religious freedoms than in Tibet. But there was no harm in on-the-spot reinforcement. A ceremony would still take place at Base Camp, with four or five lamas making the short journey up for the occasion. On the Nepalese side of Everest, expeditions would be receiving their blessing from the Rinpoche of Tengboche monastery, where I had been on my trek only two weeks earlier. Already that journey felt a long way away, even though Tengboche was just across the glaciated border to the south. The border between Nepal and Tibet runs up the East Ridge of Lhotse (Everest's South Peak), over the summit of Everest and down the West Ridge before continuing westwards across the spine of the Himalaya to Cho Oyu and beyond.

A few more kilometres in the Landcruisers brought us to Base Camp. It was quite an amazing scene. The road ended at a spring where there was a small area of green grass. On the up-valley side of the spring was a low rocky knoll, where a simple, low concrete-block building sat. This was the Tibetan Mountaineering Association office, the administrative headquarters for Base Camp. A rough track continued past the knoll on to the rocky alluvial flats which spread down the valley from the end of the Rongbuk Glacier. The beginnings of this track were flanked by a shantytown of tents, housing a motley collection of bars and restaurants. Actually, it was more of a lane than a town, but 'shantytown' sums up its atmosphere. Little did I realise how much time I would be spending here, taking a break from the tensions of our camp.

But today we were all excited. We drove past the tents, then hung on tight as the vehicles bounced and lurched across the river rocks to the flat area where Russell had established our camp. It was an impressive sight, nestled up close to the terminal moraines of the Rongbuk Glacier. Everything was set up when we arrived, with welcome drinks waiting for us. At the centre of things was the mess tent and the cook tent, with other largish tents for storage, medical needs and communications. Our sleeping tents were lined up in orderly fashion a short distance away—one person per tent, which was how I liked it. Of course, we would share tents on the mountain, but when resting it was healthy to have plenty of personal space. The Global Extremes camp was only a few minutes walk from ours, and their setup was even more elaborate, with a prefabricated hut as a recording studio, plus all our facilities duplicated.

We arrived at Base Camp on 7 April and the next day our *puja* blessing ceremony was held. Tibetan Buddhist prayers were chanted, lamps of yak butter were lit, and juniper was burnt as incense on the purpose-built stone *chorten* (altar). The chanting continued as the Sherpas positioned their ice axes and boots on the *chorten* so that they were blessed by the ceremonial juniper smoke. Some of us got into the spirit of things, dashing to our tents to get items of climbing gear, figuring that help of every kind should be embraced for an ascent of Mount Everest. I was familiar with this tradition from my other climbs, but it was still an exciting time, effectively the official start of the expedition as far as the Sherpas were concerned. This was a particularly important day on this expedition because the Sherpas were destined to play a huge role. On my other climbs I had taken an equal part in leadership with Nima and Pasang, perhaps even a stronger role at times, but on Everest I was happy to climb in the wake of the experts.

Many other expeditions had set up camps nearby, or were in the process of setting them up. Wherever possible, groups made use of any hillock or rock pile as a windbreak. Tents of every colour and shape were set in clusters across the landscape, and the expeditions ranged from those with the full bells and whistles (such as ours) to budget outfits that looked like they would be taken out by the first storm. It was quite an extraordinary sight, like a scouting jamboree that had somehow been transplanted to a bleak mountain landscape.

We spent the following week at Base Camp, getting ourselves and our equipment organised and taking a few acclimatisation hikes organised by our guide, Hermann Berie. I did not participate in these walks at first; as well as still being smitten by the flu, I was now suffering the added indignity of diarrhoea. I was quite happy to take things extremely easy during those first few days. I went on short walks to places that offered good views. One of these was the rocky knoll above the shantytown, where there was a memorial to George Mallory. It was a great place to sit and admire Everest at the head of the valley. The western flanks of the Rongbuk Valley were lined by 6000 metre-high peaks, most of them with steep scree slopes leading up to rocky bluffs and topped by summits of snow and ice. The eastern skyline was a craggy ridge of orange and yellow rock linking jagged peaks that were not high by the standards set by the mountains around us. Nevertheless, traversing the crest looked like it would be harder than Everest itself because there were so many clefts, pinnacles and buttresses that appeared insurmountable. A few kilometres up the valley from Base

Camp, this ridge finished at the gorge which drained the East Rongbuk Glacier. Beyond the gorge another ridge continued upwards, subpeak after subpeak, culminating in Changtse, the West Peak of Everest. Although we could not see beyond Changste, I knew that the ridge dipped down to the North Col. Beyond the col rose Everest's famous North Ridge, the route that all of the many expeditions here this season would be climbing.

The sight of nineteen separate Base Camps set out across the alluvial flats certainly got me thinking about the reality of mountaineering on Everest. This season was the fiftieth anniversary of the first ascent by the British expedition that put Hillary and Tenzing on the summit in 1953. Big celebrations were planned in Kathmandu, with Sir Edmund and other illustrious mountaineers in attendance. My friends at World Expeditions had organised a celebration in Nepal closer to the mountain, at Tengboche monastery. Seven trekking groups would converge there for a big party on 29 May, the date of the first ascent. Peter Hillary was to be MC at Tengboche with a satellite phone link to his father in Kathmandu. I fantasised that I might climb the mountain in May—in 1993 fellow Australian Michael Groom had reached the summit on 10 May—in which case I'd have time to scamper back to Kathmandu, fly to Lukla, dash up the valley to Tengboche and celebrate with my friends. Personally I would be celebrating more than just the fiftieth anniversary, and it would be a perfect place to party. But at this stage these were idle thoughts. I needed to focus on getting well and on marshalling my strength.

The upcoming fiftieth anniversary had been seen by many climbers as the perfect time to mount an expedition, which is why there were so many teams here. The anniversary might have helped some teams pull in a few extra sponsorship dollars, but as far as I was concerned, pre-monsoon 2003 was just when the timing proved to be right for me. Among the many expeditions, one that I found particularly interesting was a small American team of only four climbers. These were John Roskelley—a legendary mountaineer who had last attempted the mountain in the 1980s—climbing with his twenty-year-old son Jess.

They were accompanied by two other legends: Jim Wickwire, the first American to climb K2, and Dick Bass, the first person to complete the Seven Summits. At the other end of the scale was a huge Chinese expedition, reputedly with over one hundred people, including a press contingent and a bevy of scientists. The Chinese intended to make a live broadcast from the top of Everest, an aim that clashed with Global Extremes' plans to make a live cross from the summit. This issue created a political minefield that Russell had to deal with for most of the trip. The Chinese expedition was sponsored by a telecommunications company, with the managing director planning to send text messages from the summit and, while he was up there, find the time to play an electronic game on his phone with an associate at Base Camp. This was an unusual goal, and it made me think that, if nothing else, this was going to be a very interesting couple of months. With nineteen expeditions attempting the same route on the same mountain, 'interesting' would probably be the least of it.

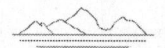

After a few days at Base Camp I felt well enough to cope with one of Hermann's day hikes. Also joining us were two of the support trekkers, Laura and Andy, who were good energy and fun to be with. 'Support trekkers' in the Himalayan Experience context were people who tagged along with the expedition, with their destination either Advance Base Camp or the North Col, the latter being a much more formidable objective. Traditionally, support treks were a way of raising funds for an expedition — if each member of the climbing team invited a few friends, and if each trekker was charged a margin above costs for the trip, the combined total could make a significant contribution to the expedition's budget. In the case of Himex support treks, the contributions were to Russell's budget, adding to this once-a-year extravaganza he operated.

My first acclimatisation hike went well, although we did not go far. The same was not true on a longer walk in the direction of Interim Camp, the next stage up the hill, and back. Altitude was a real and dangerous issue here. Having only recently arrived at 5000 metres, several people found the effects still quite severe, particularly the beginner trekkers with their limited experience. The weather was also quite bad, which meant it was very cold. On top of this, the lunch we were given to take with us was all wrong. There was a huge packet of dry biscuits for each of us, with nothing to put on them, a Snickers bar, and some fruit and nuts. Most of these foods were hard to digest and were the opposite of thirst quenching. Laura was allergic to nuts, which limited her options. I suggested people make cheese, peanut butter and jam sandwiches from the mess tent breakfast leftovers and add some Tang to one of their drinks for an energy boost. I knew the altitude would wear them out and that even the downhill walk back would take more out of them than they expected.

As the guide, Hermann needed, at the very least, to be aware of everyone's physical and mental state. I was shocked when he marched off with a couple of the group half a step behind him, scarcely looking back to see how the rest of us we were doing. From this I knew straight away that I was going to have problems with his approach to guiding. As time went on, it became obvious to me that he had a rather dictatorial leadership style, which I put down to his straight-to-the-point Germanic manner. The ramifications of this may not have shown themselves to the others, but as a guide myself I knew it was going to be a problem for me because I was determined to make my own decisions. A certain level of independence was a matter that I had agreed upon with Russell before I booked my place on the trip. However, Russell had had very little to do with us since we had arrived at Base Camp because he had been focusing on the complexities of the Global Extremes telecast. These problems proved unresolvable at Base Camp, which left him with no alternative but to make the long journey back to Lhasa. My response to his absence was to pull into my shell and concentrate on doing what I had to do, which was to get myself well and fit.

I was very comfortable in my own company, which helped. Trynt and I were getting along well, Tony was a friendly and helpful character, and Matt and I enjoyed strolling across to the shantytown to have a couple of beers and a change of scene. Gernot and I shared a passion for photography and we discussed ways of dealing with the extreme cold up high and other such matters. Dinners in the mess tent became a bit oppressive as Zeddy always took the position of Master of Ceremonies, choosing to direct the flow of conversation. I hoped that he was trying to make us all feel at home and comfortable as a group, though his approach was not the one I would have taken.

On 15 April, Chung, Tony, Zeddy and Matt felt ready to move up with Hermann to Interim Camp. Andy and Laura went with them, their ultimate goal being to reach Advance Base Camp. Interim Camp lay eleven kilometres up the East Rongbuk Valley, halfway to Advance Base. Two days after the first group set off, I followed with Trynt, Gernot and two newly arrived trekkers, Sissell and Françoise. Russell met both these women in Chamonix, where he operated an alpine guiding company called Chamonix Experience during the northern summer. The weather had been bad during our day trips, windy with horizontal sleet and very cold, but it was kinder on our walk up to Interim Camp. The camp itself was relatively basic, with accommodation being a large hoop tent with enough room to sleep ten people. Stationed at the camp during this stage of the expedition was a Sherpa with a VHS radio whose job it was to keep track of lost souls wandering the glaciers, and to monitor the progress of the yaks and yak herders who were delivering vital loads.

Although I did not feel at my best, it was good to be moving upwards at last. The twenty-two-kilometre haul from Base Camp to Advance Base Camp (ABC) was certainly hard work, though I knew it would get easier as I became better acclimatised. Nevertheless, I planned to keep the journeys to a minimum. After spending the night at Interim Camp we all made it to ABC the next day. These were hard days for me, hard but good. I deliberately carried a heavy pack of twenty kilograms, believing that a couple of tough days were in order to knock me into shape. I set as fast a pace as I could manage. This was not racing by any means—now that we were above 6000 metres, the lack of oxygen was apparent with every step I took. The views were spectacular, and it was a great feeling to be moving up the rock and ice of a glacier surrounded by mountains. Everything else to this point had been part of the build-up to the climb, but now I felt that plodding up one of Everest's major glaciers towards the great mountain was the real beginning. Everest loomed huge in front of us as we turned the final bend of the glacier. The glacier itself opened out into a huge névé, or snow basin, the scale entirely appropriate to the highest mountain on Earth.

Meanwhile, on that same day, 18 April, Tony, Matt and Chung had taken a gentle hike with Hermann up to Crampon Point, the place where the glacial terrain became ice alone, and hence more serious, so crampons were required. In the mess tent that night there was a feeling of progress being made, which lifted everyone's spirits. Zeddy started talking about his push for the summit, although that was a bit out of sequence as far as I was concerned.

The next two days were rest days for all of us. The second day had been slated as the day for our first climb up to the North Col, but the weather had other ideas. A snowstorm driven by strong winds hit the camp, destroying some tents belonging to other expeditions. I thought, *Welcome to the world's biggest mountain, and remember what the real source of power is in this inhospitable place.* The views were spectacular when the storm lifted. Extreme winds continued to rage above 7000 metres, judging by the snow trails blown from the summits of the peaks around us. Most spectacular of all was Everest.

At lunch and dinnertime on both rest days, Zeddy again instigated discussions about the summit bid. Gernot participated enthusiastically, and the two of them asked Hermann's opinion about the sequence of events, even though this was Hermann's first trip to Everest and he had not yet set foot on the mountain. Zeddy and Gernot had it all worked out on the first evening. As there was a full moon on 15 or 16 May, they decided that this would be the time for us to take our shot at the summit. They planned the minor details, then went over it all again. Imagination filled the gaps in their plan—a sure sign to me that the plan was useless because mountains cannot be climbed by supposition. Their fixation with the summit day was bad enough the first night, but it became infuriating on the second and every subsequent day. It seemed to me like planning how you were going to spend the million dollars you were going to win in the lottery—a passably interesting exercise the first time around, but totally boring every subsequent time. If we were to climb Everest it would be when conditions were right, not because we had made up our minds about the best date to do so. Gernot doggedly outlined his theories of probability and how they affected achieving the summit. From his perspective we had fallen behind the trip schedule, and the Global Extremes team was ahead of us in their acclimatisation. He refused to acknowledge any other viewpoint.

I felt I had to say something. 'I don't think the mountain is listening to us, Gernot.'

He shook his head to himself as if to say I just did not get it, which was true enough.

'It's early days yet,' I said. 'Once we've spent some time on the mountain and started climbing, it will be obvious what kind of progress we can make. By that stage we'll know who will link with whom, and how much time we'll need. At the moment we're not in a position to make a plan because we haven't been anywhere, and we don't know who's going to be fast and who's going to be slow. We haven't even left ABC.'

In response I was effectively told to shut up. As far as Zeddy and Gernot were concerned, they could discuss whatever they chose to discuss, particularly when it had to do with Mount Everest, because they were paying clients, and that was why we were all here.

Tony, the diplomat, attempted to calm things down. 'I think that what Sue is trying to say is ——'

'Thanks Tony,' I interrupted, 'but I don't need you to explain what I've just said. If they can't handle it, they shouldn't be on Mount Everest.'

This at least restored silence, though it was not a comfortable one.

During all of this carry on, Matt listened but chose not to give his point of view. Later he privately confided that his views matched mine. Trynt ignored the conversation. Chung remained a self-contained Asian gentleman throughout. I sensed that as far as he was concerned the argument was nothing more than an episode of *Days of Our Lives* playing in the background.

As I saw it, we only had second-hand accounts of the terrain ahead of us, so it was impossible to plan our summit attempt with the precision that was suggested during our dinnertime discussions. We had not even been to the North Col yet. However, this continued to be the dominant topic of conversation. Sometimes this included talking about the trip notes that had been handed out to us, outlining the expedition. The theme of this discussion was how the realities of our climb had already varied from the notes, and how likely they were to vary further down the track. As leader, Hermann should have been able to knock this one on the head by stating the obvious: that every expedition was different, that the variables were huge, and that the trip notes were an overview, not a master plan. Instead, he allowed himself to get embroiled in arguments over details, and unfortunately the rest of us had to listen because the mess tent was the only place that was heated. We could have retired to our own personal sleeping tents, but the temperatures in the evening in the early spring made this option decidedly uninviting.

At the same time, I gathered from Mark that tensions were building over in the Global Extremes camp too. So I guessed this was just how the game panned out on commercial Everest expeditions, where the participants were separated from the mountain and had too much time on their hands because the Sherpas were doing all the work.

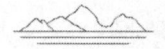

The interlude of biding our time at ABC came to an end when Hermann announced we would make our first climb up to the North Col, a day trip for acclimatisation. It was 22 April and the weather was good. It was about fifty minutes hike up to Crampon Point where our climbing equipment was stored in large, weatherproof plastic barrels. I couldn't summon much energy so I walked slowly. When I reached Crampon Point, Hermann was beginning to empty the harnesses from a barrel.

He held one up, and said, 'Who owns this old-fashioned red harness?'

It was mine.

He held it higher and repeated the question.

I said nothing. It was a perfectly functional Australian-made Vertecal brand harness. Just because I was climbing Everest, I didn't have to outfit myself like I'd just stepped out of a mountaineering equipment shop. I liked my harness and knew it was safe, and that was all that mattered.

Hermann asked a third time, obviously attempting to be funny. Nobody laughed. Still I said nothing. Trynt, Tony and Matt knew it was mine but did not comment. Eventually Hermann put the harness to one side and continued to pass out the other harnesses.

It was a minor incident, but it contributed to my decision shortly afterwards to head back to Advance Base. The others had already set off up the glacier when I walked over to put on my harness. I started to follow them at the tail end of the group, but with low energy and Hermann's petty display, I quickly decided that I could not be bothered and turned back.

I was also influenced by the fact that Hermann insisted we follow a particular procedure, one that would make us look like total novices to the other teams nearby. He instructed us categorically that we would not walk on the glacier without being roped up. Ropes traditionally link climbers together on glaciers to safeguard against crevasses. But this was an inappropriate call for the glacier above ABC, where the ice was old and stable, with no crust of snow obscuring deep chasms. There were no serious crevasses to fall into; all we needed were crampons. No one challenged Hermann's call on this, but they must have felt stupid when everyone else was simply walking straight out there on their own. Our team looked like a kiddies' party with its chaperone. Hermann never conceded that this decision was an error of judgment; he just turned a blind eye and kept going. I hoped this would not be the style of his judgment calls on the mountain. At this stage he did not seem to appreciate the severity of what lay ahead, and that all climbers would have to make these kinds of calls for themselves. Safety precautions are vital, of course, but when they are inappropriate they waste precious time and energy. Fast climbing is frequently the safest method, giving less exposure to avalanche zones and the best escape from approaching storms.

That night at dinner, after the team returned exhausted but elated, I heard about their climb. I was now wistful about not having participated, but I told myself that my time would come. Others were wondering about my plans as well. During our stay at Advance Base Camp, I had become quite friendly with Sissell. She and Françoise had just achieved their goal of climbing to the North Col, and at dinner she asked me the logical question: 'Sue, what are you going to do?'

'Oh, I think I might go to the North Col tomorrow,' I said. 'I haven't been up there yet.'

Immediately Hermann interrupted. 'Forget it, Sue. Forget it. You're not going.'

A stony silence followed. I could tell there was no point arguing because the argument would lead nowhere, and the others would probably side with him. We had completely different mentalities. He was accustomed to a very autocratic style of leadership, but I didn't play ball that way, and he just did not know what to make of it. He had never asked me anything about my capabilities or my achievements, yet he was giving me such an uncompromising order.

I went outside to get some space. *Man, I'm on the wrong trip here,* I thought.

Sissell came out as well and we talked. I had been holding back my tears, feeling very alone, so having her interest and support made a huge difference to me. She produced her VSOP Cognac and we drank some, a very generous gesture as we had more than a cap-full. It was the best medicine. I went to bed feeling much better knowing I had Sissell's support. But my problem was still not solved, and my thoughts went to home and all the hopes I had, to my father and my friends. I was definitely off track with my dream, and that was when I cried a little.

The tears were a release, and afterwards I saw that I had to find a sensible solution and get on with it. I was not going to walk away from this deadlock. I asked myself some questions: What is winning? Winning is reaching the summit and doing it safely. So how am I going to do that? I have to overrule the decisions Hermann makes about what I can and cannot do.

I decided there was no point getting into an argument and wasting energy on a useless discussion. Forward progress was what I needed, and that meant calling Russell on the radio the next morning. I knew I had missed out on the vital acclimatisation step of a day trip to the North Col, and if I didn't complete this part of the acclimatisation process I would slip behind schedule—which, when you put all the pieces together, meant I would miss my chance to make a summit bid.

First thing in the morning I went to the communications tent and said that I needed to speak with Russell, who was now back at Base Camp. I was getting on well with the Sherpas now, so this was no problem. The comms tent was close to the mess tent, so if someone wanted to listen to what you were saying it was not at all difficult. In fact, sometimes it was difficult *not* to listen if reception was bad and people were raising their voices. I was aware that I needed to express myself diplomatically.

I called Russell and said. 'Look, I haven't been to the North Col yet—everyone else has—and I don't want to come back down until I do. I don't want to slip behind in the acclimatisation schedule. I'll make a day trip up by myself, then I'll come down and I won't take any unnecessary risks. You know I've done my other expeditions safely. And I did speak to you at the beginning of the trip about being fairly self-reliant in making my schedule.'

Russell did not even discuss it. He said, 'Just take a walkie-talkie and ring at the radio scheds, which are 8 am, 1 pm, 6 pm.'

I knew there were people nearby, maybe just standing around, maybe just enjoying the gossip, so I was keen to finish the call. I added that Hermann was being obstructive by not allowing me to make my schedule, which I needed to do to progress towards the summit. 'It's been very difficult for me,' I remarked finally, 'and I'd like to report to Chris from now on, in your absence.'

Again Russell agreed without question. Towards the end of the conversation I heard Hermann's voice outside: 'Hah! What is Sue doing? She is speaking to Russell. Oh!'

When I stepped out of the comms tent there was no sign of Hermann, and I assumed he knew that something was wrong. The first thing I did was walk over to the Global Extremes camp, which took about five minutes, and found Chris. 'I've been talking with Russell, and I've come to say that from now on I'm reporting to you, not Hermann,' I said.

Chris looked at me for a moment, putting things together, then said, 'That's fine.' I knew from the way he spoke that he appreciated my predicament. I thanked him and said I was just about to head up to the North Col. I left without even looking for Hermann.

I had the most fantastic day trip. I was moving really well, feeling strong at last. The view from the North Col was spectacular. Just having a change in perspective from the views at ABC was great. The weather was marginal at the Col so I headed down almost straight away, calling in on the radio at 1 pm to say I was on my way back down and that all was well. I felt truly liberated. For weeks I had been feeling like a square peg and trying to tell myself that I could fit in. Now I knew I could do my own thing and do it well and safely. For me, this was it. The path to the summit of Everest was now open.

6

SHAKEN, NOT STIRRED

Prior to Mount Everest, and aside from the relatively straightforward trekking peaks she had guided for World Expeditions, Sue had been the leader, the troubleshooter and the person with whom the buck stopped on all of her Himalayan mountaineering expeditions. She had also been the instigator of every climb, which meant she planned every stage of each expedition. Definitely, there was satisfaction in successfully managing such complicated and dangerous undertakings, but at the same time the huge amounts of stress involved often undermined her health. On Everest in particular Sue did not want to compromise her physical and mental well-being. The mighty peak was 600 metres higher than Cho Oyu, her highest summit to date, and the immense effort and commitment required to climb in the oxygen-deprived air above 8000 metres meant that those extra 600 metres boosted Everest into a league of its own.

On Everest Sue did not want to be distracted by peripheral events that had no direct influence upon her ascent. She wanted nothing to do with logistical headaches or with offering emotional support to her teammates. Sue knew that for this climb she could not afford to dissipate her energy or lose her focus because she had taken on a role of counselling and encouraging her fellow climbers. Everest had not turned her cold-hearted; she simply wanted to focus single-mindedly on the climb.

The reason she joined Russell Brice's Himalayan Experience expedition was that she saw this as the best way to give herself the particular freedoms she required for Everest. And she had witnessed the success of Russell's approach on Cho Oyu when she had climbed that mountain from Tibet. During that expedition she had liked Russell's attitude towards his clients and the Sherpas who worked for him. As a guide herself, Sue knew the fundamental importance of having a good relationship with everyone on the climbing team — participants, Sherpas and other local staff.

However, by the time Sue arrived at Base Camp on 12 April 2003, she realised that her vision for her Everest experience was not matching the reality. She was not in good health, and it was clear to her that some of her expectations of the expedition would not be met immediately — and perhaps would not be met at all. The infrastructure and Sherpa support were there, but Sue could not ignore the fact that Russell was not about. In his place was Hermann Berie. The German guide had a formidable résumé of climbs, including the infamous North Face of the Eiger, and enjoyed a good reputation as a guide in the European Alps. He was registered with the UIAGM, the world's premier mountain guiding organisation. But he had never set foot on Everest. His lack of experience at extreme altitude may not have been a problem if Russell had been nearby to crosscheck on aspects of guiding the world's highest mountain. No doubt this had been Russell's plan. But the complications with the Global Extremes team took him out of the picture for the first stages of the expedition. During this period of Russell's absence unfortunate team dynamics developed, and the outward expression of this disharmony often took the form of clashes between Hermann and Sue.

The problems with Global Extremes did not relate to the athletes themselves but to the fact that their expedition seemed to create a bureaucratic nightmare wherever they touched down. The issues related to commitments made back in the USA by the Outdoor Life Network, the cable channel behind the Global Extremes concept. One of these commitments was that live broadcasts would be made from Base Camp, from the summit and from elsewhere on the mountain. The other commitment concerned a sponsorship agreement with Toyota USA, whereby

Toyota 4Runner SUVs would appear in the program's broadcast from Tibet. Because the Chinese authorities had their own ideas about both these matters, they became headaches that kept Russell preoccupied during the early weeks of the season.

Initially, Sue positioned herself in the background, aware that there was nothing she could do to solve the Global Extremes problem, and confident that Russell would return to the Himex team before any serious climbing took place. However, some of the other team members felt that the Global Extremes expedition was being given preferential treatment, and that this would affect their own summit chances. Unlike Sue, they could not see that these were the earliest days of the climb, and it was not surprising that such a logistically complex film expedition was encountering difficulties.

Meanwhile, with Russell out of the picture, it appeared that Hermann Berie was all at sea over the immensity of the project before him. His authoritarian style as a guide was a common approach in Europe and one readily accepted by clients there. Yet he could not speak authoritatively about the climb of Everest because he was no better informed about the mountain than the team members themselves. In fact, three of the team had climbed to significant heights on Everest during previous expeditions with Himalayan Experience. This scenario must have created a difficult situation for Hermann. His approach to the problem was to compartmentalise the running of the expedition, dealing with each day as it came and focusing on the micro issues. Perhaps he hoped that Russell would return with guidance before he had to implement the plan for the overall climb.

This tactic made Sue unhappy because of the activities she was expected to participate in. She felt she was being treated like one of the trekkers on the trips she had been guiding for the last ten years. She was at home with the realities of Base Camp, with the cold, the dust and the need to acclimatise. She did not need to be told how to walk on a glacier. She wanted to be able to acclimatise in her own way at her own speed, and spend time by herself focusing her motivation and strengthening herself for the dangers and other challenges ahead.

However, Hermann wanted her to participate in all group activities. Initially, Sue avoided confrontation by stating that she was not feeling well, which was true enough. She was regularly late for breakfast on the premise that if she slept for a few extra hours she might recover more quickly. But even when Sue gave feedback about her health and how she would manage it, she was ignored. Similarly, when she expressed her own opinions and beliefs about the expedition, Hermann's usual response was to talk over her.

Sue was accustomed to men underrating her because she was a woman. In this case, where the relationship between guide and client was a professional one, she felt Hermann had a responsibility to consider her mountaineering achievements before making judgments. She presumed he had not read her climbing résumé, which Russell had on file. His comments indicated either ignorance about her experience or denial of the fact that a woman could have achieved so much without having been guided or led by men.

Much later, Trynt told her that the group had bet on who would get together with whom and had decided that Hermann and Sue would definitely be an item. The perception was that when the sparks were flying between them it was an expression of URST — unresolved sexual tension. The expectation was that the emotions running hot would lead to a sexual catharsis, after which the group dynamics would settle down and everyone would be happy. Sue was stunned to hear this theory because nothing was less likely as far as she was concerned. She thought everyone had spent too much of their lives watching soap operas.

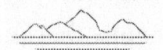

After Hermann's mockery of Sue's well-used Australian-made harness and her decision not to climb up to the North Col with everyone else, his strongly worded veto of her planned solo ascent the following day, based on his uncompromising position on safety procedures, was all that was required to spark Sue into rebellion. She called up Russell at Base Camp, who empowered her to make her own decisions and to sidestep Hermann by being answerable to Global Extremes climbing leader Chris Warner. Thereafter the expedition took a different shape. She accomplished her solo climb up to the North Col and was invigorated by finally getting to grips with the mountain.

Although Sue was now making her own decisions, she was still part of the team when it came to logistics. Three days later, on 26 April, she headed up the mountain again with the rest of the team. The aim was to climb from Advance Base Camp beyond the North Col to Camp Two at 7500 metres and to spend at least one night there to trigger the next level of acclimatisation. The brief at the outset from Russell, via Hermann, was that to have a real chance at the summit it was necessary to have gone above Camp Two on the North Ridge almost to Camp Three.

The night at the Col was uneventful apart from a few altitude-induced headaches. Sue was in good spirits until Hermann's morning briefing when he stated that everyone should wear their down suits to go on to Camp Two. On other mountains, Sue had climbed to well above 7000 metres without a down suit and had not thought to bring hers up to the Col. But here everyone except Sue had brought their suits and was now wearing them. In her absence on her solo sortie, Hermann had explained to everyone else that the wind chill factor produced extremely cold conditions on the exposed and windy North Ridge and that the suits would be needed.

Sue was furious. 'In all the discussions we've had no one raised this point,' she said. 'No one.'

'There's no way you're going up,' Hermann replied. 'What a stupid thing to do. You are a guide.'

Sue felt humiliated and angry. Several other teams were readying themselves to head up the mountain and no one was watching, but everyone was listening. Sue did not like being called stupid, and she felt that Hermann had failed in his duty of care. No doubt he felt that Sue had conveyed to him that she knew what she was doing, that she knew what to expect on the mountain, and yet now, despite this, she wanted to blame him.

She controlled her anger and said calmly, 'Good guiding is about mutual trust and respect. You haven't been clear with me—I don't know whether that's deliberate—but if we are going to work well together on the mountain, there needs to be clear communication and mutual respect and trust.'

Hermann made no comment, and this exchange was the last real conversation between them for the remainder of the expedition. Hermann led the rest of the team up the slopes towards Camp Two. Sue headed back down to Advance Base Camp. Although she remained outwardly calm, inwardly she was seething. Acclimatisation was so important, and missing out on the climb to Camp Two was a huge blow. Initially she blamed Hermann, but ultimately she knew it was her responsibility to organise herself for each section of the climb.

Up on the North Ridge, the Himex climbers struggled against the effects of altitude as they slogged up the easy-angled slope. As Hermann had predicted, the wind kept the temperature very cold. Despite this, the sun shone warm enough to soften the snow, which made clambering through it hard work. Blue skies gave way to clouds and heavy snow fell as the last of the climbers staggered into Camp Two. The tents had already been set up by the Sherpas so the climbers had nothing to do but make themselves comfortable—enough of a task at 7500 metres—and prepare drinks and meals. The wind was blowing more strongly the next day and it was certainly not an ideal day for climbing. Trynt, Zeddy and Chung decided that staying overnight at 7500 metres was all they wanted from their first climb to Camp Two, and they began the long descent to Advance Base Camp. This left only Gernot, Matt and Tony to brave the conditions and follow Hermann up to 7700 metres, a struggle they undertook to stimulate an extra acclimatisation response. By late afternoon the entire team was safely back at Advance Base Camp with Sue.

The returning climbers were all in good spirits, pleased with what they had achieved. After a day's rest, their next move was to descend to Base Camp until it was time to make the summit push. Eager to get her preparation back on track with the others', Sue had spent 29 April climbing up to the North Col in dubious weather. She carried a heavy pack, as this time she certainly was not going to be short of gear. The next morning, as the rest of the team set off back to Base Camp, she decided to head up to Camp Two despite turbulent weather. There were fixed ropes most of the way up the long snowy ridge to Camp Two so she felt quite safe.

It was a long climb and her down suit proved indispensable. Purba and some of his crew were at Camp Two stockpiling oxygen and tents for Camps Three and Four. She could see that they were keeping a quiet eye on her, which was reassuring. When they worked out that she was capable of looking after herself and was not a rescue waiting to happen—a scenario they had encountered too many times in the past—they paid her less attention and focused on their work.

Sue was self-reliant, but she never pretended to be Superwoman. She diligently fulfilled her commitment to Russell that she would call in at every rostered radio sched. Snow had fallen overnight which meant there was no question in her mind about heading further up the mountain that day. Her first night at the significantly higher altitude of 7500 metres was restless and uncomfortable, but Sue had expected this. There was a temptation to descend in the morning to avoid another bad night, and she could have used the bad weather to justify this course of action. However, she decided to spend a second night at Camp Two, recognising that this would help strengthen her ability to deal with the more extreme altitudes still to come. She wanted to compensate for the lateness of her first climb to Camp Two.

While Sue was there she could not believe the ease with which the Sherpas ran up to Camps Three and Four and beyond to deliver huge loads of oxygen and ropes, and then ran back down to Camp Two where she was. They arrived in a remarkably good frame of mind, pleasant, courteous and focused, and no doubt checking on Sue to make sure she was in good shape.

The next day, 2 May, the weather was still marginal, so Sue decided to head down. Before she did so, she attempted to dig out the tents that had been buried by the recent snowfalls rather than leaving the task entirely to the Sherpas. However, she found that her efforts were ineffectual because her muscles and lungs were not coping with the shortage of oxygen. She was not dispirited because she knew this was just part of the acclimatisation process. Past experience told her that tasks would get easier with each climb up to this height; each time she came up and spent a night at this altitude, her body would become more adjusted to the low levels of oxygen in the air. She left the snow shovelling job to the Sherpas, then heeded the advice that Russell had given her over the radio from Base Camp: 'Just come down.'

Sue arrived back at Advance Base Camp tired but satisfied. She needed to return to Base Camp where she would recuperate more quickly. The 1400-metre height difference meant a significant increase in atmospheric oxygen at Base Camp, so it was definitely worth the twenty-two-kilometre hike. But first she felt that she needed a rest day. Sue spent 3 May relaxing, and in good spirits. Not only had she done her first climbing on the legendary slopes of Mount Everest, but in doing so she had made real progress with her acclimatisation.

Also in residence at ABC from the Himex entourage was Pete Whittaker. With an ascent of Everest already under his belt, Pete was with Global Extremes as a celebrity commentator for the Global Extremes broadcasts, sharing this role with Conrad Anker, who was famous for finding George Leigh Mallory's body on Everest in 1999, and for surviving the avalanche on Shishapangma which killed accomplished American climbers Alex Lowe and Dave Bridges later the same year. Sue got along well with Pete, who was friendly and encouraging. He talked about the guiding business his family had on Mount Rainier, an impressive glaciated mountain just out of Seattle, and extended an offer to Sue to come and work there any time. Pete's dad, Lou Whittaker, was a famous mountaineer, as was Lou's brother Jim, the first American to reach the summit of Mount Everest, back in 1963. Sue talked to Pete about how she was not happy in her group. Pete was very kind and positive about the situation, saying it was early days and that the mood might change now that everyone had been part way up the mountain.

The next morning Sue woke to bad weather getting worse. She radioed Base Camp with the message that she was staying put for another day. There were areas at ABC that were relatively sheltered from the wind, but with so many expeditions converging on the spot that season, many tents had to be pitched in more exposed locations. The worst sites of all were below the main campsite, along a corridor between the ice and the moraine. Winds seemed drawn to this natural wind tunnel. Everyone at ABC who thought they had already experienced strong winds at the camp changed their minds that morning. The wind howled above the camp, but without warning dropped to ground level with the sound of a freight train approaching. The blast arrived with a 'Whoompf!' and a flattening of tents. The A-frame tents in the corridor were blown away, never to be seen again. Many tents that were solidly guyed to the ground were blown to pieces where they stood. Tents across the entire camp threatened to cut loose and take flight, and many did so, some of them full of equipment.

Sue realised as soon as the first gust hit that action had to be taken. Pete drew the same conclusion. Also on the scene were two Himex Sherpas, Lhakpa and Chuldim, one a junior cook, the other a kitchen boy, both on their first Everest expedition. They were stationed at ABC to cater for stragglers like Sue and Pete, and to be caretakers when the camp was empty. The violence of the storm had them in fear of their lives, with no idea how to respond. As junior staff they were also reluctant to show initiative because they were accustomed to responding to orders. In an emergency Sue was an expert at giving orders.

'It's no good saying you don't know what to do,' Sue shouted. 'We've got to fix the camp. We've got to do something right now.'

As she spoke more tents were blowing away. The Himex mess tent almost took flight. The back of it lifted up and the tables and big plastic barrels of food tipped over. As the tent collapsed it began to flap like a sail that had lost its wind. Sue, Pete and the others rushed around and collapsed twenty-five Himex tents, both those of Global Extremes and those of the regular Himalayan Experience expedition. The two Sherpas focused on the communal tents.

The key was to stop the tents catching the wind. This was hard work because it was no good simply jerking out the poles and dropping the tent to the ground—this resulted in it flapping itself to shreds. They had to put big rocks or loaded barrels inside every tent to hold them down. Sue's job was to receive the barrels and rocks and position them so they held down the corners of the tent, a challenging and awkward task in the confines of a flapping tent. Lhakpa and Chuldim took to the task as well, despite their fear. All around them, tents that were ripped from the ground took off across the sky like maniacal, misshapen kites. What frightened everybody was the sight of loaded barrels being lifted into the air and bounced across the landscape.

At the height of all this chaos Sue's tent blew away. Her backpack was fully loaded with the lid strapped down. Her sleeping bag was stuffed into its compressor sack. Other items of gear were shoved into tent pockets or into stuff sacks. Sue and Pete planned to move the tent and were at the point of picking it up when Pete darted off to grab a pair of gloves. Sue turned to watch where he was going, and when she looked back her tent had vanished.

She couldn't believe her eyes. A pair of Sherpas nearby were standing and watching with their hands in their pockets. 'What happened?' she asked.

'It's gone down there,' one of them said.

'Well, help us,' Sue pleaded, since this seemed a logical response to expect from anyone witnessing such a disaster.

The Sherpas just shrugged and did nothing. There was no time for a lecture on taking responsibility. Sue scampered off in the direction they had indicated, down to the end of the small valley. Another expedition was camped there, and they pointed towards an unrecognisable pile of cloth and broken poles. Her gear was strewn everywhere. Her pack was off to one side, and this amazed her—fully loaded, it had been airborne, or at least bowled along by the wind, for over 200 metres. She was annoyed at Pete for walking away when they were about to pick up the tent that she had readied to move, but she saw that it was as much her fault for leaving the zipper about one third open, allowing the wind to hook it up into the sky.

She headed across to the mess that had been her tent. A man was standing there, no doubt also coming to terms with the aerodynamic feat he had witnessed, and perhaps considering that such a wind could very easily blow him from the summit of Everest.

'So this is your tent?' he asked rhetorically. 'What are you going to do?'

His accent and the style of his down jacket indicated that he was a Russian from the team nearby.

'This is my house,' said Sue. 'I have to fix it up.'

With these words she was ready to burst into tears. The tent was completely empty. Some gear was lying around but several important smaller items had vanished. There was no one else around from the Himex camp. There was no support of any kind. The Russian man must have sensed how she was feeling.

'You need more help,' he said. 'You go and get your friend and I'll pack this up.'

And he did. While Sue trudged back up the valley, he packed up the tent and its broken poles. He found her pack of cards — non-essential but somehow reassuring. Much more importantly, he located the plugs and connective cords for her camcorder, which was a vital find. He wrapped everything up as neatly as he could, and he did all these things just because he was in a position to help when help was needed. He shrugged politely at her thanks when she returned, suggesting that he had only done what needed to be done, then strolled back to his camp.

Back up at the Himex campsite, Sue found herself another tent into which she could throw her pack and the few other belongings that she and the Russian had been able to find. Sue and Pete put away some of the equipment that had fallen out of the tents when the wind had lifted them, and did what they could to keep the flattened tents from blowing away. The wind was still blowing but at a much reduced velocity. The radio in the comms tent had been knocked around by the storm, so

Pete got it working again and put a call through to Base Camp to report on the damage from 'ground zero'.

So 4 May proved to be anything but a rest day. The final toll was sixty-seven sleeping tents destroyed or blown away, along with twenty-one large dining tents. Some expeditions had to pack up and head home because they had no equipment supplies in reserve. It was the kind of storm that appears once a decade. This year, when the fiftieth anniversary of the first ascent had attracted a record number of expeditions, the storm hit the jackpot.

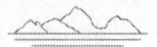

The weather had improved sufficiently by the next morning for Sue to decide to head for the relative fleshpots of Base Camp. She set off alone because she felt more comfortable in her own company, particularly after the exhaustion and stress of the last few days. She did not have the energy or the mindset for small talk, which would have been an inevitable consequence of walking down with other people.

The windstorm revealed to Sue much about the behaviour of people on expeditions. Some people immediately leapt into emergency mode. Others watched the chaos but took no action because their own tents were okay. Some who were invited to help did so; others declined. Most memorable was the man who retrieved and packed up Sue's gear. Sue had also been impressed by the two Sherpas, Lhakpa and Chuldim, who had been afraid of the storm but then got involved because Sue asked them. At one point she noticed they had cut their hands trying to move rocks in the dry cold, so she taped them quickly then got them gloves, and they were back into it.

Sue had seen these dynamics on other mountains. Some expeditions actually relied on others to step in when any emergencies arose, as Sue discovered on the journey down from ABC to recover at Base Camp.

She stopped for lunch near one of the spots that was sometimes used as a halfway camp between ABC and Base. She sat off to the side of the camp to avoid getting involved with people walking down the track.

While she munched on her Musashi bar, she noticed four climbers descending together towards the campsite. There was something odd about the group. As they drew nearer she could see that someone was being piggybacked by a Sherpa, so there were actually five people, not four. Some kind of crisis was unfolding. Sue wondered what do to — she was very tired from her climb, the windstorm and the emotional storm that had preceded these events. She was also wary about getting involved with other people's problems.

The sorry group did not notice Sue sitting on a rock eating her lunch amongst the jumble of boulders littering the glacier. She watched them make their way slowly down until they were out of sight. She finished her lunch then continued along the trail across the glacial moraine. She did not catch up to them until the point where the East Rongbuk Valley joined the moraine of the Central Rongbuk Glacier. As she approached from behind, she saw that three Sherpas were taking turns to piggyback the sick climber. A Japanese man was walking with them.

When Sue caught up she asked about the problem. The Japanese man explained that his friend was very ill. He had become incapacitated with altitude sickness at ABC. She learnt that the sick Japanese was aged sixty-five and was a heavy smoker. His face was so swollen from fluid retention that Sue thought even his mother would not recognise him. Sensibly, the Sherpas had him rigged with oxygen apparatus, but the flow rate was low. With permission, she turned it up so that he was getting more oxygen, then announced that she would run ahead to mobilise help.

The track, although rough and strewn with rocks, was gently downhill so she made good time. At Base Camp Sue gathered Trynt, who was a paramedic, and Colleen, who was a nurse, so that they could take control of the situation as soon as the sick man arrived. Chris Warner also came across. Sue was trained in wilderness medicine but she left the case to the professionals. The Americans diagnosed that the sick man had suffered a partial stroke. Sure enough, when his oxygen mask was removed and he was able to speak, it came out that he had a history of stroke. The problem was not solely due to altitude but almost certainly triggered by it.

Now that the Japanese man was in safe hands, his companion indicated that he would head back up to ABC.

'No way, man!' said Chris. 'You're going with your friend to Zhangmu.'

By this stage Russell had appeared on the scene with the two Liaison Officers who handled the affairs of all the different expeditions.

'We're not obliged to help these people,' he said to Sue, with a tone of annoyance because she had become involved.

She was surprised. 'It's a natural reaction for me that I would always help somebody.'

'But it happens every year,' he said, 'especially with the Japanese. They're always under-resourced.'

Russell was obviously frustrated by the fact that he was the net into which all problems without a solution seemed to fall. He went on to explain that this particular Japanese company was not only ill-equipped but also did not screen its customers. The current situation was living proof—barely living proof—of their poor selection process. However, after venting his spleen, Russell spoke to the Liaison Officers about how they could best evacuate the sick climber. Russell's behaviour here reminded Sue of herself—cranky at first then ready to get on with solving the problem.

It was decided that both of the Japanese should be driven by four-wheel drive to Zhangmu, the last town in Tibet before the Friendship Highway crossed the border into Nepal. Zhangmu was more than 2500 metres lower than Base Camp. With that decrease in height, all altitude-induced problems would disappear, simplifying the patient's medical condition. One of the LOs gave orders to the Tibetan driver and accompanied the Japanese to their camp to make sure this course of action was implemented.

In Nepal, every expedition had its own Liaison Officer, and often this position was regarded as a rort for the government or military official given the job. A Liaison Officer's main role there was to stop teams from breaking rules, such as climbing mountains for which they did not hold permits, entering restricted areas or crossing the border into Tibet. Usually these men knew little about mountaineering and were of limited use to the expedition, though some LOs took their jobs very seriously and were able to contribute significantly to the efficiency and success of a climb. The situation in Tibet was quite different. At the three different Base Camps where Sue had undertaken expeditions, at least one Tibetan Mountaineering Association Liaison Officer had been in attendance. Their job was to deal with whatever issues came up among all of the expeditions at the Base Camp of their designated mountain. Among their visible duties was the checking of plans and arrangements of every expedition at the Base Camp, as well as helping to resolve problems whenever they could. Sue observed that the Tibetan officials performed their jobs diligently.

She now realised that she had already met the two Everest Base Camp LOs, and they certainly remembered her from her other trips. As a woman her requests on those expeditions had been given extra attention, and Sue had been pleased to see that both men were very professional, not arrogant at all.

The evacuation of the Japanese and Sue's own role in the process set her thinking about the pressures and responsibilities of guiding Mount Everest and the other Himalayan giants. She wondered how people could do this for a living. During the most important part of an expedition, the final push to the summit and the long tiring descent, guides would be working with people pushed to their limits and not necessarily acting rationally. It was a realm where people died, or were totally stripped back to the bare bones of their character, even beyond. Sue had been on four expeditions to 8000-metre peaks. The aspect she found most horrible was that people died every season. Sometimes they died in the presence of the guide. Sometimes the guides were so caught up in the process that they died as well. There were big questions about where the lines of responsibility were drawn for a guide, and Sue was not interested in getting herself into situations where she might have to ask these questions of herself.

One of the worst things from a guide's point of view would be to have deaths among the Sherpas working on an expedition. A powerful aspect of guided expeditions is that climbers pay big money to participate — anywhere from US$20,000 to $60,000 — and with that kind of expenditure people do not want to come back empty-handed. So some take greater risks than is prudent. Evacuations are commonplace, and on commercial expeditions they almost always involve Sherpas. High-altitude evacuations are dangerous by their very nature, because the rescuers are often exposed to the same threat that made the rescue necessary in the first place. Sherpas are the ideal people for many rescue situations. As a race, they have lived at altitude for dozens of generations, first in Tibet and subsequently in the high valleys on the southern side of Himalaya. They have adapted genetically to moderate altitude and as a consequence perform strongly at extreme altitudes, making them the logical people to employ for physical work on huge mountains. High-altitude Sherpas rarely require rescuing themselves, but there is still a high death rate amongst them, largely because of the amount of time they spend exposed to the risks of avalanche, storm and extreme cold — with these risks significantly increased during rescues.

On the south side of Everest, the Khumbu Icefall immediately above Base Camp blocks access to the 'safer' parts of the mountain. It is Sherpas who fix the ropes and ladders across the crevasses and steep, unstable ice formations in the Icefall and in this way provide access to the high, glaciated valley of the Western Cwm, from where the higher reaches of the mountain are tackled. Once the route is set, expedition climbers minimise the number of times they travel through the dangerous Icefall, but during the climbing season there is a constant flow of Sherpas carrying loads and maintaining the safest possible route through the maze of crevasses. They are known as the 'Icefall doctors'. This maintenance is a huge chore, requiring the replacement of ladders that have been crushed and ropes that have been torn out of the ice by the collapse of sections of the Icefall. In this context, the Sherpas' contribution to everyone's safe passage up and down the mountain is invaluable, and comes at great personal risk. The danger of the Khumbu Icefall was one of the reasons why Sue chose to climb the mountain from Tibet, where the mountain was approached by the much safer North Col route.

On the north side of Everest in 2003, the high level of activity by the Sherpas at the Base Camps and on the mountain was obvious to everyone. Most climbers paid lip service to their contribution, but many did not appreciate the amount of sheer hard work involved in setting the route and stocking the camps with tents, food, fuel and oxygen. Most expedition members were on Everest for the first time, and they found the act of climbing so demanding that it was all they could do to look after themselves (and some could not even manage that). The climbers were very grateful to the individual Sherpas who guided them to the top, but often they did not see beyond this 'starring' role to the hundreds of hours of dangerous toil by the Sherpas that made everyone's attempt on the summit possible.

At the Himex Base Camp, some of the expedition members treated the Sherpas like servants. Zeddy was obviously accustomed to domestic staff so it was not surprising that he related to the Sherpas in a similar fashion. Gernot and even Hermann followed suit in that their relationships with the Sherpas were purely pragmatic. Personal matters were never raised by either side. And without any connection, Sue felt there could be no respect. Early in the expedition the Sherpas had kept Sue at a distance as well. It was only when she unintentionally earned their respect with her solo climbs to the North Col and to Camp Two that the barriers came down. She was never welcomed as one of the gang—a transformation she had experienced with Sherpas on treks in Nepal—but there was a recognition of some common values, such as self-reliance, and this was connection enough. For Sue, putting the billy on for others coming in from a long day or bad weather was an international, unspoken rule, so she always tried to offer drinks or food to the Sherpas in those circumstances. Usually they were perplexed or amused by the offer, but this did not worry her. After sensing acceptance by the Himex Sherpas, Sue was comfortable spending time with them. She never imposed on them, but sometimes she took the opportunity to tune into the sense of groundedness that they brought to almost everything they did.

One of the less grounded aspects of life on Everest was the shooting of films. Although the film crews work to a storyline, invariably they are opportunistic. The Global Extremes cameras came out when the Japanese man was carried into camp. This allowed Sue to see Trynt and Colleen in camera mode, emotional and expressive. Sue had been thinking that the Japanese man was ill-suited to the mountains and had pushed himself too hard but would nonetheless be okay. For Trynt and Colleen the situation became much more dramatic once the cameras were turned on, even though both of them were health care professionals who had seen people in far more critical states than the man now in front of them. The Global Extremes camera crew, with whom Sue was becoming good friends, agreed that the athletes had definite on-screen and off-screen personas. Sue did not regard this as necessarily a bad thing, but she found it curious to watch the metamorphosis.

Sue had descended to Base Camp determined to rest and regain strength. She was equally determined not to let herself get stressed about anything. This last goal proved more difficult because the same old mess tent conversations were still being conducted by Zeddy, his domineering nature only thinly masked by his joviality. To escape the oppressive scene, in the afternoons Sue often headed across to the shantytown near the Tibetan Mountaineering Association building. It was a fifteen to twenty minute walk with the rewards at the end of a drink and a different social setting. Matt often accompanied her. He was generally good company, but one thing that frustrated her about him was that he was ready to denounce the mess tent status quo when he was away from the main protagonists but never spoke up in support of her point of view. He was a senior figure in the shipping industry who was in charge of several hundred people. This was obviously a role of great responsibility, and yet he was prepared to spend ten weeks on Everest. So he must have really wanted this summit. For this reason Sue did not push him too much about anything.

Sue had voiced her opinions during the first few weeks of the expedition, but she was no longer prepared to do so. She and Hermann had established their lines of non-communication and it was easier to extend that silence than to take part in discussions that did not interest her, particularly as she had set herself the goal of avoiding stress and confrontation. Although Sue was still part of the Himex team in many ways, at a personal level she had broken free.

Unfortunately, the notion that mountaineering was a noble pursuit whose practitioners rose above the petty follies of humankind was sadly out of touch with what was happening at Base Camp. There were nineteen expeditions on the north side of Everest during the spring season in 2003, which should have been enough for their expedition to maintain its anonymity among the crowds. However, sometimes a person or a group of people stood out. Many of the guides on Everest that season also guided the other peaks that made up the Seven Summits, and Zeddy had become well known on this circuit during his pursuit of the high points of each continent. His reputation preceded him, and the Himex expedition was judged accordingly before the team even arrived at Base Camp. The entire team became known as a trophy hunting crew, people only interested in ticking off a list of summits. This certainly was not justified, but any incident which supported this point of view was capitalised upon by the gossip merchants.

The normal strains of expedition life added to the equation. There were well over two hundred people tackling the Tibetan side of the mountain. During recovery time or bad weather periods at Base Camp, many of the climbers were lonely, vulnerable or overawed, and they were looking for scapegoats to cover up these weaknesses. A very common reaction to the stresses of altitude was irritability, and in order to maintain group harmony scapegoats were found in other teams. This was not a predetermined strategy; it was merely how the dynamics took shape within some expeditions. Certainly this was the approach Zeddy and Gernot adopted with the Global Extremes team. And many other expeditions saw Global Extremes and Himalayan Experience in this light as well.

Global Extremes was particularly criticised for bringing American reality television to Everest. The complaint had very little substance. Many climbers who knew nothing about the Global Extremes expedition regarded the concept as a manufactured cable TV product that was out of its depth on Everest. There was a general attitude that the adventure athletes were Baywatch babes and hunks who could lift heavy weights and run fast across the sand but who would not be able to cope with climbing the world's highest mountain. The truth was that most of the athletes had a strong mountaineering background and had trained hard in the disciplines appropriate for the climb. Among the OLN film team were some of the most accomplished climbers in America. Many wrong calls were made about Global Extremes, and many of these came from the people who were closest to them — the Himex expedition.

A variation on this theme came from some of the low-budget expeditions at Base Camp. They had a 'sour grapes' attitude towards the better resourced, more professional outfits, mocking the comforts and facilities available to the top expeditions. Sue was well aware that physical comforts meant very little when interpersonal relationships were tortuous, so the gripe was irrelevant to her. And while the small expeditions might badmouth Himalayan Experience as elitist because of their heated mess tent, hot showers and communications tent, they had no qualms about asking Russell for free weather reports. Russell paid large amounts of money for specialist weather information sent via satellite from Switzerland. His years of familiarity with Everest enabled him to interpret these reports very accurately. This was definitely one of the factors that had led Sue to his expedition in the first place; she had looked at the history of Everest climbing and had found that the main death traps were picking the weather incorrectly or ignoring it. Himalayan Experience also had caches of oxygen high on the mountain to cover unforeseen circumstances. Often this oxygen was used to rescue ill-equipped or unprepared climbers from other teams, and rarely did thanks come back to Russell for his commitment to safety, which sometimes came at considerable cost to his business. Russell certainly did not regard his outfit as elitist; he simply believed he had found the formula for safety and success on the highest mountain in the world, and the formula did not come cheap.

Every season the Himalayan Experience Sherpas set up the most difficult sections of fixed ropes, and usually set a greater proportion of the fixed lines than any other single operator or expedition. The other major expeditions usually contributed by setting some lines of ropes on other parts of the mountain, generally in consultation with Russell. These were the ropes that everyone depended upon to make their ascent of the mountain, and they were essential. Most of the climbers did not have the strength or the solid basis of skill needed to climb a mountain without fixed lines — not only the climbing skills, but the knowledge to assess which slopes were prone to avalanche or rock fall, and where deep crevasses might lie hidden under a crust of snow.

This season the Chinese team and Himalayan Experience were slated to fix the ropes to the North Col. Many teams were running to an earlier timetable, passing time at ABC while waiting for Russell's Sherpas to move up from Base Camp. Meanwhile, a large Russian expedition which planned to climb the mountain without oxygen arrived at ABC. They were strong climbers not afraid of hard work. They were also keen to make progress, so over the next two days they climbed up and secured a line of fixed rope all the way to the North Col. The following day dozens of climbers and Sherpas from other expeditions clambered up the ropes to secure good campsites at the Col. Some saw this behaviour as parasitic. Others saw it as a case of the smaller teams saving time and money by taking advantage of resources laid out by the larger expeditions. In fairness, many of the smaller teams would have been happy to fend for themselves if the route had not been inundated by the Sherpas and climbers of the larger teams. It was a complex social environment, not the kind of issue one expected to be dealing with on Mount Everest.

Sue was disconcerted to find that this 'soap opera' attitude of the Base Camp scene extended beyond the unfortunate mix of people who made up her team. Mark Whetu began to visit the Himex mess tent after mealtimes. Later on, at ABC, Russell and Tony usually joined in.

When Sue heard of the death of Paul Carr on Cho Oyu, Mark was very supportive, and that put the seal on their developing friendship (Paul had been a guide for World Expeditions whom Sue had known well). Mark often visited Sue in her tent during the afternoon when she was avoiding the social morass of the Himex mess tent and Mark had had enough of the Global Extremes camp, where the Americans talked endlessly about America, things American and American adventure racing. It was natural for the easygoing antipodeans with a similar sense of humour to gravitate to one another. Unfortunately, it appeared to be equally natural for others to assume that Mark and Sue had a sexual relationship, which was untrue.

Assumptions at Base Camp were not limited to relationships between people. Many negative things were said about the huge Chinese expedition, an amazing extravaganza involving thirty climbers and over seventy others. Sue was surprised when a well-presented Chinese woman walked into the Himex camp. She introduced herself as Xinmin Yan, a journalist, and then asked Sue in excellent English if she would like to be on Chinese television. Two trucks full of television transmission equipment had made the long journey from Beijing, and now the China Central Television producers wanted someone from each of the nationalities present at Base Camp to make a cameo appearance. Sue immediately agreed to represent Australia. Many of the climbers refused to participate because of the Chinese occupation of Tibet. Xinmin had not been born when the Chinese invaded Tibet, so she did not buy into their argument. Sue too thought that refusal on the basis of Chinese history was a narrow-minded reaction. She made a general comment that everyone should be good spirited about what they were trying to do, which was to promote adventure to one billion people who probably knew little about what happened outside their own province. Her protestations were in vain. Many climbers saw no point in participating.

As it was to be a live broadcast to the whole of China, a rehearsal was definitely in order. Sue thought this would be an easy way to meet climbers from the other teams, much simpler than wandering into an unknown camp and saying, 'Hi, I'm Sue' and waiting for whatever response she might get. She was surprised at how small the turnout was at the practice. She thought it was ridiculous since nobody had anything much else to do.

When her turn came, Sue quite happily chortled, 'Hi! I'm Sue from Sydney, Australia. This is my third 8000-metre peak, and Tibet is very different from the beaches at home.' It was brief and painless.

Afterwards Sue gave Xinmin and her associates some advice: 'If you want to get cooperation from these people you've got to put on breakfast for them. Specially prepared food is valuable currency here.' They laughed at her suggestion but took it up, which was easy for them because they had several trucks full of food. Word was sent out to all expeditions that breakfast would be provided for those who participated in the next day's broadcast. There was a much better turnout, not only because of the food itself, but because it could be used as an excuse to participate. However, even then the body language of many climbers conveyed that they were not comfortable. Several were quite aloof, with 'Do you know who I am?' looks on their faces. Some were high profile sports stars wearing personalised badges on their jackets who were big news in their own country. They would come across as nobodies on Chinese television and did not seem happy about it. Sue found the whole performance amusing, with these climbers reminding her more of awkward school boys than legendary mountaineers. She doubted whether the personalised labels would help them get up the mountain.

Sue admired the way Xinmin handled the situation. She did not worry about the concerns of others, whether it was the 'Chinese' issue, the fact that she was woman, or the fact that she was not a mountaineer. Much later Sue was invited as a guest of her Himex teammate Chung to the Chinese mess for lunch, and she was treated very well and welcomed to return at any time.

In the rugged and dusty setting of Base Camp it was easy to forget how sophisticated modern China had become, though it was evidenced in the nature of the Chinese expedition. The Chinese climbing team was sponsored by SOHU, a telecommunications company, and was led by Wang Yongfeng, whose climbs of the Seven Summits had led to his appointment as Assistant Secretary-General of the Chinese Mountaineering Association. Second in charge of the expedition was thirty-eight year old Zhang Choyang, the Chairman and CEO of SOHU. His unusual goals of having the mountaineers play the Internet game 'Chivalry Online' and send text messages and photo phone images across China from the summit were designed to promote his SOHU brand. In the build up to the expedition—and no doubt in the aftermath—he used the symbolism of 'higher challenges' and 'mountains of achievement' to motivate his staff. Enthusiasm and hyperbole, once the domain of the Motherland, had indisputably gone over to the private sector.

At the other end of the scale was the four-person American expedition consisting of Jim Wickwire, Dick Bass, John Roskelley and his son Jess. Jim was famous as the first American to climb K2, the world's second highest mountain and one with a reputation for being harder than Everest, while John had been the leading American mountaineer of the 1970s and '80s. In 1982 both Jim and John had attempted to climb the Great Couloir, a direct route up Everest's formidable North Face. The route was subsequently climbed for the first time in 1984 without oxygen by the first Australian Everest expedition, and had not been repeated since. Dick Bass climbed Everest in 1985 at age fifty-four, setting the record for being the oldest person to have summitted. Over the intervening decades the record was pushed well into the sixties, and now at age seventy-three Dick planned to regain his title.

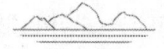

Sue found that Base Camp was an interesting experience in some ways, but its appeal lessened as the days passed. Tensions were building up within the team, and within the other expeditions as well, as the time drew near for a summit push. She devised diversions for herself, such as leisurely excursions with a packed lunch. She would walk across to the Mallory memorial or to one of the pubs in the shantytown, armed with her book *Holy Cow* by Sarah Macdonald. These humorous tales of travelling in India were a bright light in the dusty, windy drudgery of Base

Camp. She now opted not to get into making the rounds of the other camps, something she had done earlier in the expedition with Trynt, when she realised that one advantage of being women in this male domain was that they were always invited to stop by for a coffee. Sue also elected not to spend her time ringing or emailing Australia. She could not afford the satellite phone charges, and she also knew that if she got into the habit of making contact with friends and family back home, she would only want to do it even more, and that might weaken her mindset.

One morning, however, Sue needed to speak to a friend, someone who valued her companionship, who valued her as a person. It was a need too great to resist, so she rang her old World Expeditions friend Megan. Megan picked up the phone and squealed with delight. She lived at Newport, one of Sydney's most northerly beaches and a healthy distance from the bustle of the city. It was a glorious day in Sydney and she had just come back from the beach. The phone had rung just as she sat down to breakfast.

Sue huddled in the comms tent while she listened to this information. Outside the landscape was windswept and freezing. She was wearing baggy fleece clothes and sneakers. Every item was permeated with dust, as had been the case for weeks. The image of swimming at the beach, dressing in clean casual clothes, then sitting down to a real coffee made with real milk and picking at fresh fruit glistening on a plate was a picture of unattainable paradise. The scene was so appealing, so apparently carefree, that it made her incredibly homesick. At first she thought she could be down in Kathmandu in two days, back in her favourite hotel under a shower and away from the harshness of everything to do with Everest. But of course she knew that ten minutes after arriving in Kathmandu massive regrets would kick in. Everest was the ultimate project, one she had been leading herself towards for years. The decision to come this season, during this historic year, to this side of the mountain had only firmly been made a few months earlier, but the roots of her Everest climb ran much deeper than that. These thoughts pushed any ideas of quitting out of her head.

She continued to chat eagerly with Megan, not saying much about Everest, only promising that she would be cautious, that she would take care of herself, that she would stay strong. Megan was very encouraging, emphasising that success, or resolution at least, was very close now. Then they talked about other things, just illogical girls' talk mostly, but it was hugely fulfilling—as fulfilling as the plate of fresh fruit and the real coffee that lay on the sun-dappled tablecloth on the opposite side of the world.

There was no discussion about how long they were talking or of what it was costing. It was a simple matter of two friends chatting, each of them just wanting to know how the other was travelling through life at that time. When Sue hung up after forty-five minutes on the phone, she thought, *Yes, this conversation is my bright light shining on what I have to look forward to, shining on the joys I can indulge in at leisure when I get home.*

She took that light and shone it on her current circumstances, standing at 5000 metres in the barren Rongbuk Valley, her hands in the pockets of her down jacket, her back to the wind. Against the bigger picture, this waiting time on Everest was a short-term issue. The climb itself was huge beyond conception, but the timeframe was finite. She told herself, 'I can manage this.'

7

DOWN BUT NOT OUT

On 14 May the Himalayan Experience and Global Extremes teams left Base Camp to begin their summit climb. Most of the Himex team had been at Base Camp for two weeks and were definitely ready for a change of scene. The first stage was an easy hike to Interim Camp, though Global Extremes continued through to Advance Base Camp. This was to be as far as Troy Henkels was to go. The Alaskan decided to give up on the climb and head home, despite his mountaineering background. Meanwhile, Trynt Young, eliminated from the Everest squad in the final round of the Global Extremes competition, was as motivated as she had always been.

The teams were pleased to be moving upwards again, but for Sue things began to go wrong almost immediately. Everyone was in their own little bubble, and this included Matt with whom she had agreed to partner. Less than a kilometre from Base Camp, Sue tightened her waist belt and to her horror the buckle broke. This may not seem like a huge calamity, but for Sue it was. Her greatest strengths were her mind and her legs. Her upper body was not designed for carrying heavy packs, and yet carry them she did. Today she was carrying twenty kilograms. Her technique had always been to bear the weight on her hips, so the buckle of her waistband assumed greater importance than it did for most people. Sue did not feel she could ask for help from Hermann or Gernot because by that stage communication had completely broken down. She spoke to Trynt and Tony when she caught up with them at a rest stop. Tony was the Mister Fix-it of the expedition, and after considering the options he improvised a closure using the Velcro strap designed to attach an ice axe to her pack.

Everyone continued up the valley at their own pace. Sue was the last to arrive, with her heavy pack the main reason. At Base Camp she had told herself that carrying a big load was no longer a good idea strategically, but unfortunately she felt that once again she had no choice. Strong winds had lashed the North Col camp, and several of the Himex tents had been blown away, including the one where Sue had slept and stashed her gear. Some equipment had been salvaged as it spilled out of the different tents, but in the process everything was mixed together, and the Sherpas who had been on the scene were unable to confirm that her gear, pivotal to her summit bid, was still there at the North Col. This issue weighed heavily on her mind, just as her pack weighed heavily on her hips, full as it was with spare 'just in case' items.

When Sue pulled into Interim Camp the tension in the big tent was palpable. Gernot was not there and she gathered from the conversation that he had decided to go ahead of the group. Sue was surprised. Apparently he had expressed his right to climb the mountain without having Global Extremes ahead of him, so he was pushing on to ABC in order to climb the mountain with the Global Extremes team.

Sue was about to say that this was a selfish and unrealistic course of action on Gernot's part, but as soon as she uttered the world 'selfish' Zeddy interrupted.

'Gernot is anything but selfish,' he said. 'You have it all wrong, Sue. He is anything but selfish.'

Hermann agreed, which astounded Sue.

'His action is selfish because he has left us,' she replied. 'We no longer know where he is. By the time he gets close to ABC it will be dark, unless he really hurries, which could be dangerous. The people there might have to go out and look for him. He could walk off a cliff or among dangerous seracs. It's just not a good idea.'

Sue expressed these views but held back from commenting further. Gernot was extraordinarily determined, and it was this, more than expert skills, that enabled him to climb. Determination was vital on Everest, but so was good judgment.

Russell was already at ABC, and he immediately expelled Gernot from the trip. He saw Gernot's actions as the height of irresponsibility, and inappropriate as well. Global Extremes was a separate entity, and with its video broadcasts, interviews and celebrity commentators, it was not in a position to take anyone else into its charge. The fact that Gernot survived heading off on his own impetuously did not mean he would survive if he attempted it again.

When Sue arrived at ABC early in the afternoon next day, Russell and Gernot were talking earnestly, not far from where her tent was pitched. Eventually Gernot indicated that he understood the issues, made the appropriate assurances to Russell and was reinstated on the team.

At a group meeting at ABC later that evening, however, Gernot defended his plan by outlining his theory for success. Everyone had heard it before.

'The maximum probability for me to summit Mount Everest is for me to go at the first opportunity,' he argued. 'The first opportunity is on the full moon, as Russell said, and the first group going is Globex, so I must go with them if I want the maximum probability of success.'

At that stage it seemed that Global Extremes would push for the summit first, and that the Himex team was likely to have better weather on the chosen date of 22 May. But Gernot would hear nothing of it.

'No, that's reducing my probability for success,' he replied. 'The theory of probability is that you have to make it the maximum, and you do that by maximising the opportunities.'

Sue thought to herself, *Do you think the mountain is listening to theories of probability?* When she voiced the question, Gernot did not even look at her. He was so worked up, so emotional, that she thought he was going to cry. He had undergone such a change from the affable and helpful man she had camped beside at Base Camp, who had shared things from cough lozenges to camera equipment with her. She was amazed by the transformation. She definitely did not want to climb on the same rope as this man, but there was little chance of that in any case because Hermann had Gernot and Zeddy under one wing, and Sue certainly was not going to be invited under the other.

Everyone in the mess tent wanted to know when the best time would be to go for the summit. It seemed that Hermann did not know which way to jump. Russell was across with the Global Extremes team, so Hermann called for Purba to come into the tent. He sat the lead Sherpa down and essentially asked him to sort out their disagreement. Purba was baffled and did not want to buy into the dispute. Instead he gave minimalist answers, limiting himself to yes or no when he could. He was very happy to leave the tent at the earliest opportunity. Sue found it a very embarrassing episode, which served to polarise the team. Purba's role was certainly not to settle pointless arguments, and she said as much.

Sue was perplexed by the situation. The rest of the team must have realised that Gernot was obsessed with the climb—which was a dangerous state of mind—but no one else spoke up. She figured that this could only happen on Everest, where the stakes were so high, where decisions were clouded by money and pride. Everyone had their own little canoe to paddle and they were not sure of their own positions, so they did not want to deal with anyone else's.

Russell did have a plan, of course, and Hermann related it to the group. It was to kick into action immediately. Over the next four days they would move up from camp to camp towards the summit, a day at a time with no rest days. By 19 May they would be at Camp Four, ready for a summit push on 20 May.

Everest had other ideas. Bad weather hit, and the move up was put on hold. The mountain called the shots here and showed that the tortured debate about which summit date was the right one was a farce. The Himex team did not move up from ABC to the North Col until 18 May, which meant their chance to go for the summit was put back to 22 May. Meanwhile, the Global Extremes summit push and live broadcast was rescheduled to 23 May. Sue had been right when she had repeatedly stated during the mess tent conversations that you could not plan an attempt on Everest's summit by logging it into your diary like a dinner party. The overall schedule now had the Himex team a day ahead of Global Extremes, so all the angst and argument and resentment were a waste of breath.

While they were sitting out the storm at ABC, no one was able to give Sue a precise answer about whether the gear she had stashed at the North Col was still there. Both Mark and Russell had told her independently not to worry, that she would be able to borrow what she did not have. This was not a satisfactory answer for Sue, particularly in regard to her down suit. Sue's suit had been personally designed. It was made to measure—which was small—and worked perfectly for a woman needing to urinate because of the cut and the way the zips worked. This was more than a matter of convenience because the extreme cold on these high mountains could be very dangerous if insulating garments had to be removed in foul weather. Sue had found that men really did not appreciate how important this was. The Himex suits did not work well for Trynt, who had needed Sue to help her unzip and un-Velcro when she needed to urinate at the North Col. Success on Everest came from paying attention to detail, and staying warm in extreme conditions was a very important detail. When at last they did head up from ABC, her pack was still heavy with gear to replace the items that may have gone missing. She was very concerned about the things she would not be able to replace.

The scene at the Col was chaotic. With both Himex and Global Extremes in residence, there was two teams' worth of gear at the camp. Confusion reigned because the gear that had been recovered when the tents had blown away had been distributed not only among the replacement tents but also among those that had not been disturbed by the storm. Sue had a frustrating time going from tent to tent in search of her belongings. Everyone was focused on getting themselves comfortable, and at first they did not take more than a cursory look in their tents before telling Sue that nothing was to be found. As the team leader, Hermann was the logical person to approach. Sue asked him directly and he made some effort to look and then went back to what he was doing, which was getting Zeddy and Gernot set up in their tents. She then realised she herself needed to look inside every single Himex-owned tent—and there were eight of them awkwardly pitched around crevasses and other tents. The issue was worth making a pest of herself over.

Eventually her search yielded some results. The most important gear turned up, namely her down suit and her goggles, but other items that had been packed in the same bag had disappeared. The missing items included her brand new headlamp, two pairs of Thorlo Extreme Weather socks that had never been worn (she had been saving these for the summit), her Outdoor Research insulated gauntlets, plus the Musashi bars she had set aside as the major food items for the highest and hardest days on the mountain. Sue believed that someone had helped themselves to the socks, the food and her down mitts because they had been clearly visible in the same transparent, unsealed plastic and unlabelled bag that contained her down suit and her goggles. Her goggles had been wrapped inside a hat, and she guessed that they had not been taken because they were hidden from view. Her new heavy duty thermals had been left because they were too small to fit anyone else. The lesson for her was that she should label her stuff, just like at school. There were common brands, so one person's set of gear could look much like someone else's. Sue's Mountain Designs down suit was unique, which perhaps saved it from getting lost.

It was a sorry turn of events if the gear had actually been taken. Perhaps climbers or Sherpas from other expeditions who had lost equipment in the storm had desperately looked for replacements. This would have been no excuse, of course, but it would have provided a powerful incentive for breaking the rules of mountaineering conduct, and indeed the rules of society.

Elsewhere on the mountain, one other climber had been more fortunate. When John Roskelley was gearing up for his second load carry up to the North Col in mid-April he realised that two days earlier he had left his brand new Gore-Tex gloves on the rock where he had taken off his crampons. He cursed his forgetfulness and blamed it on being exhausted. At this time virtually very expedition was making its acclimatisation climbs up to the North Col, which meant that over one hundred people walked past that rock during those two days. When John hiked back up to Crampon Point, he was surprised and delighted that his gloves were exactly where he had left them. Some kind person had tucked them into each other and placed a stone on top so they would not blow away.

While John had been reassured about the essential goodness of humanity, Sue could not help but feel demoralised, despite having located her down suit. Once she had accepted that nothing more was likely to surface, she headed to the tent she was to share with Matt. He had made himself comfortable and was waiting for Sue for the next step. Sue knew he expected her to light the stove and melt some snow for food and drinks. During their first overnight at the North Col, Matt had shown few self-management skills when it came to snow camping. She had done all the melting of snow, cooking and washing up. Sue was disappointed that as her partner he had not added to her strength by sharing the load, but added to the load by doing nothing. She was not surprised to find herself in the same role again, but she hoped he might be able to pull his weight in other ways.

She showed him what she was taking in terms of food, then said to him, 'I think it's too heavy.'

'Well, if you're taking all that then I'll leave my stuff behind,' he replied.

He made no offer to carry anything of hers, nor did he suggest that she leave her food and that he carry his instead. Sue attempted to push the point.

'I'd like to take less because I have to take other things, too,' she said. 'My gear might be missing from Camp Two, as well as from here, so I have to carry extra stuff.'

But Matt chose not to buy in, using the non-confrontational approach of saying nothing.

At first Sue felt dispirited, but then she realised that he just did not get it. She was worried that she would not be able to make the climb with so much to carry and with Matt to look after as well. But as she melted snow and enjoyed a hot drink—Matt was quick to say how fantastic the drink was that she made for him—her motivation returned, and the fire returned to her belly. She thought, *Yes, I can do this.*

The next morning they set off early for Camp Two. It was quite windy, but at least this time Sue knew that the climb was much further than it looked. Again she was slow because of the weight of her pack. She wondered how it was that the others were climbing so fast until she realised that most of them had passed some of their heavier items to the Sherpas to carry. Sue was still troubled and weakened by diarrhoea, so she regretted not handing over some of her belongings as well.

When they finally arrived at Camp Two, Matt wriggled into his sleeping bag, pulled it over his head and started to go to sleep. Before he was entirely cocooned, however, Sue said, 'You're going to have to get some snow if I'm going to cook.'

'It's okay,' he said. 'I don't want anything.'

'But you have to have drinks tonight and fill your water bottle.'

'You've gotta get the snow from over there where it's clean.'

Sue realised there would be no help from Matt, only an apparent denial that the pair of them had needs and that it was only fair to share them.

Sue melted the clean snow that had blown against the side of the tent and used the water to cook some instant noodles. She then melted more snow for drinks and for their water bottles. It was not arduous work in itself, but the altitude and the cold made it so. The wind which had been blowing all day grew stronger in the late afternoon; she snuggled into her sleeping bag and dozed for a few hours until the sound of it lashing the tents woke her in a fright. It was dark and she wondered if the tents would blow away. For the rest of the night the wind blew strongly with frequent gusts of terrifying force. Sue knew they would not be able to move up if the winds continued at this strength. She thought that if she tried to leave she would get blown away because she was so lightly built.

By morning the gusts had diminished in force, but the wind was still blowing hard. At around seven o'clock Sue unzipped the tent door and stuck her head outside. She could see Hermann up at a tent with some others. As he turned downhill to move across to another tent she called out, 'What's happening?'

'We're going,' he called back.

No qualifications, no comments about the weather, nothing about a strategy. It was already late, and Sue felt there should have been clarity about procedures—stop, go, wait—with all members of the party at first light. But she had no walkie-talkie, which would have given her more independence, so felt she just had to tow the line and move with the group up the hill. She and Matt readied for the impending climb to Camp Three. He crawled out of the tent fifteen minutes before she did because he left her to dismantle the stove and pack the pots and food. The wind was gusting strongly again when Sue eased her way out of the tent, crampons already clipped to her boots.

As soon as she was outside, the strength of the wind sent a shiver of fear through her. *I don't like this,* she thought, *I could get killed in these next few days.* She lifted her pack on to her shoulders and immediately felt it was too heavy in the wind. What could she leave behind? All of the Sherpas had set off already, so she could not pass anything to them. She could not give anything to Matt either, not only because he was sure to refuse but also because he had disappeared. He had set off without her. She was on her own now and very nervous. She could not think of a worse combination.

As she took her first steps up the slope she was surprised how weak she felt. She wondered how she would be able to balance with such a load on her back. The only answer was to keep moving and find a way to manage as she went. She slowly made her way past the tents pitched in tiers up the slope above. Near the top tent she came across Matt leaning on a rock slab facing into the wind. His water bottle was hanging from his hand with the lid open. He showed no signs of recognising her.

Chung was just above him. 'What's with Matt?' Sue called. 'Is he all right?'

'No,' Chung replied. 'He's lost it. He dropped his other water bottle.' He turned and headed upwards.

Sue spoke more loudly. 'Matt, are you okay?'

'I'm fine,' he said.

'Your water bottle's undone.'

'Okay.'

Goggles obscured his eyes, which were the best quick test for lucidity.

Slowly Matt screwed on the bottle lid and began to lift himself up out of the snow. Sue started walking. She looked up and saw Hermann setting off. He did not look around to check that Sue and Matt were okay, which was very disconcerting, especially in these marginal conditions. Sue watched him walk up the snow slope to a nose of rock beyond which lay the fixed rope. He moved easily across to the rope, clipped into it with the cord from his harness, and then continued upwards. Again Sue encouraged herself, *I can do this; everyone else has.* But she followed slowly, and when she came to the nose of rock, she hesitated. The rope was out of reach and the few steps in between did not look secure. There was a huge drop below. She summoned her courage, but when she stepped out to begin the sloping traverse across the rock, a gust of wind caught her backpack and unbalanced her. For a split second she thought she was going to fall. Instantly she stepped back, then retreated a few more steps until she was out of the full force of the wind. She was still not near any fixed line and felt unsteady.

As she stood contemplating the possibilities, Matt came blundering past, now a man on a mission. He said nothing but immediately stepped out on to the traverse. His longer reach meant he had to take fewer steps before he could clip his sling onto the fixed rope and be safe. He made it look easy, but Sue still did not feel comfortable.

Fear is commonplace in mountaineering, a signal to assess the risks then take appropriate action. Sue analysed her feelings. She knew her pack was too heavy, to the point where she had let the wind catch it and almost topple her down the slope to her death. She could see now that she was weaker than she had realised. And she was totally without support from her team, or at least that was how she felt. She knew that in dangerous conditions it was easy to decide the risks were too great and convince herself that the wise decision was to retreat. She was not going to make the decision she now faced lightly. Her life was at stake, but so was her first chance to summit Mount Everest—and it might be her only chance. For half an hour she procrastinated, and then it all became clear to her. The fact that it was taking so long to make the decision about whether to go up or down was a sign that she should retreat.

Sue also remembered what Russell had said about the weather forecast, that the meteorological information indicated the best weather window of all would be at the end of the month, a whole week away. Russell had been quietly confident about that. She trusted both him and her own instincts about her capabilities right here and now.

She made up her mind. She realised that she could not be sure of completing another three days of climbing all the way to the top and back if no one was even looking to see where she was. And the climbing was only going to get more difficult. She acknowledged that she did not feel strong enough to manage her own safety, and in such a marginal environment the result could be death.

One of the Himex Sherpas manning the camp had a radio, so she borrowed it and called Russell at Camp One on the North Col.

'It's too windy,' she said. 'I don't think I can do it.'

Russell's answer was predictable. 'You're going to have to push through bad weather to get to the summit.' He said it very calmly. 'You're not going to get good weather all the way. And it's only a short bit you've got to deal with now. You're going to have to push through it.'

'I don't think I can do it,' Sue repeated. 'It's too much for me.'

'Do what you think is the right thing, but remember, it *is* windy on that corner—it's just one of those places.'

Sue could tell that Russell really wanted her to succeed, but he did not know how she felt. He did not realise how strongly she doubted her ability to push through the difficulties on this day, under these conditions. Nor did he know that turning back was never an easy option for her. She was very clear about not wanting to be rescued. She looked down the huge sweep of the North Face to the upper reaches of Central Rongbuk Glacier where she would land if she slipped. She thought about people back home. In particular she could hear Sue Badyari's words: 'You know it doesn't matter if you come back empty-handed. We'll still love you whether you make the summit or not.'

Sue continued staring down the face, imagining the mess there would be when they came to pick her up—if they came. And how angry all her friends and family would be because she had felt she had to push on. She cleared the image from her head. *No, it doesn't have to be today,* she thought, *I can come back up here in better weather, when I'm in better shape.*

She went back to the tent and called Russell again. He told her, 'If you're going to come down, do it straight away. You're only going to feel more tired if you stay there. Come down now because you need lots of rest.'

Sue packed a few small items and left them in the tent, a token of her faith that she would be back, then headed down the broad, snowy ridge. She met a huge line of people coming up, including Ted, Colleen, Petit and Jesse from Global Extremes. Next in line was Mark, who was devastated when he saw Sue coming down. He knew this could be the end of her Everest attempt. But Sue did not want to talk to anybody. She felt ashamed because she had ruined her chances. She had been overly ambitious. She had been feeling weak and yet had carried too much. She had made the mistake of being tough and ignoring the signs. Everest allowed no leeway with these factors. Everest allowed no leeway with anything.

It seemed to take such a long time for her to climb down. She rested in the sun at Camp One then descended the fixed ropes from the North Col. Back at ABC she listened to conversations on the radio until the news of progress by the others on the mountain upset her too much. She wondered whether she would have the strength to go back up, and whether the weather would cooperate.

Chung soon arrived at ABC, having followed her footsteps down from Camp Two. At least now she was not alone in having turned back. On several previous expeditions Chung had retreated before the summit, so he was well aware of what Sue was feeling now. His presence here on his fourth expedition to Everest, fresh from another setback halfway up the mountain, made Sue appreciate that there was life after retreat from Camp Two.

Intellectually she knew that she need not be finished with the mountain yet, but her heart was heavy with a sense of failure. The heaviness was because she had not pushed herself to her limits before retreating. She reminded herself that she had turned back because she had not felt strong enough to convert the opportunity of being at Camp Two into a safe and successful ascent. She reminded herself that Everest could still be climbed this season, and that if she refused to acknowledge the possibility she was just finding an excuse to avoid the ultimate confrontation with the mountain. She did not like that idea. She had told everyone — herself, her friends, and her memories of her father — that she was here to give it her best shot.

While Sue and Chung were weighing their options at ABC, over the next two days the remaining climbers on the Himex team continued up the mountain according to their plan. On 21 May, after two or three hours sleep at Camp Four, they were ready to head for the summit at around 11.30 pm. Some were more prompt in getting away than others. Weather conditions were not ideal — the wind blew constantly, and the occasional stronger gusts were even more intimidating in the black of night. Some of the climbers considered turning back, but the winds eased and everyone continued upwards. The pace was slow not only because of the darkness but also because of the restricted vision caused by oxygen masks, and the cumbersome task of clambering over downwards sloping rock shelves in heavy plastic boots equipped with crampons. The crampons were necessary for the infrequent patches of ice and snow that needed to be crossed. The extreme cold combined with the rigours of high altitude made it totally impractical to take crampons on and off, so this was not even an option.

It soon became apparent that another difficulty they would face was the sheer number of people attempting to reach the summit on the morning of 22 May. Hermann, Gernot, Zeddy and Matt had managed to leave with their three Sherpas immediately before a group of thirty climbers from other teams. Tony and Trynt were unlucky and were caught behind the crowd.

At the point where the North Ridge intersects the North-east Ridge, climbers turn right and follow the North-east Ridge for about one-and-a-half kilometres to the summit. This is a huge distance to travel when above 8500 metres, as it means spending a dangerous amount of time at this extreme altitude. Along the North-east Ridge there are three famous obstacles, each of them a steepening of the ridge. These three short cliffs are known as the First Step, Second Step and Third Step—not particularly imaginative names, but imagination is in short supply at those heights. Each of the steps created a bottleneck as climbers waited for their turn to tackle the difficulties.

By far the most challenging was the Second Step. There was only room for one person to tackle the intimidating rock wall at a time. The steep cliff is only four or five metres high, but there is a further exposed traverse up to the bottom of it. After climbing a ladder tied to anchor points on the cliff, each climber had to swing out and traverse to the right because a big protruding boulder blocked the route straight up. These last moves were over a huge drop and often climbers hesitated here, making several half-hearted attempts before taking their courage in their hands and committing themselves to the last two metres of rockclimbing. While Tony was waiting, a climber fell and dangled in space until Tony grabbed the rope and swung the man back on to the rock. Tony watched two other climbers fall off, twice each. All of this took time.

The day before, an American climber had slipped and fallen to the bottom of the Step when his rope came loose. He escaped injury because his fall was broken by a British climber. Unfortunately, the impact broke one of the legs of the British man he landed upon. The American was shaken but okay.

A plea came across the radio waves from the British man. 'They've broken my leg! Everyone's climbing past me! They're not stopping to help!'

At the North Col where he was stationed for the Himex summit bid, Russell grabbed his radio. 'You're going to have to crawl,' he said. 'Don't wait for help. Keep moving because we can't get someone to help you straight away. You're going to have to crawl.'

There was a silence, perhaps because the man could not believe the instructions he was being given. Russell repeated himself. 'You've got to crawl.'

The advice seemed so harsh, so Russell added, 'Crawl like I did on Kanchenjunga. You have to get down off the ridge in whatever way you can.'

For Sue listening in at ABC on a walkie-talkie, it was unimaginable that a man with a broken leg would be lying there while others walked around him. Then she heard Russell commissioning some of the Sherpas at Camp Four to help bring the climber down. It would take even these fit and acclimatised mountaineers two hours to reach him.

That was the day before. Today, as the Himex team climbed upwards, the issue was not accidents but the sheer numbers of climbers. It was chaos at the base of the Second Step. Some people realised that their chances of reaching the summit and returning safely were now very small because so much time was being wasted by nervous and exhausted mountaineers fumbling their way up the cliff. The entire Swiss expedition led by Kari Kobler turned back after witnessing the crowded scene and thinking through the implications of spending another hour or more in the queue.

It was bizarre to think that at this most remote and inhospitable spot on Earth, people were forming a queue. It had been exactly this scenario that had turned into disaster on 10 May 1996. There had been a similar traffic jam at the Hillary Step, the equivalent of the Second Step on the climbing route from Nepal. Because of delays at the Hillary Step, climbers had still been heading for the summit when their agreed upon turn-around time had passed. The turn-around time was set by the leader of each expedition. The rule was put in place so that climbers would be able to make it back down to 8000 metres or below in daylight after climbing as far as they could towards the summit. The veto on climbing upwards after the turn-around time was also to prevent people from being caught high in the mountain in the cloudy or stormy conditions which commonly occurred in the afternoon.

On Everest on 10 May 1996, over a dozen people were converging on the summit at turn-around time, and several more were already descending. The weather was worsening, but the summit was very close and its lure was very strong. When the storm hit with sudden force, everyone struggled to get down from the peak. But for eight people on the Nepalese side and three on the Tibetan side it was too late. Among those who died were New Zealander Rob Hall, owner and chief guide of Adventure Consultants, and one of his assistant guides, Andy Harris. Rob's American client, Doug Hansen, was unable to move up or down despite Rob's greatest efforts. When their oxygen supplies were exhausted, Doug died, and Rob found that he no longer had the strength to move from where they had been crouching together at the South Summit, only fifty metres below the peak. In a tent on Everest's lower slopes was Ed Viesturs, the most accomplished American high altitude mountaineer of his generation, who spoke at length with Rob by radio to motivate him to make the superhuman effort needed to drag himself down the mountain. But it was to no avail. Rob survived the night, but because the storm continued to rage unabated, no one could reach him with more oxygen. Any attempts to reach the summit in such violent weather would have been suicidal. Rob's last words on the radio were patched through to his wife, Jan Arnold, in New Zealand via the satellite phone at Base Camp. Jan had climbed Everest with Rob in the spring of 1993, three years before, so she could visualise exactly where Rob huddled in the snow. It was a brief, appalling and public farewell during which the couple chose a name for their unborn child.

Rob had ignored the turn-around time he had put in place by over an hour because he felt there was still time to take Doug to the top and back in safety. He had misjudged the weather. It was a tragically bad call, one that was mirrored by Scott Fischer, leader of the Mountain Madness expedition that had been climbing parallel with the Adventure Consultants expedition since Base Camp. Scott also extended his curfew time and as a result died in the worsening storm. Others died as well, and the death toll would have been even higher if not for the brave rescues accomplished by guide Anatoli Boukreev and the Sherpas who were at the highest camp on the South Col.

That same night Michael Groom, an Australian working as a guide for Rob Hall, was able to bring help to a group of climbers disorientated in the darkness on the storm-swept South Col. Michael was urged to set off from the group to fetch help because he was the strongest among them, and was more familiar with the terrain as this was the second time he had summitted Everest. The situation was desperate because their camp was pitched somewhere on the wide expanse of the Col, but if Michael headed in the wrong direction he would plummet off the mountain. He made it to the camp with barely enough strength to tell the Sherpas where to find the group of climbers huddling in the storm.

Every climber on the mountain in the spring of 2003 would have known the details of the 1996 disaster. It was the ultimate Everest tragedy, which prompted commercial operators to follow much stricter guidelines for their clients and their guides. In this context, the bottleneck at the Second Step was a very serious setback. The decisions of many climbers to turn around at that point were a matter of following the procedures that had been put in place by the expedition leader. The weather was far from ideal, and for many this was another factor in the decision to retreat.

Trynt was very aware that the bottleneck at the Second Step might cost her the summit. She had seen the many headlamps of the climbers in front of her when she reached the North-east Ridge—Russell watching through a telescope from the North Col below counted close to fifty—and so she made a concerted effort to overtake as many people as she could between the First and Second Steps. She moved across this section very fast, making up time and overtaking by not pausing when the climbers in front of her rested. She reached the infamous Second Step before a big queue of people had accumulated and was able to climb it without too much difficulty. She set off along the ridge but the wind became so strong that she decided it was foolhardy to continue.

Trynt was very clear-minded when it came to safety, and although she did not like the decision, she turned around and headed back towards the Second Step. Suddenly the wind died down, not completely, but enough to make her feel safe again. She turned around and headed back up the mountain. It took her almost an hour to get back to her high point, but from that moment there was no stopping her. She reached the summit at 9.11 am on 22 May, sharing her special moment and the small space with her climbing partner, Dorje Sherpa, and about ten other people. (Over the course of the expedition Dorje, Purba and another Sherpa, Dawa, climbed with Sue and twice went to the summit or near it, as well as involving themselves in rescues.)

Among the people who made it to the top of Everest that day were two members of the Chinese team. The SOHU members celebrated by making mobile phone calls and sending colour images from the summit. They had followed in the footsteps of three of their comrades who had summitted the day before, on 21 May. Those first summiteers had been congratulated by the Beijing Olympic Organisation Committee, then told that the Olympic flame would be brought to Everest. Live broadcasts were made from the summit. By way of contrast, John and Jess Roskelley, fifty per cent of the four-man team, also summitted on 21 May. They were a bit perplexed by the large Chinese contingent high on the mountain, many of whom were part of the crowd problems when the two Americans descended the Second Step.

Meanwhile, Trynt felt a huge sense of urgency about getting down to safer altitudes as fast as she could, so she and Dorje spent only ten minutes on the summit. Her major difficulty on the descent was finding a way around the unbroken line of people making their way up the ridge. When Trynt reached the Exit Rocks, where the North Ridge met the North-east Ridge, she came across a body in a sitting position near the fixed rope. She had not noticed it on the way up, so she attempted to revive the person. She quickly realised that whoever it was had been dead for a considerable length of time—four years, she later found out—but had been perfectly preserved by the intense cold.

A crowded trail to Camp Two, Mount Everest

At 8600 metres, the crux of the Mount Everest climb is this 'step' of about five metres using a ladder placed by Chinese climbers in 1975

Courtesy Ted Mahon

Me on the ridge, about 15 minutes from the Everest summit

Courtesy Tony Kelly

The view from the ridge of the final dome of Mount Everest ahead. You can see the ceremonial prayer flags left by the Sherpas hanging down the Kangshung face.

The final steps to the summit of Mount Everest

On the roof of the world! Dawa and me on the summit of Mount Everest at 7.15 am, 31 May 2003.

The view of Makalu and Makalu 2 from the summit of Mount Everest

Gasherbrum 2; following the left-hand ridge, it took eight hours of climbing through an icefall to get to this point, Camp One, at 5900 metres

Camp Three, Gasherbrum 2, at approximately 6900 metres

Me in my tent at Camp Three, Gasherbrum 2. You can see there's not much room once you've squeezed in all your gear, sleeping bags, suits and cooking utensils!

Beginning our final ascent of Gasherbrum 2 in the pre-dawn light

On top of the cornice of Gasherbrum 2; we considered it too dangerous to go even a metre or two further along because the whole cornice could break off underneath us

On top! Me standing on the fine ridge of the Gasherbrum 2 summit at 10.30 am, 26 July 2004, with Masherbrum in the distance behind.

When she had climbed past in the dark that morning, she simply had not noticed the body.

Tony was not so lucky at the Second Step. He spent so much time waiting that his oxygen supplies were severely diminished by the time he reached the top of the Step. He struggled upwards but his oxygen was running critically low. Forty-eight metres below the summit he wondered whether he should turn back. He radioed Russell, who told him what he did not want to hear but what he knew was common sense — that yes, he and his Sherpa, Dawa, should retreat. All three knew how narrow was the margin between life and death at 8800 metres.

Hermann had left Camp Four with Zeddy, Gernot and Matt before the major exodus from the camp, and to do this they had to leave well before midnight. They were among the first climbers away, which put them at the head of the queue. It was just as well they made an early start because they climbed very slowly, slow enough for Trynt to overtake them on her way up while it was still dark, but just fast enough for them to avoid the traffic jam at the Second Step. Even before they reached the that point, Russell had radioed Hermann to say that they should consider turning back because they were not climbing fast enough to reach the summit before the turn-around time of 11 am.

Hermann and the Sherpas managed to get Gernot, Zeddy and Matt up the Second Step before the huge wave of climbers launched themselves up the fixed ropes. As they got into the rhythm of the climb, they all moved less slowly, except for Zeddy and Purba, who dropped gradually behind the other three Sherpa–climber pairs. Russell was still worried that they were climbing too slowly. He calculated that if they continued to the summit, they would not get there with enough time to make it back to Camp Three safely. This meant they may have to stop at Camp Four, something he definitely wanted to plan against. After such a long and debilitating day, Camp Four was just too high for safety. Some climbers suffered from such deep post-summit exhaustion that it was almost impossible to get them awake enough to mobilise themselves in the morning. One short night at 8300 metres on the way to the summit was more than enough.

Russell kept trying to make radio contact but could not get through to them. He could contact the Sherpas up on the ridge very clearly but could not pick up even a squeak of static from Hermann. From the North Col he radioed Sue at ABC to see if she was getting reception, but she had heard nothing from Hermann either.

Then a call came through, and it was Hermann. 'Yes! Everything is okay. We made the summit! First me, then Matt and Gernot.' There was a pause. 'And Zeddy is still coming ... just now ...'

By this time it was 11.30 am, half an hour after the turn-around time, and visibility was poor. Russell spoke with urgency. 'You have to get down. You must come down now.' There was no response. Hermann had turned off the radio.

Suddenly Russell realised that Hermann must have had it turned off during the climb as well, which was why contact had been impossible. It was the height of irresponsibility as far as Russell was concerned — an unforgivable breach of safety procedure. Had he been able to speak to them earlier he would have ordered them to turn back at the turn-around time. Tony had played by the rules and had turned back. But Russell now knew that Hermann and his crew would make it only as far as Camp Four that night. This would put them in a very marginal state and in very poor condition for the long descent the following day. It was under these conditions that an accident could happen. An added complication was that the Global Extremes team, with their cameramen, was scheduled to spend that same evening at Camp Four before beginning their summit bid before midnight. Now there would not be enough tent space at Camp Four.

Russell realised that he might have to radio Global Extremes and ask them to wait at Camp Three. Meanwhile he had a crisis on his hands.

Russell was aware now that Hermann and his crew would run out of oxygen. They had been on the move for so long already, with a considerable distance still to descend. Once their oxygen supplies were exhausted, their rate of descent would slow dramatically — if they were able to continue at all. He sent two Sherpas up from Camp Four to make sure that the Sherpas with the climbers had located the caches of oxygen for the four descending climbers. Matters were made even worse by the fact that Zeddy was going snow-blind. He had taken off his goggles before dawn because they had iced up, making it impossible for him to see through them properly. As soon as the sun rose, the glare plus the reflection from the snow began to burn his eyes. It was many hours before he began to feel the damage. There was a lot of pain and then he went fully blind. Though his eyesight would gradually recover in a day or two's time, this fact was of no help at all when he was at 8500 metres, staggering with exhaustion, running low on oxygen and unable to see.

Even Tony, who had made the right decision to turn back, ran out of oxygen on the descent between the Second and First Steps. He began to hallucinate, and then slipped and found himself dangling on the fixed rope. Dawa anxiously came to Tony's aid. Hermann, now on his way back from the summit, caught up with the pair as they moved very slowly along the ridge. Hermann insisted that Tony use his own still functioning oxygen bottle. Tony refused, but Hermann disconnected his bottle and handed it over. It was a very generous act. Now Hermann had put himself at great risk.

Somehow Tony and Dawa managed to climb down to Camp Three at 7900 metres before exhaustion stopped Tony from going any further. Hermann waited at Camp Four for Gernot, Matt and Zeddy to arrive. They staggered into camp too late and too exhausted to go any further. Matt had frostbitten hands and frost damage to his face. So did Gernot, only not as severe. Zeddy was being led by three Sherpas now. The Global Extremes climbers were already in residence at Camp Four, having moved up quickly, but Russell had asked the camera crew to remain at Camp Three on standby. There were not enough sleeping bags for everyone, so cameraman Ken Sauls and stills photographer Jake Norton carried loads of sleeping bags up to Camp Four and then returned to Camp Three for the night—a huge effort and beyond the call of duty.

At Camp Four, the Global Extremes athletes and their leader, Chris Warner, were not in a good frame of mind. The previous afternoon the British climber with the broken leg had been brought down to Camp Three by Sherpas and several climbers, ready to be taken the rest of the way down the mountain the next day by a team of British Royal Marines. It was an efficient rescue, but a disconcerting sight for the Globex athletes. Now, on 22 May, they had heard constant radio conversations among the different teams about the chaos at the Second Step. They witnessed the arrival of Hermann, Gernot, Matt and Zeddy in turn, each of the four looking worse than the one who preceded them. During their arrival, when several of the climbers as well as some Sherpas were moving around all at once, an oxygen bottle was dislodged. It bounced a short distance before striking Chris Warner on the head. It was a heavy blow, and Chris was lucky not to be concussed. He realised he needed to head down the mountain immediately, so he grabbed his gear and carefully set off down the fixed ropes. His vision in one eye was compromised and he wanted to get the best medical advice as soon as he could. Sue met him briefly at ABC but could not say much except to wish him well. When he reached Base Camp he grabbed his gear and a Chinese jeep to Zhangmu. Within a few days he was back in the USA.

The Global Extremes athletes did not have quite the same degree of urgency, but they decided on the spot that they needed to head down as well. At extreme altitudes you either went for it or you came straight back down. They chose to wait until the morning. Both Petit and Colleen vowed that this was the end of the show for them. Summit day on Mount Everest was a different ball game to the adventure racing at which they excelled. Enormous demands were made of them physically and psychologically during multi-day races, but the dangers here were incomparably greater. On Everest it was very easy to die. Lying in the tents next to them was proof of the severity of the summit climb. The four Himex climbers were totally exhausted, yet they still had two vertical kilometres of the mountain to descend before they could regard themselves as safe.

While Petit and Colleen were no longer interested in continuing with the climb, Ted and Jesse withheld their judgment. They agreed that now was not a good time to go for the top. Apart from the frenzy of activity and the sheer numbers of people attempting to climb the peak, there were now major logistical problems. The Sherpas who had planned to climb with them that very night had been forced to move into rescue mode because Hermann and his crew had put attaining the summit ahead of everything else. This decision led to snow blindness, frostbite, shortages of oxygen, extreme exhaustion and a perilous mismanagement of time. Any form of incapacity was a dangerous development on Everest's highest ridge, and whenever it occurred Russell's policy was to send backup—provided conditions allowed. In this case, the essential safety procedures were to Global Extremes' detriment.

The next day the two teams headed down the mountain. Three Sherpas assisted the snow-blind Zeddy for the entire descent. Gernot, and particularly Matt, needed considerable help as well. During the past few days, too many people had been trying too hard to get to the top. Had a storm blown in at this time it may well have been 1996 revisited—chaos and multiple deaths on the mountain's highest reaches. In these circumstances it made much more sense for Global Extremes to retreat, regroup and then consider their options. The pieces of the puzzle had simply not fallen into place for them, not yet at least.

No one mentioned the irony that Trynt, who had been voted off the Global Extremes Everest Expedition, was the first and only athlete to make the summit to date. Without articulating it, Trynt had put into practice a maxim used by Michael Groom during his oxygenless ascents of the six highest mountains in the world: 'You make your own luck.'

8

SUMMIT FEVER

When I heard that the rest of our team was coming off the mountain after reaching the summit, I could not decide what to do. Should I to go up to meet them? I did not agree with the way Hermann, Zeddy, Gernot and Matt had tackled the climb. Trynt and Tony and been much more responsible. Trynt had done everything in her power to get the mix right, and had managed it well. Tony had been on target, too, but there had been a problem with his oxygen. Details were sketchy, but I gathered he made the decision to turn back while he still had some oxygen left, which was the only safe course of action. The others, however, had pushed on regardless of their circumstances. In fact, I felt embarrassed to be part of the same expedition because of the risks they had forced the Sherpas to take in their efforts to get them down safely. I was also appalled by the fact that they had inadvertently destroyed the summit chances of the Global Extremes team.

For most of the last forty-eight hours, Chung and I had been sitting at Advance Base Camp with the cook, Chuldim, and the kitchen boy, Lhakpa, listening to the walkie-talkie communications between Russell at the North Col and the teams up on the mountain. Chung and I had heard everything: our team members climbing up and then coming down very late, arriving at Camp Four at eight o'clock at night with Zeddy unable to see because he had taken his goggles off up high. The situation worsened with the shortage of oxygen and the need to source other bottles. Then there was the final crunch of them requiring the tents at Camp Four so that the Global Extremes team could not move up. If it were not for the strength of the Sherpas and for the film crew members who took up sleeping bags, there could have been deaths. Also important in preventing disaster was a clever damage control plan instigated by Russell and Swiss commercial expedition leader Kari Kobler. It could have been catastrophic, but because nothing really dreadful happened, no one fully appreciated how much respect this mountain should command.

The truth remained that whatever the conduct of Hermann, Zeddy, Matt and Gernot, this day was a special time for them. Each man had achieved his dream of climbing Mount Everest, and I was not going to let my personal feelings tarnish their moments of triumph. I went to each of their tents and tidied them to create a welcoming ambience. While I was about it, I laid out their sleeping bags so it would be easy for them to crash out when they collapsed in their tents. My actions were all part of my resolve to be positive and supportive, which I felt was the right stance to take. Personally, I was happier knowing that no one was aware I had prepared these subtle welcomes since their return to Base Camp was about them, not me.

On a pragmatic level, it made sense for me to stay put rather than head up to meet the summiteers. Recuperation was my number one priority. This was difficult enough to achieve at 6400 metres and would not be helped by the extra exercise of the fifty-minute slog to up Crampon Point.

It certainly proved easy to be positive and supportive with the first person to come off the mountain and into camp. Chung and I were still in the kitchen tent when Trynt shrugged her pack off and came inside. As she walked in I went straight to her and hugged her, lifting her up.

'Power to you!' I said. 'Power to you, ma'am!'

I was so pleased for her that she burst into tears. 'Everyone has said such great things to me,' she sobbed.

'They're not just saying it, you know. You have every right to be so proud of what you did, of how you climbed. You never compromised safety. You climbed with integrity. And you just kept going and going.

You totally hammered it. You pulled it out when it counted. You did it. And you got yourself off the mountain independently. You ought to be bloody proud of yourself.'

Of course, these words only led to more tears. Tears of happiness and release. This was her moment, and I wanted her to bask in her achievement and not let it pass by in the chaos of what had unfolded up there, and what might unfold down here as well.

She looked weather-blasted and deeply tired, but glowing. We had hot drink after hot drink so she could rehydrate. It was cosy in the kitchen and much more personal than in the mess tent. Chung headed up to meet Tony mid-afternoon, as he and Tony had been on Everest together in the past and this was the second time that both of them had turned back.

Meanwhile Trynt talked, and Chuldim, Lhakpa and I listened. It was wonderful. At dusk the others came in, and not just the climbers from our group. People from other expeditions were staggering in all afternoon, heading for their own camps. I did not notice Hermann or Gernot's arrival, but I certainly remember Matt appearing just on dark with Sherpas at his side. He had a wide stare and I was not sure if he was all there. He looked a hundred years old.

'Matt!' I cried.

He looked at me. 'Did I do good, Sue?' he asked. 'Did I do good?'

I couldn't answer at first because I was so shocked. Not only did he look a hundred years old; he looked like death.

'Yeah, Matt,' I said finally with warm pat on the back. 'You did okay, mate. But we'd better get you inside.'

As we walked to his tent next to mine, he looked at me vacantly and asked again, 'Did I do good?' He was a real mess. His fingers and toes were frostbitten, some so badly they would possibly have to be amputated (eventually they were). His face was frostnipped though the damage was superficial. For the moment he was absolutely shattered.

'Sure you did,' I reassured him once more. 'Sure you did.'

An hour or so later, when it was dark, Zeddy staggered in with four Sherpas helping him because of his snow blindness. He had torn a huge hole in his down suit when he had fallen while descending the Second Step, and one panel was now empty of feathers. He said he couldn't see anything. From what he and the Sherpas described, he certainly didn't exaggerate the difficulties of climbing down without being able to see. His descent sounded truly horrific, not only for him but also for the Sherpas. As well as being in charge of the climbing route, Purba was as strong as a horse, able to carry Zeddy around the camp, even though he, too, had just returned from the summit of Everest. I walked with Purba and Zeddy to his tent and gave him my water bottle to use as a urine bottle for the night.

The climbers from other teams were all back in camp by now as our team was the last. For hours they had been wandering past in disarray. It seemed to me there were too many inexperienced people who had overstretched their capabilities and were now barely able to function. That might seem an easy judgment coming from someone who had yet to climb the mountain, but I had seen enough competent climbers after they had returned from an 8000-metre summit to know that you could be exhausted and still in control. Trynt was an example, as were some of the climbers from the International Mountain Guides team camped nearby.

Mario from the Swiss team was one of the very capable European guides whom I crossed paths with many times on the mountain. In fact, I crossed paths with him as many times as I could because I found him very attractive. It seemed to me that the men looked appealingly weather-beaten and macho after a month or more in the mountains, whereas the women simply looked tired and unkempt. Perhaps there was something appealing in this as well, a kind of bedroom look, but be that as it may, I felt that Mario was able see past the unflattering down jacket and the wind-blasted cheeks. I was shocked and disappointed when I heard his story and why he was not able to summit. He told me that he and his clients had waited two hours at the Second Step but for safety reasons could not wait any longer. The weather was not good, and the queue progressed too slowly, so they had to turn around and come back empty-handed. It was a courageous decision to make because they were very disappointed and had come so close to achieving their goal.

The Global Extremes team had made it down much earlier in the day, but I didn't get to speak with them. And they certainly weren't rushing over to congratulate Zeddy, Gernot, Hermann and Matt, whose very late return to Camp Four cost them their shot at the summit. Our team had caused more disruption high on the mountain than any other. Only the British man with the broken leg created an equal stir, and his injury had been inflicted by someone else.

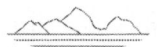

The next day at ABC was interesting. Everyone had either summitted, failed in their attempt to summit and was going home, or failed and was planning to have another shot at reaching the top. The range of emotions encompassed triumph and euphoria, intense disappointment, and a gnawing nervousness at the prospect of heading up the mountain again.

The divide between these emotional states was best illustrated by events the next morning. In the light of day you could see the full extent of the damage exacted by the mountain. Our four male summiteers shuffled over to the mess tent in their bivvy boots and half done-up trousers. Their faces had been hammered by the wind and sun, and their fingers were cracked and split from the cold. Trynt was better presented, but she had been more in control — as had Tony. He had the same weather-beaten look but his fatigue had not been by lightened by euphoria. The comment was innocently made at breakfast, by Matt I think, that the Global Extremes team was not happy and that it was our team that had cost them their summit bid. Zeddy, Gernot and Hermann pointedly refused to acknowledge the comment and kept eating. I said nothing.

After breakfast there was a call for a photo session, instigated by Zeddy, as most things were. The eight of us wandered over to the spot he had selected. The most important thing was Zeddy's flag, 'Forever Everest'. As the group assembled, Zeddy cried, 'Only summiteers!'

Inwardly I sighed. After all this time together, it came down to this.

'All right,' I said. 'I'll take the pictures.'

At this point I was still half a dozen metres from the group, and Chung was with me, but Tony was already among the group so he had to come out. He had climbed all but the last fifty metres of the mountain, yet his teammates of the day didn't want him in their photo.

I collected everyone's cameras and took a shot or two with each of them. The wind was extremely cold and my hands felt freezing as I snapped the photos. The whole exercise seemed hollow to me because we had not gelled as a group and the climb was not one to be proud of. Yet people wanted it to look like a heroic team event.

Zeddy made another announcement. 'Now I think we should have everybody.'

Hermann volunteered to take the shots, so I handed the cameras to him and joined the group. Giving the cameras to Hermann was my first contact with him for quite some time, and insubstantial though it was, it was also my last. We all huddled together as he took some shots. There was a call for Hermann to be in the photo as well, so the camera was handed to Lhakpa. In that group photo, I am nestled in with 'those three', Zeddy, Hermann and Gernot, in the front row. Our arms are around each other. I really don't know whether or not it was now a case of 'no hard feelings'. It did not matter. They were going home.

There was no real hatred directed either way between us; it was just that we had such different outlooks. I think that perhaps I annoyed Hermann, Gernot and Zeddy at times because in their cultures women were supposed to keep quiet, do as they were told and be in total admiration of men who go to the mountains. At least, this was the feeling I picked up from them, and the only explanation I could think of for their behaviour towards me. I challenged them not for the sake of it, nor because I thought women should be allowed a say. I spoke up because I thought they were talking nonsense. My opinions were dismissed so readily I could only assume they regarded me as speaking out of place. Not only was I a woman challenging Hermann, the accomplished and renowned guide, about how to climb Mount Everest, but I was also an Australian woman, a woman from a country where there are no mountains. How could I possibly know anything about how to climb the ultimate peak?

But today I had no reason to confront Hermann. It was his last full day at ABC, and really there was nothing I needed to say to him. Russell, however, had a great deal to say. Hermann went over to Russell's tent, where Mark joined them. I knew they would be talking about what had happened up there. They sat among some rocks next to the tent with both Russell and Hermann talking earnestly. The two men certainly had different approaches to guiding mountains, as well as how to relate to the clients in their charge. And I imagine that from Russell's point of view their quarrel went further, into the realm of Hermann failing to respect the trust Russell had extended to him. I heard nothing of what was said that day, but I had picked up on Russell's strong feelings when the problems had been unfolding up high and Hermann had ignored the turn-around time and switched off his radio.

Meanwhile, the climbers who were leaving were busy packing their belongings ready for departure the next day. Yaks were on their way up from Base Camp. Matt would have to ride one of the yaks because he could not walk on his badly frostbitten feet. Twenty-two kilometres sitting on a yak was not a journey I wanted to experience, but Matt had no choice.

I spent most of the morning chatting with Trynt in her tent as she packed. Some of it was just girls' talk, but she also told me everything she could about the route and the obstacles I should look out for. She gave me details of how she had worked her gear: water system down her front, gloves and socks with heat packets, how the oxygen mask bothered her, how she dealt with the cold. She offered to lend me almost everything she had, which was great given that I had lost so many things when my tents had blown away. I wore her socks and her gloves to the summit, and used her catalytic hand warmers. I also thought I should try her water system to see if this would work better than using a bottle, as it would save me stopping (in fact I found it did not work for me and I did not attempt to use it on the summit climb). Among Trynt's things was a fleece hat that turned out to be Sissell's, who had long since left. All the girls had helped each other, which was nice form. I gave Trynt my special Mountain Designs 'Go' good luck T-shirt, which she loved. I really admired how she had taken on board my advice to forget the men she had been flirting with and instead focus on the climb. The impression she had unwittingly created around the camps of being a Baywatch babe was blown out of the water when she changed her attitude and climbed the mountain in better style than anyone else on our team. She did the women's side proud, and she was over the moon with happiness about her success.

When I talked to the two Global Extremes women about their experiences, they were in a completely different headspace. The sight of Zeddy and Matt, physically incapacitated because they had pushed beyond their limits, turned Petit off the climb. She told me, 'I never want to be part of that scene.'

I looked at Petit. Younger than I was, she also appeared much stronger. And Colleen was very strong as well. She had competed in races that went for hundreds of kilometres. She was incredibly tough, but she felt the same way as Petit. My response to both of them was the same: 'Don't make any decision now. Just wait and see.'

Colleen dismissed the suggestion with a shake of her head, and said, 'Oh, I don't know at this point.' But this answer told me that she did know. The decision to climb Mount Everest is seated much deeper than a shake of your head. You have to want it with all your heart. That much I knew. I thought, *This is how we are different, these women and I.* I think Colleen had been totally shocked by what had happened up high, and not just by the fact that the actions of Hermann and the others had cost the Global Extremes team their summit chance. The precarious nature of climbing Everest hit home, literally, when Chris was struck on the head by a falling oxygen bottle. The fact that he had to leave not only the mountain but also the expedition gave their descent a feeling of finality, even though the rest of the Global Extremes support structure was still in place. All this was on top of the intimidating winds, the cold and the huge scale of Everest.

The next day the Himex summiteers prepared to leave. Other teams were moving out as well. Jess Roskelley came up to our camp, endeavouring to find out some information about yaks. I talked to him for a while and had to admire both him and his dad. They had run their own small expedition, which had shrunk to just the two of them after Dick Bass and Jim Wickwire had gone home. They had climbed the mountain safely, despite the chaos around them. But then John was one of the most accomplished American mountaineers of his generation, to the point that if there had been guides on their trip, he would have been giving them the instructions rather than the other way around.

I took the time to say goodbye to Kari Kobler and the Swiss crew, including Mario. I also farewelled the IMG team, with whom I had got along well. When our phone was out of action, IMG allowed me to make a call from ABC to Sue Badyari in Australia after I aborted my first summit bid.

There must have been 200 to 250 climbers on the north side of Everest over the season, but the mass exodus that was happening now left few behind. Most of the smaller, budget expeditions had been forced to leave after the first violent storms when all their kit blew away, and those remaining certainly met their match after their first summit push.

I said my goodbyes to the team, managing to miss out Hermann. I was busy in my tent when he left, and that was not entirely an accident. Gernot I was never able to work out; he had momentary acts of enthusiasm and generosity towards me, but more often he was laying down intensely strong views, then steamrolling if I made the slightest comment. Nevertheless, he asked for my address, and so did Zeddy. We exchanged details and then they were off.

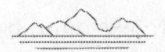

For the first time since we had arrived, peace reigned at ABC. Yet it was an uneasy kind of peace. I was feeling weaker and weaker by the day.

It was an effort to walk to the mess tent and the toilet tent, which made me wonder how I was going to manage climbing. I told myself to stop having such stupid, unproductive thoughts. Instead, I had to direct all my attention to recovering as much strength as I could in the short time before the next summit bid.

I knew I had to guard my attitude. The social make-up of the team improved dramatically with the departures, and the Sherpa crew at ABC relaxed as well, sharing stories and chores. They still worked as hard, but the atmosphere in the camp changed dramatically because there was no one left to order them around. But though the feel of the camp was now much more supportive, I still had to fire up my motivation and belief in myself. I knew that the Tibetan name for Everest is Chomolungma, meaning Mother Goddess of the Earth. This was a woman's mountain, which I had to see as an advantage. I could do this using straightforward stubbornness, refusing to go home until I had exhausted all possibilities.

The expedition was only another week, and I would be here until the last day. My dad would have expected no less, and my brothers, too. In our family, we had learnt to have no malice, to not quit on our goals, to give everything our best shot and to not get distracted. I learnt from triathlons in my twenties that you should finish your race having fully utilised every drop of strength and skill you have, and finish knowing you have given it your all and did not quit early because you talked yourself out of it. Mount Everest was something beyond a triathlon, but the principle held true.

I set about eating well, doing my stretches, getting restful sleep and willing my body back to strength. It helped to work on other people's will as well. I had many conversations with Chung. I liked him. He was much smarter than people took him for, and much more committed as well, but he had talked little when the entire group had been present. Instead, he tended to do his socialising in the kitchen tent with the Sherpa crew, many of who he knew well from other trips. This was Chung's fourth expedition to Mount Everest, which said everything about how badly he wanted to reach the top. It also said something about his approach to the climb. He had many other mountains under this belt, and he was passionate about his climbing, but he choked under the pressure of Everest. He had lost a substantial amount of weight during our forays to high altitude. He knew this was normal, but he kept saying, 'My legs are so skinny! How can I do it?'

I felt that Chung wanted an excuse not to go up again. 'Stop fussing about it,' I said. 'The climb is all in your head. If your legs aren't strong enough, you'll find out when they stop working. Then you turn around, but not before. You want to climb this mountain, so why would you turn around before that?'

Tony was also having doubts because he was understandably exhausted after all but reaching the summit. I told him what I had told myself. 'It's only another week, mate.'

'But I'm so run down,' he answered.

'You might feel bad now, but think about how bad you'll feel in two weeks' time when you bump into Chung and me in Kathmandu and we've both reached the summit.'

This seemed to do something for him. I twisted the knife. 'And you know you can do it, and do it safely. Common sense saved you last time, and it will see you through again—you know that.'

Tony had the goods, there was no doubt about that, but it was really going to hurt to do it all again. So now he was on board as well. And in the Global Extremes camp next door, Jesse and Ted were preparing themselves with obvious determination.

Mark was a great help to me during this time. We kept each other's spirits up. He knew that throughout the trip I had been carrying too much weight, so he went through everything in my pack.

'You've got too much shit, Sue,' he said, holding up my two sets of spare gloves. 'We've got to take some stuff out.'

Rather than letting me just stuff my pack with what I thought I needed, Mark made me consider every single item. And the weight of what we eliminated was definitely worth losing. The angst over leaving such good performance gear behind was the hardest thing I had done to date. It meant goodbye to insurances and backup, but going lightweight was so important. I had made the mistake of carrying too many heavy loads all through the trip, thinking I would get stronger, but living at 6400 metres, with diarrhoea, I did not. This was my last chance to give myself a break.

Tony, Chung and I decided to head up on 27 May. The program was that we would climb on 27 May to Camp One, 28 May to Camp Two, 29 May to Camp Three, 30 May to Camp Four, and 31 May to the top and back down to Camp Two. The first of June would see us at ABC, 2 June at Base Camp and 4 June in Zhangmu.

The weather was not inspiring, but with the windows of good weather being so narrow, we knew we would have to leave in marginal conditions to get the best day for the summit. Russell's forecasts promised good weather for the last days of the month, but we were impatient and we didn't want to get caught out too low on the mountain if a fine spell appeared unexpectedly.

On 27 May Chung and Tony headed up early, with Mark and me two hours behind. Jesse and Ted had headed up the day before with cameramen Mike and Ken, plus Jake, the stills photographer. Mark knew the route well and was confident he could catch up with the Global Extremes group before he was needed, wherever they happened to be on the mountain. We reached the North Col in good time. I felt stronger than expected. My pack was lighter not only because we had trimmed it down but also because I had given a small sack of odds and ends to one of the Sherpas to carry. Others did this and I saw no reason to be stoic. At this point I didn't care about being one hundred per cent self-sufficient. Whatever it took me to get myself up, within reason, I would do it.

We relaxed in our tents at the North Col, with one special, good luck beer for the road. I felt renewed enthusiasm and excitement, emotions I had not felt much on this trip. Then we set off to Camp Two. I felt okay except for a profound feeling of tiredness that stayed with me the whole way. Four hundred metres height gain does not sound like much, but it is a huge effort above 7000 metres. The weather was still turbulent which made the day less pleasant.

Not everything was as it should be at a practical level. I had trouble with my oxygen. I was only using oxygen at this height because there were spare tanks and Russell advised us to utilise them. I cursed myself for not experimenting with the set more thoroughly when I tried it out at ABC. As I had never climbed with oxygen before, I had yet to learn to troubleshoot. The problem was that somehow the oxygen was causing my sunglasses to fog up. I could not quite work out what was 'normal', and conditions were too difficult to stop and have a mothers' meeting about it. I told myself just to keep going and work it out en route.

Meanwhile, as Tony and Mark climbed on through to Camp Two, I felt disappointed that I had let them get away so early. I thought it was my chance to show Mark that I could set a steady pace, but it was not to be. The last little bit coming into Camp Two was horrible because it seemed to go on forever. It was a trick of the mind, of course—to the ascending climber, the camp looks close and so your mind signals you to get ready to relax, but at 7400 metres that short distance takes a lot of effort and a lot of time.

I rested just short of camp and looked down at Chung about thirty metres below.

'Sue! Sue!' he called.

'What's wrong?' I shouted back. 'What's the problem?'

'Give me some encouragement!'

I laughed. 'Okay. You're almost here.'

I was delighted by the interchange as it showed we were unified, we were working well together. But also in Chung's eyes I was performing better than he was, which made me think maybe I had been judging myself harshly.

I turned back to struggling up the slope. I could not help but wonder how I would climb the remaining 1400 metres to the summit. I knew the answer was to take it one day at a time. If the goal for a day's climbing seemed too daunting, I would take it hour by hour. The trick of altitude was not to let yourself be hypnotised into resting for too long. You must fight that lethargy. All good high-altitude climbers are able do this. The weather was on our side. Although it was a little turbulent, I could feel it coming good, and it was much warmer than during my last climb to Camp Two. The signs looked positive.

A few minutes later, I looked up the ropes. Camp Two was in sight and the Sherpa Dawa was coming down towards me. Soon he was standing next to me, offering to take my pack. This was obviously his purpose in coming to meet me, so I readily handed it over. Swinging it off my shoulders reminded me that I had neglected to put my oxygen mask back on after exchanging comments with Chung. Surprisingly I felt no difference between using the oxygen and not using it.

Two weeks earlier on my first foray to Camp Two I had felt okay at this height, a bit weak from diarrhoea but not exhausted, and certainly not ready to have my pack taken from me. Today I felt like one of the dozens of struggling trekking clients whose packs I had carried into camp, and it was good for me to experience that same relief and humility. This time the summit was at stake so I had to make things work, and not get too hung up on the purity of doing it all myself. That was only an illusion anyway, with the Sherpas right at my side. However, I remained strong in my resolve to be accountable for my own safety without impinging on the safety of others. If I could not meet these requirements, I would go down.

At Camp Two, I tumbled into a tent with Tony and Mark. When Chung arrived he bunked in with the Sherpas. The wind had picked up and was blowing horribly. It was only after I stripped down to my thermals and wriggled into my cozy sleeping bag that I noticed Tony and Mark were still in their down suits and harnesses, ready for anything the mountain might throw at us. When I arrived I had been so focused on getting into my sleeping bag and resting that I had not paid any attention to how my friends were reacting to the conditions outside. I took notice when they began to contemplate putting their boots back on. The wind got stronger and stronger, to the point where I was worried that we would be blown away. I was very comfortable in the warm cocoon of my sleeping bag, wearing only a thermal top and bottom, but much less comfortable in my mind. I deliberated about what to do. My tiredness and the cosiness of the sleeping bag answered the question. Ignoring the wind, I pulled the hood of the bag around my face and snuggled up at the far end of the tent away from the door and furthest from the gusts.

When the tent showed no signs of becoming airborne we accepted the horrific winds as just being part of our current reality. We began to chat about nothing in particular. As we talked, Mark took my harness and the loop of cord attached to it which I used for clipping into fixed ropes. He unwrapped some of the gaffer tape he used to hold the karabiner in place on his clipping loop and taped it to my loop to fix my karabiner in position. This meant that the karabiner would no longer slide loosely along the loop, hence making it much easier for me to unclip from one fixed rope and re-clip to another while wearing my cumbersome gloves and mitts. Although I did not appreciate it at the time, Mark's attention to this detail greatly smoothed the passage of my climbing over the vital next few days, and it was something I should have picked much earlier.

No sooner had he finished with my harness than a call came through from the Global Extremes camp at ABC. It was from Peter Engelhart, the OLN manager heading up the Globex expedition. He asked Mark to move up to Camp Three to take live footage of Ted and Jesse. I could not believe the request so late in the day, but then Peter had never been on the mountain so he had no idea of what the words 'strong winds' meant at these heights. Mark did not seem too concerned. The sun was shining and that was good enough for him. He knew the mountain well and there was fixed rope all the way, so he put his boots on and left.

Tony and I were now getting on really well, and we were feeling as good as one could feel at 7500 metres. The Sherpas were also ready for some serious action. It had been agreed in the days before we left ABC whom we were to climb with. Tony would be paired with Dorje, and I would be with Dawa. I did not know Dawa particularly well, but I did know he had almost reached the summit with Tony the preceding week. Chung was to receive special treatment. Because this was his fourth attempt to climb Everest, Russell was determined that he would succeed. To increase the odds, Russell assigned three Sherpas to climb with him—Purba, Tsering and Datenji. As well as being our *sirdar*, Purba was one of the best climbing Sherpas on the mountain. The plan was that we would climb independently but loosely together up the fixed rope to Camp Four, and from there we would partner with our Sherpas.

Meanwhile, Tony and I concentrated on keeping ourselves warm and hydrated in the tent. The wind maintained its strength during the night and into the next day, and we decided that the sensible thing to do was sit out the weather. Meanwhile, the Global Extremes team and their Sherpas pushed on to Camp Four. Time dragged, with nothing to do but lie in the tent and brew the occasional soup or drink, but it was not as arduous as might be expected. High on a mountain you become involved in the needs of the situation, and when that means lying in your sleeping bag that is what you do. For one thing, at 7500 metres, mental functions are slowed down by the shortage of oxygen, so time seems to pass twice as fast. Other worldly concerns are in another world. It did not occur to us at the time that the date was 29 May, the fiftieth anniversary of the first ascent. Our minds were focused entirely on our own ascent.

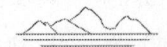

By the second morning, 30 May, the wind had eased so we set off early for Camp Four. After two nights at Camp Two we wanted to keep to our schedule by leapfrogging Camp Three. We were setting ourselves the task of completing two days' climb in one, then after a few hours' rest, heading for the summit.

I set off enthusiastically, determined not to encounter a psychological barrier at the windy corner where I had turned back the preceding week. I now knew that this section immediately above Camp Two was renowned for gusty winds, unpleasant sloping slabs of shale and the huge drop into the Central Rongbuk. After running these thoughts through my mind, I stepped onto the rock and without hesitating rounded the corner to the fixed rope.

I continued up the slope but found that soon I was being overtaken by everyone else. This had never happened before. I was wearing my oxygen mask and the system was turned on, but I had to take my mask off regularly to catch my breath—which logically did not make sense. Dawa was above me. He looked back regularly to make sure I was climbing, then he turned back to scrambling up the rocky slope, so I was unable to catch up and tell him I had a problem with my oxygen.

I told myself to stop being a girl and get on with it. I had been in other situations where things had not been quite right with a piece of equipment—like a sharp item in my pack poking me in the back—and I had made myself push on. This was what I did now.

It wasn't until I was fifty metres from Camp Four that I saw a climber whom I recognised as Dr Jon Gibons, the doctor from the American Ski Everest Expedition. The first time I met him was when he came over to help with the sick Japanese man I had escorted to Base Camp. As he came down towards me I ripped my mask off and gasped, 'I don't think this is working. Can you please look at the dial?'

He gave a positive gesture immediately, and then paused to look at the set-up poking out of the top of my pack. It took him only a few moments to get it functioning. With my mask on again, I immediately noticed the difference. There was a clear, hollow sound, the gushing of the oxygen as I breathed. My voice echoed when I thanked him, an effect which I soon realised was an indication that the oxygen system was working well. It had only taken him a moment to fix it, then he was on his way, his hand raised in farewell. *What a nice man*, I thought as he headed down, comfortable in his skin after having summitted Mount Everest.

There was a dramatic difference with the oxygen flowing properly. Immediately I felt less lethargic. I was now fifty metres below Camp Four, and I had climbed all this way without any oxygen because the regulator had not been properly set. How stupid to have put myself through all that extra effort because I didn't understand the technology properly, when I could have been saving energy for the big climb tomorrow.

I came into camp feeling a lot better, but this was short-lived. I started losing vision in one eye. Tony and one of the Sherpas were chatting about the next day's program. I said with some urgency, 'I think we should get the stove on and get into the tent.'

'Okay,' said Tony. 'We'll do it in minute.'

My left eye was starting to go black, and I recognised this as a symptom that I might faint. Dehydration had caused me to faint in my earlier life as a competitive sportsperson. Today I had drunk nothing since leaving the tents because I had been trying to catch up, and now I desperately needed to rehydrate.

'Tony,' I said with a greater degree of urgency, 'I'm losing my vision. I have to have a drink.'

He took notice of this. 'Put your oxygen back on and keep it on,' he said as he unzipped the tent for me. I crawled in and hauled my pack after me. I did not worry about getting comfortable but immediately pulled out my drink bottle and drank from it. At 8300 metres it is hard to function properly, and I knew I had to tend to my needs quickly or I might crash and burn and ruin my summit chances entirely.

I took care not to drink too much water at once in case I brought it up again. High altitude puts such a strain on you that it is not uncommon to vomit. I alternated taking a swig of water with breathing oxygen and soon was feeling more normal—or as normal as I could expect to feel. We were camping higher than the summits of Shishapangma and Cho Oyu. Only the summits of Everest, K2, Lhotse, Kanchenjunga and Makalu were above us. Tomorrow, if the weather was good, K2 would be the only one of these peaks I would not see.

Tony clambered inside as well, got himself organised and set about trying to fix his headlamp, a vital piece of equipment for our midnight departure. I made myself more comfortable and then focused on melting snow. This was more awkward now that I was breathing oxygen; the mask blocked part of my field of vision, the hose got in the way, and when I moved I had to move the bottle, which was no longer in my pack on my back. I filled the water bottles, topped up the pot with more snow, and made a few more drinks for us, as well as some soup with noodles. That was all either of us could bear, yet we knew eating anything would be difficult tomorrow and we needed calories.

'Hey, I'm doing all the chores here,' I remarked to Tony, but actually I did not mind the drink-focused work because I was quite efficient at it after lots of practice. Tony eventually managed to repair his headlamp. He had a couple of Musashi bars which I had given him ages ago and he had saved for the summit bid. They now became our dinner. I rued the fact that many of mine had been looted from my caches at lower camps or been blown away in my tent during the wind storm at ABC two weeks before.

We tucked ourselves up in our sleeping bags at around three o'clock and rested until we heard some discussions outside Chung's tent about three hours later. A Romanian climber had appeared out of nowhere, very late in the afternoon given that we were at 8300 metres. It was a startling development. At first we thought he was looking for a tent in which to sleep, but he was actually looking for another Romanian who had died somewhere on the mountain. We couldn't help him. He settled in the tent of a group next door, also eastern European. He was dressed in very basic clothing and was entirely by himself on his sad mission. Later I learnt that the body of the Romanian he had been looking for was found on the glacier, his position indicating that he had fallen from Camp Two. The fact that he was wearing only socks on his feet suggested that he had stepped outside his tent to urinate and had slipped. It was so easy to die up here. Constant vigilance was the key to survival.

Luckily for our visitor, and for us as well, the weather was now crystal clear. There were amazing views from our tent door. We could look west along the Himalayan Range, past Cho Oyu, with peak after peak disappearing beyond the horizon. After taking our fill of the view we zipped up the door and snuggled into our sleeping bags again. It was only 6 pm but this gave us four hours to relax before we started readying ourselves for an 11 pm departure—the time suggested by Purba because the weather was so good. I did not expect to sleep properly because at these altitudes the effort of breathing keeps you awake. We used oxygen at a low flow rate, which made me feel more comfortable.

At 10 pm we roused ourselves and checked the weather. It was absolutely perfect. This was an amazing moment for me. I knew we had a real chance of reaching the summit. I had dreamed so many times of this occasion, the big day out on Everest, and how it would be for me. The weather was on our side; the rest was up to us.

We got ready as quickly as we could. Years of guiding had made me very efficient with mundane matters such as this, but tonight I was stymied by not being able to find the battery for my camcorder. I spent twenty or thirty minutes searching for it. Tony got himself totally ready while I was conducting this search.

In good humour, he asked, 'Do you know the story of the yak that was early and the yak that was late?'

I looked at him and smiled. 'No, but we better be the early yaks.'

I still don't know the story of the yaks. I was distracted by finding my battery in the crotch of my down suit, where it ended up after slipping out of an internal chest pocket. I had not felt its presence there and only found it after eliminating all the other possibilities. By the time I was out of the tent, with my pack shouldered and my gloves and mitts on, the others had already left. Only Dawa was waiting.

Tony had headed out first with Dorje, but they were quickly overtaken by Chung, who was being hussled along by Purba, Tsering and Datenji. I was determined to catch up, to Tony and Dorje at least, because staying with them would help pull me along. I was feeling good and stronger than expected. More than anything I was determined. It was a pitch black night, millions of stars and not a breath of wind. These perfect conditions turbocharged me to make the best of this day. It was good to be climbing in the dead of night as it forced me to focus on where I was putting my hands and feet, rather than worrying about the huge drop below me.

Climbing not far behind Tony worked well because it meant that he and Dorje led the way. With fixed ropes lying across the slope there was no chance of getting lost, but Tony and Dorje did the decision-making about whether to cut left around a particular block or boulder or go over it. I was perfectly comfortable with making such decisions—to me it was an enjoyable part of climbing—but at midnight on Everest I was happy to make up time by following Tony and Dorje's lead. In any case, there were plenty of times when I tackled an obstacle differently because I took smaller steps. I also had less strength in my arms, which meant I used techniques involving balance and raising my body by pushing down with my hands.

I enjoyed climbing with Dawa. We didn't tie a rope between us at any stage, but he was a strong, reassuring presence. He observed my climbing style and judged when to offer advice and when to watch in silence. He assisted me a few times, with things like switching oxygen bottles and other tasks that climb partners do for each other. I felt very comfortable in his company, safe and not under pressure to perform. He did not need to encourage me to climb or keep moving because I was doing that for myself.

The powerful beam from his halogen headlamp was also of great benefit. I was using an LED light that would last me many dozens of hours, but it had much less power. My own halogen lamp was one the items that disappeared when my tent blew away. I could see my hands and feet well enough with my own headlamp, but sometimes when I was deciding which way to move I needed to call for light. It is true that I wasn't demonstrating total independence, but that was because of the cards fate had dealt me. However, fate had also dealt us a beautiful night, so I was going to make the most of everything that providence put on offer.

It was a long night, but I was totally engaged with performing every little task. One particular annoyance was the water bottle I inherited from Matt after mine had disappeared, again in the windstorms. It was a copy of a top-line Nalgene bottle but had the problem of leaking unless the lid was screwed down very tight. This tightness, combined with the lid freezing on to the bottle mouth, meant that the only time I could have a drink was when I passed it to Dawa so his strong hands could open it. Because of this extra step in the process, I did not drink as much as I should have. But at least my oxygen was working well. The only problem was that the mask was bulky and prevented me from seeing my feet properly, but this was a restriction I had to live with.

These little issues might seem trivial compared to the great feat of climbing Mount Everest, but the reality of such a harsh environment is that dealing with fiddly pieces of equipment is an extra challenge on top of coping with the shortage of atmospheric oxygen, the threat of frostbite, and the lack of appetite, sleep and a fully functional mind. As for the climb itself, technically it is one step after another, like any other climb. The difference with Everest is the extra effort that has to be put into managing the threats around you. I was well aware that Zeddy had not managed the threat of snow blindness, Matt the threat of frostbite, and Tony the damning reality of not having had enough oxygen in his tank.

The climbing itself was sufficiently demanding. At sea level, wearing shorts on a sunny day, I would have regarded the challenges of Everest's upper slopes as nothing more than a fun scramble, with the exception of the Second Step. But the cold, dark, oxygenless air, all the bulky clobber, ice on the rock, and the ever-present threat of a deadly storm blowing in, made everything different.

Abandoned sections of old rope lay strewn across every serious obstacle on the upper mountain, attempts to make the climb more manageable. Where ropes had been tied to a piton hammered into the rock, bunches of ropes hung like huge tangles of spaghetti. Some of the ropes had obviously been there for many years, with new ones added because the old ones were no longer to be trusted. After reading a tag that said 'October 1988', I always took care to grab or clip into the newest looking rope. I did my best to avoid putting my weight on these fixed lines because there may have been some hidden damage to the rope, or perhaps an anchor might be loose. It is standard mountaineering practice to minimise your reliance on equipment that you have not put in place yourself. I had the added advantage of being one of the lightest people to climb the mountain, and I figured that if burly men had survived these ropes then surely they would hold my weight.

Every time we paused for a moment Tony would pull out a gel sachet and squirt it into his mouth. It was the logical food up here where water froze and chocolate could only be broken with an ice axe. There were barrels full of goodies including gel sachets at ABC, but I had not thought to bring any as I had never used them before, considering them a bit of overkill. What had I been thinking? This hadn't been discussed at ABC, but of course I should have known, especially as I knew my Musashi bars had been raided by others on the mountain. Tony disposed of one of these sachets in ten seconds, and I must have seen him pop four or five. He didn't know that I didn't have any, and I did not mention it. I just cursed myself for not thinking thoroughly about my important needs and how to satisfy them.

Despite these glitches I felt that we were making good time—not that I had any real idea where we were on the mountain in the dark. I figured that I could pull out my one scavenged protein bar and have a bite when we reached the Exit Rocks, but when we stopped there it was frozen and threatened to break my teeth. I gave up and accepted this would be a long climb with nothing to eat but the odd handful of snow. Urgghh! The plusses I was experiencing easily outweighed the negatives. My oxygen set-up was working perfectly, the weather was perfect and the gloves I had borrowed from Trynt were perfect, especially with her hand warmers inside them. I had been very worried about how cold a night it would be, but in my thermals and fleeces and down suit I was actually sweating. This was not a problem I expected to have.

The hours slipped by as we climbed and climbed. In the darkness there was no confirmation of progress, no appreciation of how far we had come or how far we had to go. The terrain was almost entirely rock, generally shale that mostly sloped downwards, yet there was enough snow to warrant us wearing crampons the whole way. On a snow slope you can switch into plodding mode, which is virtually autodrive, because you are just lifting one foot and putting it down again higher up. Very repetitive, often boring, but at least you can get a rhythm going. Moving over rock in the dark on Everest was a different story all together. Every step had to be carefully considered, as did every handhold. Quite often I needed to plan the sequence of movements so I didn't end up with my left foot where I needed to have my right one. Although this was mentally more taxing than climbing snow, it was also more absorbing, particularly as we were constantly moving diagonally to the right, which was more difficult than climbing straight up. The upshot was that we had less time to think about what hard work it was as we rock-scrambled our way towards the very top of the world.

There was nothing much to say, and less breath to say it with. I did not need special guidance, and I certainly felt that Dawa and I were climbing as partners, which felt really good. I realised that there were no plans to stop for a rest. Wherever there was easier ground I tried to speed up, and because I did not want to scare myself, I never looked down, even though there was nothing to see except blackness.

We approached the Second Step in the dark, which is the best way to tackle it. The notorious obstacle was frightening enough without being able to see its full airy setting. This was the hardest part of the climb, even though a ladder surmounted most of the steepest part. I had heard about this famous ladder, placed by the Chinese in 1975, but knew little of it. I preferred not to over-analyse how I would approach it as I might choke when I got there, rather than go with my rockclimbing instincts. The problem was that the ladder stopped short of the top of the cliff. We approached it along a tongue of snow up to the base of the corner, and from there we were to clamber up it, one at a time. Dawa climbed up rung by rung then near the top moved off the ladder on to the rock wall. Almost without pausing he was over the lip and out of sight. Of course, he had climbed it before, and I didn't expect to mirror his performance.

My heart was in my mouth as I stepped off the snow and on to the ladder. It wobbled a little, which was disconcerting, but otherwise it was just a ladder. I climbed to the bulge of rock at the top. Dawa had muscled his way up and over, but I tried this and could not manage it. I retreated and reassessed. If I could not climb this section, it would be the end of Everest for me. To avoid the bulge I would have to traverse to the right across the wall with my feet on tiny ledges. I knew I had to make this traverse using balance, not strength. I stepped across, looked at the problem, stepped back again. Across again, then back again, each time trying to figure out the best sequence of moves with my feet and hands.

After a few half-hearted attempts, I thought, *Okay, do it this time and don't muck it up.* I moved up and across again. My crampon found purchase on a little ledge, which allowed me to get my body weight in the right position. I took my other foot off the ladder, stretched across with my right hand, grasped an edge which held my balance, and then clambered over the top. I had worked out the right positioning, and as is often the case when you finally master a climbing manoeuvre, I wondered why I had found it difficult.

I felt a great sense of relief because I knew that the terrain ahead of us was easier, or at least less intimidating. Excitement replaced relief, the highest level of excitement I had felt on the whole trip because now I knew I would succeed. Darkness was giving way to dawn. It was just beautiful. I looked to my left across to Makalu and beyond to see if clouds were coming upon us, but it was perfectly clear and still, as it was off to the west towards Cho Oyu. Light was coming quickly now. I looked along the summit ridge and thought, *I'm so close; here is the summit pyramid.* But I soon realised I was wrong. First we had to traverse the ridge to the Third Step.

Now that it was light I could see how slowly we were moving. Of course, we were climbing as quickly as we could, but at 8700 metres nothing happens fast, unless you make a mistake. The cloak of darkness no longer hid our extraordinary position on the exposed ridge. I chose not to look down the huge drop of the North Face, but I could not help but be aware of the huge space that lay below me in both directions. I proceeded along the ridge with even more caution.

As we reached the Third Step I saw a half-buried body lying face down in the snow on a slope fifteen metres below me on the North Face. It appeared that the person had tried to avoid the steep beginning of the step by traversing to the right but had slipped, fallen and been unable to haul himself up again. Earlier in the morning, when it was still dark, we had to step over the body of another dead climber. He looked like he was still alive, just sleeping. This was the man Trynt had attempted to revive ten days earlier but then realised there was no point. I recognised his boots as a good brand, but lightweight, the sort that few would wear to these heights, and a Russian-style down jacket, quite distinctive because of its basic design. The climbing Sherpas who knew the upper reaches of the mountain well, and who coped best with the high altitude, could have spared the energy to move the bodies away from the climbing route. However, their religious beliefs prevented them from doing so. It was only with great reluctance that they would agree to a request to bring down a body. Of course, these grizzly reminders of the dangers only made me more determined to stay focused and clear-headed.

The Third Step was not very steep, a manageable mix of snow and rock. When we surmounted it we could see Chung and the Sherpas coming down the snowy slopes of the summit pyramid. When our paths crossed a little later, Chung looked hammered but elated. We barely stopped as all of us had unfinished business.

We then climbed the snow slopes of the summit pyramid. The sun was reflecting brightly from the snow now so I changed my goggles for my sunglasses. In the process I knocked the nosepiece out my good Oakley glasses and watched it slide down the slope and disappear down the North Face. Dawa immediately gave me his spare pair of goggles.

We traversed around to the North Face again, on to loose scree in a very exposed situation, but not difficult. We then came to a big slab with cracks in it that required physical strength. I attempted to surmount it using my preferred balancing techniques, but Dawa said, 'Sue *Didi*, just do it.' He sounded like a Nike ad, but what he meant was: Don't worry about style, just haul yourself up. So that's what I did.

Strength worked for me that time. I readily acknowledge that men are stronger than women, especially in upper body strength. I have seen too much proof of this to change my view, and I regard the very strong women I know as exceptions.

After the rock slabs we came out on to a snow slope. The dome of the top was very obvious from here and Tony and Dorje were just reaching the summit. I knew I was going to make it. Excitement was welling within me but I kept it at bay so I would not lose my concentration. *Just take small, slow steps and pay attention,* I instructed myself. I climbed carefully and steadily up and across the snow. The last real obstacle was an icy traverse where some fixed ropes had blown away and others were frozen into the ice. A slip here would be very serious so I took great care. I stepped firmly, making sure my axe and crampons took firm purchase in the ice. After this it was a few minutes traverse and up a dozen bucket-sized steps cut in the snow that everyone who had come this way this season had used. I did not look up until I reached the last bucket step.

Then Dawa and I took the last few paces to the summit. I had been forewarned that the area was not big, but I was still surprised by its size — no larger than two table tennis tables. Tony and Dorje were there, and one other person stood near them. Although I did not recognise him in his oxygen mask and down suit, I realised later that the extra person was Jamie McGuiness, a New Zealand guide whom I knew. The protective gear hid our features as well as our emotions, so it was impossible to know who was in tears. I was not, but I was certainly one happy woman.

I pulled off my oxygen mask for an uninterrupted look at the world's ultimate panorama. 'That's not a bad view,' I said. It was completely clear.

The time was 7.15 am and I was on top of Mount Everest. So much of my energy had been directed to getting me here. Now that I had arrived at the summit I felt I was in a vacuum, and not just the vacuum effect of the thin air. I was bewildered to be here at last. It was a momentous occasion for Tony and me, and significant for Dorje and Dawa as well, particularly as it was Dawa's first time right up to the summit. The four of us hugged, yet we did not really talk to each other. Tony and Dorje started down after a few minutes, as they had arrived before us.

I had been so focused on reaching the summit I had not considered what to do when I got here, apart from shooting some video. *It doesn't really matter,* I thought, *just enjoy the view.* I looked down into Nepal but did not process what I was seeing. I could barely recognise any peaks. To the south was a jumble of little white bumps that could be Ama Dablam, Thamserku, Kang Taiga, Cholatse and Tawache, all the peaks I knew so well from below. From two kilometres above their summits, they were indistinguishable. But I did recognise the peaks that were above 7000 metres; there were fewer of them and they were more obvious: Cho Oyu, Gyachung Kang, Shishapangma, Pumori, Makalu and Makalu 2. Kanchenjunga lay to the east, and Changste splayed right out in front of us to the north, dividing the Rongbuk glaciers.

I was on top for about twenty minutes, but I did not think to drink or eat anything. There was no time. I needed to take photos and get footage, both for myself and for my sponsors. I needed to check my oxygen then work out how much I had left for the descent. And I wanted to enjoy where I was; I wanted to lock into my mind the image of the prayer flags Dawa put up for us, as well as the view and the situation we were in. I felt like I was in a crow's nest looking out over a sea of mountains, and beyond them the world. My mind did not process anything else; it read each minute as an hour, blocking out the whisper of urgency that was somewhere behind me, reminding me how quickly the weather changes and that I could get caught out trying to get down. I allowed myself those few minutes of tuning into the reality that was the summit of Mount Everest—the peak itself, the cold, the view, and the ethereal quality of perception that came from the lack of oxygen. It was a unique combination, a unique take on the world. Then I let myself listen to that whisper of urgency; it was louder now. We had to leave as soon as photos were taken.

The expectation came from somewhere in my mind that a climber would appear from the Nepalese South Col route at any minute. The tracks there were fresh and numerous, but no one manifested while I was there. I had a feeling for a moment, when I looked out and could see the whole 360 degrees, that someone or something was above me smiling down, really wanting me to have good luck, whatever force it was: God, Buddha, Allah, Mother Nature.

Although I had been breathing bottled oxygen, my mind was not working anywhere near full speed. But it was still quite clear. I looked up and said out loud, 'This one's for you, Dad. The next one's for me.' I was honouring my dad but already projecting myself forward. It was what both of us would expect, nothing less.

Jamie headed off next, leaving Dawa and me with the summit to ourselves. There was nothing to say, and no one else to spoil those special moments. No one was intruding with phones or radios. This was no place to get emotional; there were too many practical matters to consider. But it was a moment of joy totally uncorrupted. I knew how lucky I was.

I was just beginning to follow our tracks back down the bucket-sized steps in the snow when someone else arrived. He announced himself as Banjo, Jamie's client, and it seemed strange even at the time that a client should summit Everest by himself. He asked me to take his photo, but Dawa stepped in to perform the task. He wanted me to start down the mountain immediately.

My mental processes may have been slow, but I was now fully aware of the need to begin the descent. I knew I had a very, very long way to go. I also needed to urinate. The first few minutes were easy, but I paused when I approached the icy traverse which led back to the crest of the North Ridge. I could feel my confidence ebbing because a slip here would have severe consequences, so I committed myself immediately. I stepped across carefully—perhaps too carefully since moving slowly made it harder to balance on the slippery ice. When Dawa came down he scampered across the icy section, not giving his feet time to slip.

Now that we were on the ridge again the terrain was easier, for the time being at least. Jamie was a short distance ahead of me so I was able to see him bend down and pick up a few shards of rock before moving on. This seemed like a good idea, so when I reached that same spot where the ridge was clear of snow, I pocketed a few rocks myself.

I felt pleased to have the souvenirs for my young followers at home, but I was also very conscious that I needed to keep up the momentum of my descent.

The next challenge was to climb down the Third Step, which proved to be more straightforward than I had feared. When we were clear of the Step and on an easier section, I spotted some clean snow, without grit, and shoved a handful into my mouth.

'Sue *Didi*, why do you eat so much snow?' Dawa asked. 'Have you no water?'

I told him the lid of my bottle was still frozen and we did not have time to stop.

'Yes, we do,' he replied. 'We have lots of time.' He reached for my bottle and unscrewed the iced-up lid. I drank from it gratefully. The Tang in my drink gave me some much needed calories and the sweetness made me thirsty for more. The bottle was still half full yet we had been on the move for almost twelve hours. It was little surprise that I felt very tired.

We continued down along the gently sloping ridge. I became especially nervous about getting down the Second Step safely. However, as I approached the top of the step, my immediate preoccupation became the need to urinate. By now I thought I was going to explode. I found a place were I could step to one side, and I felt immediately grateful that I had not lost my custom-made Mountain Designs down suit. The process of relieving myself was so much easier when wearing a suit designed for and by a woman, especially when that woman was me.

As we approached the lip of Second Step, I thought, *This is the big one. Let's get it right.* It was a vertical descent which I knew would be a challenge at this extreme altitude. Strong men who did not want to risk their lives on ropes of uncertain age and reliability chose to down-climb the Step, but I knew I did not have the strength to do this. My best choice was to abseil. I reassured myself with the thought that because I was a lighter person, the ropes were less likely to break. At the edge of the drop I took a moment to rest. *Just a breather*, I told myself, then again, *Let's get this one right.*

I realised how much the high altitude was interfering with my mental processes when I attempted to attach my descendeur to the rope. A descendeur is a simple device that, when clipped to both harness and rope, allows you to slide down the rope in a slow and controlled manner, even over vertical drops. In other circumstances I could have attached the rope to my descendeur in my sleep, so often had I performed this routine task. But here, at the top of the Second Step, suffering from the low level of oxygen and a touch of fear, every time I attached my descendeur to the rope I saw that I had set it up for my left hand. With my degree of physical exhaustion I really needed it to be controlled by my much stronger right hand. At last I got it right—much to Dawa's relief, I am sure. Now that I was ready, there was a single moment when my heart was in my mouth as I stepped over the edge and put my trust in the two frail ropes I had chosen. The abseil came easily and I slid down the rope completely under control.

At the base of the Step I felt an enormous sense of relief. From here onwards the risks were miniscule by comparison. But I did not let down my guard. I knew that I would not be safe until I reached Camp Four. From there an almost continuous line of fixed rope placed by our Sherpas led all the way down the mountain.

Time became a blur as I forced myself slowly downwards. I was devoid of energy but had to keep going. Dawa went ahead once I was down the last rockclimbing obstacles, and I felt enormous relief that I was not going to die in some nasty way. At last I arrived at Camp Four, feeling that I had climbed well all day. Never in my life did I think that one day I would feel I had found refuge by arriving at 8300 metres, but the word on my lips was 'Hallelujah!' Two of the Sherpas who had been with Chung were still there and they greeted me with a cup of tea. I could not think of a better welcome. I gulped down a second cup and a few shortbread biscuits, but stopped there. I knew I needed litres and litres of fluid, but I also knew that if I drank too much at once I was likely to throw up everything I had swallowed.

The Sherpas had already pulled the tents down and were packing up food, sleeping bags and used oxygen cylinders. Dawa encouraged me to head off while he helped clear the site, but I sat there for a few minutes longer. What a great day's climbing it had been, and not only because it was Everest—all the major aspects had gone smoothly. And there had been a good, positive mood amongst the four of us.

Chung was already well down the mountain by now, and Tony and Dorje were just dots on the rope below. It was time for me to get moving again. Now that I had a reliable fixed rope as a safety line, I did not need to focus quite so keenly on getting every footstep in exactly the right place. This freed up my mind to notice other things, such as the soreness of my toes, and that my ankle ached where I had broken it a year ago. Down-climbing only made both these things worse because my toes were pushed to the front of my boots and my ankle was under constant tension. But it didn't matter.

I told myself that I would stop at Camp Three, but when I reached the spot where Camp Three had been, there were only a few tents packed and ready to be carried down by the Sherpas as they came through. I was disappointed that I had to keep going, but I consoled myself with the thought that I would be more comfortable at the lower height of Camp Two. There was no way I would go further than that because I was totally shattered. I was so thirsty that I needed to sit down there, melt a mountain of snow and make litres of drink.

Dawa caught up with me and we descended together, scarcely bothering to speak. As soon as we arrived at Camp Two, he said, 'Come on, let's go.'

'No,' I said. 'Not me. I can't.'

But he was persistent. I repeated that I no longer had the strength to stop a fall if I slipped, but I don't think he believed me. I must have looked tougher on the outside than I felt on the inside. 'Please don't ask me,' I said, almost in tears. 'Don't ask me anymore. Please go on, and I will come down tomorrow morning.'

He sensed then that I was on the verge of breaking down. 'Okay, we will stay here,' he said. I thought he was a real gentleman about it, quietly revising his plans to insist on staying with me in the tent next door.

It was time to let Russell know what was happening, so Dawa called him on the radio. 'All's well,' I said when Dawa passed the walkie-talkie across to me, 'but I'm calling it a day here at Camp Two.'

'Okay,' Russell replied, the tone of his voice telling me my decision was fine by him. 'Come down tomorrow morning. I'll probably have to leave at noon to head down to Base Camp.'

I really wanted to see Russell before he disappeared into the preoccupations of packing up Base Camp, because I knew that amid all the busyness the moment would be lost. I did not really need to say anything much; I just wanted to share a moment of celebration with him. So the next morning I needed to make the 1100-metre descent from Camp Two to ABC in time to arrive before midday. But that was tomorrow.

It was around three o'clock in the afternoon and I had been on the move since eleven o'clock the previous night. Dawa had done the same, of course, but he was more accustomed to the process. I crawled into the tent with food and drink foremost in my mind. At first I could see nothing there in the way of food, but with a bit of fossicking I managed to find some instant noodles and some lime guu powder (a kind of rocket fuel for athletes, concentrated carbohydrates with a few other nutrients thrown in). I lit the stove and began melting snow. I also discovered a small packet of alcohol wipes, frozen because water had leaked into them. I lay them in the setting sun that was shining in through the door of the tent and they thawed quickly.

For five days I had been wearing the same clothes, and now was the first time I had the mental space to think about how rank I felt. I took off my boots and cleaned my feet and it felt fantastic, then I cleaned my face (not with the same wipes!). I felt like I was in heaven. I laid back over the pile of sleeping bags and other stuff in the tent, looking down at my toes and the wet wipes and the sunset out through the tent door, waiting for the billy to boil and enjoying the fact that I did not have to walk another step for today. And I had done it. What would the others think? Then I realised that nobody back home knew what was going on. I really did need to get down to let them know that everything was okay, that everything was very much more than okay.

Soon I had enough lukewarm water for a decent drink so I cooked up the noodles. The combination of relaxing, having food and drink in my belly, and being clean (around the edges at least) made me feel much, much better. Yet I still felt so tired that it was beyond me to do anything but doze in the shelter and security of the tent. When the sun moved behind the mountain, the sudden drop in temperature woke me up. I looked out through the tent flaps at the amazing view across the mountains.

The thought came to me again that nobody knew about my success. For the first time I remembered the huge party that World Expeditions had just held at Tengboche to celebrate the fiftieth anniversary of the first ascent. *Well, I've missed that one,* I thought. And by the time I got out of Tibet, everyone would have left Kathmandu as well, including Sue Badyari and her son, who had come to Nepal for the Tengboche celebrations. But there would be plenty of time to celebrate.

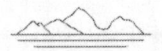

The next morning Dawa woke me at six o'clock and passed a warm drink into the tent. It was a very welcome gesture which saved me an hour of melting snow. I had slept very well, given the altitude and the fact that I had stopped using oxygen when I pulled into Camp Four.

Russell radioed just as we were walking out of camp at seven o'clock, eager to confirm that we were on our way. I felt chronically tired but at least it was now all downhill, and I was certainly moving much faster after a good night's sleep. At the North Col there were a couple of little humps that blocked the way to Camp One, and the effort of clambering over them made them feel like whole mountains in themselves. I had to stop at the camp to collect the small amount of personal gear I had left there. Thankfully one of the Sherpas was happy to take a small sack of odds and ends down for me.

From the North Col it was a long way down to the glacier floor, so constant vigilance was still in order. At the first steep slope I got a wake up call. My ice-axe was in a holster on my harness, and as I moved hand-over-hand down the rope, the axe caught on the slope, pushing me off balance. A quick rush of adrenalin had me correcting my balance immediately and shoving my axe out of the way. This was enough to snap me out of my tiredness. There were gaping crevasses just below me, and it would have been messy even though I was clipped to the rope with a karabiner and sling.

When at last I reached the glacier I found it very hard work, as did almost everyone else after the climb, because I could no longer let my boots flop forward with each step. On the snow slope above, gravity had effectively led me down the mountain. Now I had to raise my foot with every step, and my legs felt as heavy as lead. I forced myself onwards. As I approached ABC I had a surge of energy and almost ran the last kilometre, arriving at midday for my promised meeting with Russell. We were all smiles. He handed me one of the last beers in the camp, one that he had saved especially for me.

'This will finish me off,' I said with a laugh. 'But who cares?'

I had arrived at ABC and had nowhere else to go that day. What a good feeling that was. However, Russell had to hike the twenty-two kilometres down the valley that afternoon to make sure the dismantling of Base Camp proceeded according to plan. We talked briefly then he had to go.

I had an urgent need as well, before finding some lunch to wash down with my beer. I went to the comms tent and tried to ring Australia, but nobody was picking up their phones. It was very frustrating. I was keyed up to share my success and there was no one to listen to me. I tried again after lunch and managed to get through to Grahame, not saying much more than that I had summitted and was safely back at Advance Base Camp. I really did not know what to else say; I had been away so long that I could not think what was of interest or importance. I explained that conditions had been perfect on summit day and on the top, that it had been hard and that I was tired and glad to be coming home. After this the satellite phone was packed up and was not brought out again for the rest of the trip. I found out later that many people tried to get through, including the media, but no one managed it.

The next morning it was time to head down to Base Camp. I knew it would be a big day. Chung had left the previous morning so Tony and I walked together. I started out feeling really good, but I gradually ran out of energy. Summer had arrived, which meant monsoonal storms were hitting Everest and the surrounding mountains. It also meant higher temperatures, resulting in more melt-water filling the glacial streams. In a few places the path was no longer usable because it had been washed away. Elsewhere the streams were too wide to jump across. In both cases we had to backtrack to find alternative routes. Had we been feeling fit and fresh, it might have been fun to find our way around the obstacles, but as exhausted mountaineers with muscles wasted away by the ravages of high altitude, diversions were the last thing we needed. In one particular place the river crossing was quite dangerous—had we slipped in we may have been carried away or drowned.

Once we put the glacier behind us, the track was in much better shape. Tony gradually pulled away from me. My toes hurt, and I knew I was going to lose the big toe nails, but I kept kicking rocks because I was too tired to lift my feet properly. Now at least all I had to do was to keep walking. After everything I had put myself through during the past week—during the past nine weeks, in fact—surely I could manage to walk for a few more hours. I gained a new lease of life when one of the Tibetans arrived from Base Camp with a thermos of tea. The hot liquid was the nectar of the gods. I kept walking but soon I was feeling weak again. Every step became an effort. The only way I could maintain my morale was to walk looking down at the track and my feet so I couldn't see how much further I still had to go.

At last when I arrived at Base Camp, it was almost as though nothing had happened. I was last in and was barely noticed. People knew I was reliable by that stage, and I was doing no more than turning up on schedule.

Everyone there had climbed Everest, so no one could brag to anyone. We laughed about it, but it was quite an extraordinary situation. This was our second last night in the mountains, which meant it was party time. Russell produced bottles of Moet and delicacies such as pâté.

I didn't care about anything so long as I did not have to walk anywhere. Mark was there, which was great; the only time I had seen him since he left Tony and me at Camp Two was when our paths crossed briefly on my way up to Camp Four, as Mark came down with Jesse and Ted after they had summitted. That was just a case of quick hugs for their success, and to wish me well.

The party was short-lived because most people were overtired, and I was certainly one of them. Sleep didn't seem to make any difference to my tiredness.

The next day I sat outside the mess tent, mostly with Mark, Tony, Chung, Jesse and Ted, in mild weather and no wind. There was nothing to do but relax. The tensions and the 'crowds' were gone. Even Russell, who was packing up, had time to sit with us for a chat.

The following morning we woke to foul weather. Everest was invisible in the clouds; snow was everywhere. At Base Camp the snow melted when it landed on us, making everything wet as we attempted to pack. It was a miserable morning for packing but we had no choice. Worst of all was a decision to defer breakfast. Instead we were to eat at Tingri, which was several hours drive away. I couldn't believe it. I was thirsty and hungry, but the decision made some sense. We wouldn't have to eat in the storm, nor would the kitchen staff have to spend time cleaning it up, and so we could get away sooner. The Sherpas wasted no time, and sure enough, we were soon driving down the road towards Rongbuk monastery.

It was strange to be in a vehicle again, travelling so effortlessly. But while it may have been effortless, it soon became uncomfortable as we took a short cut across some very rough country in rain and sleet. The short cut began with a crossing of the Rongbuk River, then we headed over the Nam La Pass. This route did bring us to Tingri more quickly than the route we had taken into the mountain two months earlier. We stopped at the roadside town only long enough to eat, but at least when we clambered back into the vehicles we were fed and watered and on the main road again.

We had a long day of driving still ahead of us, but there were reasons for the urgency. Most of the climbers had flights home within the next few days. More than anything we wanted a serious change of scene. Kathmandu was the perfect place to relax and celebrate. I knew there were spectacular sights to be enjoyed along the way because I had travelled here on my expeditions to Cho Oyu and Shishapangma, but today no mountains were visible because of the bad weather. Nevertheless, it was good to see a different landscape and to think that this was our last full day in Tibet.

We drove and we drove, and at last we reached the town of Nyalam and began the long descent down to Zhangmu, the town on the Chinese side of the border. The road followed the course of a gorge, and as we zigzagged down into it, for the first time in months we were surrounded by greenery. All the barren fields we had seen post-winter were now full of crops ready to be harvested. It took less than an hour to drop from the barrenness of the Tibetan plateau to the jungle near the Nepalese border. It was a visual feast, and the air felt like honey—moist and rich. Spectacular waterfalls plunged hundreds of metres into the gorge. There was the potential for our vehicles to plunge over the drop as well, so close was the edge of the road to the precipice, but danger had become such a part of our lives over the last two months that we didn't even think about it. This was my fourth trip down this road and I enjoyed it every time.

It was late afternoon when we reached Zhangmu, and the border was closed. We had to spend a night here, which was fine by me as I had done enough travelling for the day. There was plenty of food, plenty of drink, and a good time to be had at the Zhangmu disco. Despite my tired legs and sore feet, dancing was a great way to burn off the lactic acid that had accumulated in my muscles after my recent exertions. However, the late night did nothing to alleviate the tiredness we all felt; this was quite obvious the next morning waiting in the queues at Chinese immigration.

The border crossing was reasonably straightforward. There was the usual slowness of processing a large group, and there had just been the outbreak of SARS, so all of us had to be tested for temperature. I was the first in our group, and when the guy put a gun up to my forehead I got a real fright because I had not seen a temperature gun before. I was diagnosed too cold and had to stand aside and wait to be retested. It was a real test of my patience too because I was so keen to get down into Nepal after so long.

We continued down the switchbacks to the Friendship Bridge over the river which marked the divide between the Tibet and Nepal. As we crossed the bridge we looked down to the left and were startled to see the Global Extremes Toyota 4Runners behind gates in a holding yard, still impounded. Russell just shook his head and smiled as we drove past. Somebody else's problem now.

There was a delay getting the gear through customs but Russell knew the game well, which made things easier. Finally we were on the road again. It was fantastic to be driving through Nepal. I felt like I was back home. The air was so warm that we were wearing virtually no clothes. It had been months since we had been able to do that. I was travelling in a Landcruiser with Russell and Mark, and it was great to be talking and laughing, having no worries ahead of us. The beers in our hands definitely helped with the relaxation process. After under-populated, treeless Tibet, the green, peopled landscape was friendly and inviting.

It was mid-afternoon by the time I was dropped at the Radisson. I rushed into the lobby. None of my friends from World Expeditions were there, so there was no one I knew with whom I could share my success. There were not even the usual staff from the hotel who knew me. Every year the trekking season finishes at the end of May and everyone leaves town. That was only a few days ago, but it appeared the exodus had already happened.

I had to tell someone, so when I spotted an unsuspecting World Expeditions client wandering through the lobby I bailed her up. 'I've just climbed Mount Everest, and you're the first person I've told,' I said. She appeared vaguely interested, but she was looking for her partner. It was not quite the reception I had hoped for.

I collected my key and caught the lift up to my room. All my luggage was still coming but I had one small bag left in storage with a clean

T-shirt and shorts. What a treat it was going to be to wear something so lightweight and different after months of wearing bulky clothes full of dust. I kicked off my shoes and pulled a beer out of the bar-fridge. I thought how good it would be not to have to lie in a narrow sleeping bag but in a bed with clean, crisp cotton sheets where I could sleep thoroughly spread out. How good it would be to go to the toilet without having to put on warm clothes and boots, how good it would be not to puff and pant after performing the simplest actions. I would shortly have a shower with hot water pouring down over my head and no concern about getting a chill. I would be properly clean after weeks and weeks of my daily ritual of washing from a cup. I chose to do this because the shower at Base Camp was either always in use or too damn cold because the hot water had run out, and I felt I was sure to catch a cold. Life was looking rosy. To me, my return to my familiar routines in the Radisson signalled full circle—the expedition had come to an end.

I switched on the television and jumped on the bed. I thought to myself, *Indulgence, here I come.* Then the phone rang.

It was Sue Badyari. She told me she had left Kathmandu only a few days before, after anxiously looking for me at the Tibet Hotel and leaving feeling very worried about what might have happened to me.

My friend's voice at the other end of the line was like a switch turning on the tap of my euphoria. I had bottled up so much inside me during the expedition, and although all the stresses and dangers had gone, my triumph had somehow stayed contained within. Now, talking to Sue, who understood so much about me, I found suddenly that everything came pouring out. There had been so much rubbish, but what I babbled about mostly was the good stuff—my success, the perfect summit day, that I was tired but not destroyed, my video footage, my friendship with Russell and Mark, and more besides. I was looking forward to coming home as always.

Sue and I must have been talking for over ten minutes when there was a tap on the door to my room. The knocking became insistent so I interrupted our conversation to answer it. A young bellboy stood there in his uniform.

'Excuse me, madam,' he said. 'You are wanted on the telephone.'

'Thank you, but I'm already on the phone.'

He hesitated for a moment, then said, confidently but politely, 'But other people want to speak with you. Not just one person. More persons.'

Please ask them to ring back.'

He looked at me quizzically, implying that my suggestion did not solve the problem.

'Look,' I said, pleading special circumstances, 'I've just climbed Mount Everest.'

He beamed a huge smile at me now, as if this was the best excuse a hotel guest could have.

'Okay, madam,' he said, with a bow of his head. 'I will tell them that.'

9

Ms EVEREST

By early June 2003, journalists were wondering what had happened to Sue Fear. Those most keen to know were the journos who had elected to report on Sue's expedition stage by stage. They had taken the trouble to interview her in Australia, and again when she had passed through Kathmandu after her acclimatisation trek to the Nepalese side of Everest. The press had been sent email updates from Advance Base Camp at first, but a long silence followed. At last they received a call from World Expedition's Steph Hammond after she heard the great news from Grahame Fear. But all Steph could tell them was that Sue had summitted on 31 May and was now safely off the mountain. Many calls were made to the expedition's satellite phone by Linton Besser from the *Today Show*, by Simon Marnie from ABC radio, by *The Panel* and by others, but the sat phone had been packed up, shoved in a nameless barrel and forgotten about. The show was on the road home.

So it was not surprising that when Sue arrived back in Kathmandu she was besieged by the media. She gave interview after interview. She spent her first morning at the Radisson drinking coffee with Russell, Mark, Highland Expeditions director Meraj Din, and Lhakpa from the World Expeditions desk, frequently excusing herself to take phone calls. All she was doing between interviews was waiting for the next one, and enjoying occasional calls of congratulation. She had no opportunity to walk even fifty metres up the road to her favourite supermarket to buy herself a few treats or pick up some mandatory gifts for the kids of her friends at home. The response and the interest were overwhelming. The expedition's last bottle of Moet had at some stage been put in Sue's care, so she broke it open that night with Russell and Mark as a last farewell. The next morning she left the country.

When Sue arrived in Sydney on the evening of 8 June, she was unaware that the preceding week had seen a media blitz focused on both Mount Everest and Sir Edmund Hillary. The coverage was timed around the celebration of the fiftieth anniversary of the first ascent on 29 May 1953. On the day of the celebration, Sue had been at Camp Three on her way to the summit. Meanwhile, in Australia there had been television documentaries and feature stories in newspapers and magazines. A rash of books about Everest were published or republished around this time. Then along came Sue, fresh off the top. No other Australian had reached the world's highest point that season, so the media had no one else to talk to who was 'newsworthy'.

At Sydney airport Sue was met by thirty people—friends and family who wanted to whisk her off for celebratory drinks at a nearby hotel. But first she had to accede to a request from the ever-enthusiastic and unrelenting Linton Besser from Channel Nine, who had come especially to collect Sue's camcorder tape for some broadcasts the following day. After almost three months of getting up early and being ready for action, her first opportunity for a sleep-in next day was foiled by an early appointment for a television interview.

The next morning at half past six a limousine pulled up outside Sue's apartment and she was driven ten minutes up the road to the TCN 9 studios. She was looked after from the moment she arrived by a lovely young woman called Gerry, who took her to the Green Room (the name given to every pre-interview waiting room at every television station). The most obvious feature was a table spread with croissants and fresh fruit, orange juice and fresh coffee. Sue snapped into reverse culture shock and tucked in. Suddenly getting out of bed early did not seem so bad. Soon she was bustled into the studio where her interview with Steve Liebmann seemed to last less than a minute.

Back in the Green Room, the producer spoke to her about her plans for the day. 'Can you stay around this morning?' he asked. 'You can come on Kerri Ann Kennerley's show.'

At first Sue thought he must have been joking. 'I want to go home. I've been away three months,' she said.

It was the producer's turn to be puzzled. He was not accustomed to people shunning an opportunity to be on national television.

'What do you have to do at home?' he asked.

'About three months' worth of laundry, watering my pot plants — and sleeping.'

'Well, why don't you pop home, do a load of laundry and come back in an hour or so. We'll have some nice snacks here and you can relax.'

Sue smiled. How could she say no? She went home, which took more than ten minutes this time because the morning traffic was building, put on a load of laundry, then returned to the television studio for an interview with Kerri Ann Kennerley. Sue and Kerri Ann talked for ten minutes about all sorts of matters. It was a much more satisfying experience than a moment in the news segment of the *Today Show*. Afterwards the producer was very appreciative of Sue's patience. With a smile, he suggested that she take home some of the lovely salmon and cream cheese sandwiches she had been devouring. He had obviously tuned into her impressive post-expedition appetite.

Sue's first day in Sydney set the pace of her life for the next few months. There were more television appearances, radio interviews, newspaper and magazine articles. She was the second Australian woman to climb Everest, but she felt it would not have mattered if she had been first, third or tenth. She had not anticipated such recognition by the public. She had wanted to climb Mount Everest because it was the world's most famous mountain, and because she wanted to see how far she could take her mountaineering. The climb was for her father and, through him, for her mother. These were private reasons, and yet Sue now found that the public at large wanted to hear about her climb.

One topic of conversation that the media regarded as particularly interesting was Sue's surname. Her response was to say that Fear was short for Fearless, which had been her nickname for years. She soon understood that the media focused on her name and other trivial matters because they had no clue about mountaineering. She learnt to steer interviews towards the things she wanted to say. She related a few obligatory anecdotes about the cold, the danger and what it was like on top, because this is what everyone wanted to hear. Then she moved to the heart of the matter—the achieving of goals by working towards them consistently, the importance of having a passion, and the value of self-reliance.

The publicity from the first flush of interviews had the benefit of priming the general populace for Sue's nationwide slide presentations. She had agreed to present a series of slide shows for World Expeditions and Mountain Designs as part of her sponsorship agreements with them. The first show was scheduled for two weeks after her return to Australia, so there was barely enough time to have her film processed, get her slides sorted and run through a couple of rehearsals. Her first 'live' performance was at the national conference of the Duke of Edinburgh Award Scheme, as this organisation was another of her sponsors.

Before Sue headed off on the Fearless Everest Tour, she threw an open-house party at her place. It turned into an amazing celebration. She was overwhelmed by the gifts and the luscious food that people brought. When the party atmosphere was building, but before it was time to turn the music up loud, Sue gave a brief slide show about her climb, as a window into her world of Everest.

The dramatic tales and images of the slide show prompted some of her friends to share with her privately how her expedition had quietly changed their lives. When everyday challenges such as childbirth, marriage and career change seemed overwhelming, her friends had thought of where Sue was, and of the dangerous and desperately difficult task she had set herself. Her example had given them strength to tackle their own, non-geological Everests. When Sue heard this from her first confidant she was surprised, but she was stunned when others stepped forward with their own versions of the same scenario. These confessions were precursors to similar stories that people would soon be telling Sue at the public slides shows. She was amazed at how she was able touch people's lives through her adventures, simply because she was not afraid of pursuing big goals.

The first of her public slide shows was in Canberra, and it did not go as smoothly as she hoped. She found that every talk had at least one mishap — there were delays while light switches were located or extension cords hunted down. At other times the equipment would malfunction. The Mountain Designs staff assigned to monitor the projectors would forget their jobs and get drawn into watching the show. Sue could not be cranky about this misplaced enthusiasm because she realised these young people were bursting at the seams with excitement about adventure, just as she had been at their age.

Sue had given dozens of slide presentations to potential World Expeditions clients, but marketing adventure travel destinations was a different kettle of mountains. The Everest show was about Sue. It was about her thoughts, how she overcame setbacks, her greatest moments, her deepest lows, her feelings on the summit. These were personal subjects close to her heart, and they were not easy things to talk about to huge, anonymous audiences. Passion and energy were needed to speak to crowds of two to three hundred people, which was the size of the audience she drew every time. Each session drained her of energy, and it became increasingly hard to regain that energy level for the next show.

Sue's Everest evenings were more than lectures illustrated with slides and a five-minute movie clip of her summit footage. She raised money for the Fred Hollows Foundation by signing and selling Everest posters sponsored by Australian Geographic. Sue had a long history with the Foundation, having worked for the organisation for six months in 1995. She welcomed the opportunity to use her Everest success to raise a substantial amount of money through poster sales, and her contribution was acknowledged when she was made a Fred Hollows Foundation Ambassador. Sue was also raising money for the Australian Himalayan Foundation by auctioning special edition photographic prints, supplied by Vision Graphics. Her evenings involved much more than merely talking about herself at length, and because she was busy with these activities before and after her talk, as well as during the intermission, she was unable to be timekeeper and master of ceremonies. She came to accept that occasional glitches and delays were not major disasters, particularly when she realised that the audiences loved every talk and really just wanted to meet her personally.

After her first shows in Canberra and Sydney she flew to Brisbane for an evening presentation, then caught an early flight back to Sydney so she could give a talk at Abbotsleigh, one of her old schools. The assembly hall was packed with students, as was a second hall where the event was broadcast live on a big screen. It was the school's Foundation Day, and 1300 Abbotsleigh girls listened to Sue's story.

Before the first week of the tour was out, Sue was reeling from the scale of her activities — not just the size of the audiences and the amount of travel, but also the fact that she had no time for anything else, except sleep. The second week involved shows in Adelaide, Melbourne, Hobart and Launceston. After Everest she had planned to have a holiday, but that was nowhere in sight.

As well as presenting three or four shows a week for six consecutive weeks, Sue faced travel and media interviews every day. The publicity led schools of all shapes and sizes to request that she pay them a visit so she could share her experiences. She squeezed these talks in when she could because she felt she could make an important contribution. Regardless of her day's program she always finished late at night, exhausted. There was no one to act as minder who could lessen her load, and the tour became a marathon as hard to face as Everest itself. She grew chronically tired. Although her increasing familiarity with her material made each talk easier than the last — and although she came to appreciate which parts of her story elicited the best response from audiences — yet the stress of the tour was almost overwhelming. There were times when she was on the verge of tears from frustration and weariness. She got to the point of wanting to phone Steph to pour out her feelings, and by accident she let it slip one evening on a call. Although Steph was supportive, Sue realised there was nothing to do but make the tour work, to do her best right to the end as she had on Everest. The tour may have seemed more taxing than the expedition, but it was all relative. The reality was that the stresses she now faced were different from the ones she had endured on the mountain. The reason she found the tour taxing was that she had not been able to take time to revitalise her innermost resources after the exceptionally tense months of the climb.

The stress came not only from the huge work load she had to cope with, but also from the way that people perceived her now that she had climbed Mount Everest. In a way she had become public property. This was because Everest had been the ultimate symbol of adventure for the best part of a century. She began to appreciate that she would be wearing this symbol as a badge from this point onwards, whether she wanted to or not. And the 'Ms Everest' badge was not always a pleasure to wear. At one dinner party, twelve months later, the boyfriend of one of her friends began to expound his strong views about how Everest should be climbed, and he indicated that Sue had not fitted into that mould. His views were taken from reading John Krakauer's *Into Thin Air*. Yet compelling as it was, that book told the story of just one episode in Everest's long and varied history. Sue could not believe what she was hearing — she was at dinner with friends, had no intention of discussing Everest at all, but this unknown man was airing his ego and demanding from her opinions and justifications on a topic he knew next to nothing about. This was one end of the spectrum. At the other end were the huge numbers of warm responses to her success by many people.

The horizon was opening up in front of her. Because of Everest she was approached by people whom otherwise she would never have met. It was not that she had been reclusive; in fact, she was a social animal who enjoyed spending time with her friends. Included among these were the girls she had first connected with in the mainstream travel industry, girls who loved parties, buying clothes and ogling men, and hated wearing sensible shoes — such as those worn outdoors. Sue delighted in the contrast of this with her outdoorsy friends of both genders, whose ideal dinner party was a bottle of red outside the tent as the sun set over the wilderness. But now new people would approach her after her talks or would telephone her out of the blue, somehow having found her phone number. She took little notice of those who regarded her as a freak show and simply wanted to know more, but she welcomed people who were drawn by her spirit or by elements of her character that had somehow struck a chord.

Among these were people from the corporate world who recognised some common thread between their workplaces and Sue's attributes — perhaps her habit of setting precise goals or her unshakeable determination. It was during her lecture series that Sue was first approached to give corporate talks. Her tactic in life had always been to make the most of every opportunity. Although she felt burnt out by the tour, she knew the corporate speaking market was potentially very lucrative and that now was the time when she needed to capitalise on the interest she was receiving. Once again Sue stepped out, just as she had on the frightening windy corner above Camp Two on Everest.

A persistent cause of stress during the Fearless Everest Tour was the slide projector she had used. This technology suited the simple, in-office presentations she had given for many years for World Expeditions, but it was quickly becoming an anachronism in the digital world of conferences and corporate presentations. Sue realised that the digital path was one she must follow. Her brother John was able to tell her everything she needed to know, to the point of giving her a shopping list. She upgraded her computer, bought a scanner, a laptop and the appropriate software, and after a few late nights working it all out with John, breathed a huge sigh of relief. She immediately realised that the digital world was going to be so much easier to manage than the cumbersome world of slide projectors. This was just as well because she was aware that the corporate scene would be entirely new to her. There was a whole dimension of difference between talking to a receptive hometown audience who were attending because they were interested in a girl from the suburbs who had made it to the top, and a corporate group who were in the auditorium because Sue was the next item on the agenda.

Her first talk came about because a senior manager who had attended one of her public talks approached her afterwards. 'Our staff need an injection of enthusiasm,' he said, 'something from left field to rev them up again. You're just perfect for the job.'

Sue was flattered, and she felt a little less intimidated about being 'next item on the agenda' because she was not being asked to deliver a particular corporate message. The staff of that company proved to be very responsive when she told her story without embellishment. Nothing extra was needed to keep them mesmerised. They were an intelligent audience, able to see in their workplace both good and bad parallels with Sue's dramatic story, one where more than monthly targets were at stake. Despite her exhaustion, her first corporate talk was a success, with a good dose of first-time adrenalin carrying her through.

Sue found that most of her corporate engagements took the same course — simply telling her story as it occurred, including her feelings, motivations and doubts. As in her public talks, she found that people wanted to know what really went on during the seventy days of the expedition. The realities of climbing Mount Everest are clouded by myths and melodrama, and Sue hoped that, if nothing else, people would understand something of her experiences, compare hers with others' and read more about Everest. In her corporate talks this goal had to be modified because usually there was no time to cover the whole board game. Sue learnt to focus on a few key events and issues to convey the essence of her experience.

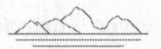

After those first crazy months, Sue desperately needed a break. She was not the sort of person to take a regular holiday. Instead, she flew to Sabah in Malaysian Borneo to climb Mount Kinabalu, at 4090 metres the highest peak in South-east Asia. She also visited orang-utan and turtle sanctuaries, and snorkelled the reefs on a tiny, remote desert island dive resort. It was here that she found some time out — no phones, no cold weather, no place to rush to. It was ten days of heaven, and just what the doctor had ordered.

To this point Sue had had no time to consider the impact of Mount Everest on her life. She had tackled the mountain because it was a climb she wanted to do for herself, a goal she wanted to realise. Now she found herself famous, with all sorts of opportunities coming her way. Corporate speaking offered her a way of funding expeditions which, despite the bleak simplicity of life in the mountains, were expensive undertakings.

She wanted to climb more mountains, and she realised that Everest was going to open all sorts of doors in that department. She had also discovered the satisfaction of sharing the wisdom she had gained from her time on the highest peaks. She accepted now that many people were genuinely inspired by her achievements (her first reaction had been disbelief), and the majority of these people had no interest in climbing. Rather, they were inspired by an Australian woman with a regular suburban upbringing who had been able to overcome huge obstacles to achieve a dream.

Sue knew that her father would have been proud of her ascent of Everest because he had watched her work diligently through a training course of mountains, culminating in attaining the summits of two 8000-metre peaks without the use of supplementary oxygen. Her mother would have been surprised at these achievements because she had died before Sue had embraced an ice-axe as her tool of trade, but Joan Fear too would have been proud. At her father's funeral Sue had read a eulogy in which she pledged she would make a difference in the world, and already she had raised significant money for two charities close to her heart. Charities were a convenient conduit, but she also wanted to make a direct difference to the way in which people approached their lives. She had witnessed the transformation of clients on treks in Nepal, but adventure travellers formed a very small percentage of the populace. By bringing her adventures to school assembly halls and town halls around the country, Sue was able to reveal unknown dimensions to many, many hundreds of people. She had seen this for herself and, in less stressful circumstances, she was willing to continue this spreading of the word in the future. Her presentations were not the tightly edited product of the National Geographic Channel and its ilk, but instead were the raw voice of a woman who spoke with the passion and conviction of recent experience.

That voice of hers struck a particular chord with women, which was not surprising. Sue inspired women partly because she had found success in this most macho of male domains, where suffering and surviving the wrath of nature and the elements was all in a day's climbing. Her aim had not been to thumb her nose at men and say, 'I can do this, too.' She simply wanted to climb mountains. In fact, she preferred the company of men in the mountains because they were prepared to take more risks than women, and if they came unstuck their way was to laugh it off, provided they survived.

At the same time, being with men was not always easy. To succeed as a mountaineer, a woman had to be very self-contained emotionally, physically and psychologically. This was not something appreciated by most male climbers. For instance, it was challenging for Sue to be a guide and leader in Pakistan because in this part of the world, being in charge was not a woman's role. One jovial Pakistani Liaison Officer had once asked her a curious question.

'Do you know the problems of the world, Sue?'

'No, I do not.'

'Wine, women, and wealth!'

'Oh, really?' she said. 'And you're telling that to a woman?'

Another LO, a young major from an upper class family raised in the seaport of Karachi, had said about Sue in her absence, 'Women should not be in the mountains; they should be in the home. There is no place for them here.'

In this context Sue had to find ways of respecting local culture without giving up on her goals, and at times it seemed almost impossible.

Sometimes there were also difficulties on the mountains with men from the home front. There were many occasions when Sue shared a tent with male mountaineering friends. Sometimes she would snuggle up to someone she regarded as a good friend so that both of them could be warm in the freezing conditions of the high Himalaya. There was no subtext intended, but sometimes sexual advances were made.

Sue recalls a time on the snow slopes of Cho Oyu when she was sharing a tent with a friend who was guiding a separate team of climbers on the mountain. Sue and this man had snuggled up together in a small tent that offered little alternative. Soon he asked the question, 'What would you like me to do?'

'What do you mean?' she asked. 'Put the milk bottles out?'

He repeated himself, saying it slowly. 'What would you like me to do?'

It gave Sue a chill when she realised what he meant, and a feeling of being alone again. He wanted her to initiate the first move in order to shift the responsibility away from him.

She replied, 'What would your wife like you to do?'

Sue had nothing against sexual encounters, but not here, not now and not on this mountain. In this particular instance it was the man who became offended, implying that Sue had broken the rules by bringing his wife into the picture. Sisterhood could be practised remotely.

The worst aspect of such scenarios was that the instigators were nearly always married or in a committed relationship. In such get-togethers, the woman was always seen as the 'tart' while the man came away as the 'stud'. From Sue's point of view, it was demeaning for all involved. Sue could identify with Elle MacPherson as a magnet for men, but Sue only had to deal with the problem when she was in the mountains. The rest of the time there were plenty of other women around to share the burden.

Another boring facet of male company in the mountains was the 'Do my muscles look good in this?' syndrome. Mountaineers need to be precisely aware of their capabilities in order to survive. However, sometimes self-knowledge became self-absorption. Sue was prepared to endure such characters because of the truly good men she met along the way. She had many great and enduring friendships with male mountaineers, men who shared her passion for the mountains, welcomed her as someone who had taken charge of her life, and valued her eagerness to be a team player, especially when the chips were down. She felt empowered by the enormous support she was given by many male climbers, without a trace of judgment.

Men also found Sue's mountaineering achievements remarkable because she had succeeded in a male arena. She was slight enough in build to be blown off a mountain by a big gust of wind, and her upper body strength was not a strength at all. Nevertheless, she had proved herself to be as resilient as anyone else on the mountain, whichever one she was climbing. She may not have been as strong or skilled a climber as some, but she was as tough and as independent. There is a saying that behind every great man is a surprised woman. Perhaps equally likely is the dictum that behind every successful woman mountaineer is a hundred surprised and sometimes confused men.

Away from the mountains, Sue gave little indication of her true mettle. Her inclination had always been for actions to speak louder than words. There was more to her than she chose to reveal, and she liked it that way. Everest had made her famous and so perceptions of her were suddenly different. Now she was an enigma, and that fascinated people.

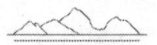

As Sue matured as a speaker she became more involved in the corporate market. She grew more adept at identifying parallels between the challenges of climbing mountains and those of being successful in business. Clarity of goals, perseverance and good leadership were keys to success anywhere.

There was no corporate ladder to ascend in the adventure guiding industry. Sue had taken the 'alternative path' of climbing to the summit of Everest, and in that way she had unwittingly gained access to the most exclusive of boardrooms and the ears of the men who sat there. One advantage of sidestepping the ladder was that she avoided the politics, the glass ceilings, the gossip and the ruthless compromises demanded by business. She had taken other risks, purer ones of life and death, so in the corporate world she arrived directly at the cutting edge. That edge was where Sue had always sought to be in life, from her childhood vision of sailing the world to her young woman's dream of climbing the highest mountain in Africa. She had done more than think about options when she had searched for what might bring her the deepest satisfaction in life; she had sailed those boats, run those triathlons, chopped that wood in the snow, sat at that desk in the travel agency. And at last she began to climb those mountains.

Everest was a high point along the path, no question about that, but the path led onwards to new mountains. Her Everest climb had been hugely satisfying, and more than anything else it was confirmation that she had the ability to cope with the enormous scale and hardship of the world's highest peaks. But the largest crossword puzzle is not necessarily the hardest, and she knew that while Everest's 8850 metres offered the biggest challenge in some respects, there were many mountains with a much lower success rate, many mountains that had repelled all attempts to climb them.

Sue particularly liked the extended challenges of the 8000-metre peaks. The shortage of oxygen added a level of difficulty that was inconceivable to those who had not experienced it for themselves. Anyone can imagine the shortness of breath that comes from the lack of oxygen; much harder is to imagine the extraordinary effort required to perform any physical task, and the almost overpowering sense of lethargy that comes with a decrease in mental functions. When extreme cold and volatile weather are added to the mix, the oxygenless climber faces the toughest of all physical challenges. Oxygenless climbing is hard enough at any height above 7900 metres, but there is a dimensional change above 8300 metres. This is why there have been fewer than one hundred oxygenless ascents of Everest out of close to two thousand total ascents. Sue was keen to establish her own safe limits about oxygenless climbing on other 8000-ers. She knew that the capability to function properly varied enormously among the people brave enough to try it, and so she planned to proceed cautiously. There are fourteen 8000-ers, and for the moment she was leaning towards tackling one of the lower of these giants. Her oxygenless ascents of both Cho Oyu and Shishapangma were proof that she was not being reckless beyond her means, and the extraordinary feat of endurance in climbing Everest, even though it was with oxygen, would stand her in good stead.

Success on Everest often leads to invitations to join expeditions to other 8000-metre peaks, and the first of these was not long in coming. Sue's friend Zac Zaharias of the Australian Army Alpine Association invited her to join an expedition to Gasherbrum 2, the second highest peak in the group of four mountains of that name in Pakistan's Karakoram Ranges.

Sue had been thinking about this mountain as her next climb anyway, so she jumped at the chance. The trip involved a small but enthusiastic team of AAAA climbers who had climbed together in the past, so Sue looked forward to an expedition where the team dynamics had stood the test of previous challenges.

The idea was to leave Australia in July 2004, which left Sue with only a few months to get ready. She found alternative leaders for the two climbing trips she was scheduled to lead during this period and intensified her training routine. The Army climbers continued with their preparations. Everything was falling into place until one of the climbers realised the drastic implications of an Australian government warning that Australians should not visit Pakistan because of the tensions of terrorism and the Gulf War. For Australian citizens in general this was only a strong recommendation, but for military personnel it was a clear directive. The consequences of not complying would be severe. Suddenly the expedition was cancelled as no exceptions to the ruling were entertained.

Sue was shocked at this development. What annoyed her was that the warning itself had been in place for some time but had been virtually the last formality checked, rather than the first. The news came through after she had already given away the guided climbing she had planned for the year, leaving her high and dry.

Within a week of the cancellation, however, Sue was introduced to a man in the Sydney Mountain Designs store who had some interesting news. He told her about an Australian-organised international team of climbers heading to Gasherbrum 2. Circumstances had changed for this expedition as well, and now they were looking for a replacement leader.

Sue realised this could be exactly the opportunity she was looking for, but she was very wary of the dangers of guiding an 8000-metre peak. She followed up with some enquiries and learnt that the team consisted of accomplished climbers—according to their CV's—and that her role, should she decide to take it, would not be as a guide but as the team leader, a very different set of responsibilities. She was confident she could handle this, having led four high-altitude treks to the Karakoram mountains in the mid-1990s. However, she knew that being a woman leader in this part of the world was hard, and that her lot would be even more difficult when leading a mountaineering expedition. It did not take her long to weigh up the pros and cons. The cons were quickly put aside. She knew that Gasherbrum was a beautiful mountain in one of the most magnificent settings imaginable. Psychologically she had already prepared herself to climb this peak, and so she made the vital phone call of acceptance.

Sue had no concrete plans for what might happen after Gasherbrum 2 because for her it was always one step at time. Her long-term habit was to keep one eye on the big picture, but the other mountains she was interested in climbing were now just ideas to put away until after Gasherbrum 2. Many high-altitude climbers had their most successful years in their forties, which Sue found encouraging. She was also aware that forty years is only halfway through life's quota, and she was open-minded about the direction fate would lead her. The hardship of mountaineering might lose its appeal sooner rather than later; the right man might modify the course of her life; there were other unforeseen possibilities. There was no fixed path, and she would make her choices when the time came.

And so, after a year of post-Everest hullabaloo, Sue was heading off to another major climb. Everest had taken over her life in ways she had never imagined possible. Her Everest experience had given her a voice, opened up a new income stream and cemented her commitment to climb more mountains—and there were other subtle changes as well. Now at last it was time for her to dust off her down suit, sharpen her ice-axe and pack her bags. Her attempt on this huge mountain—when she would be in charge of a small team, without Sherpas, in the face of the notorious Karakoram weather—would show her how much she had grown, or otherwise, from the Everest experience. She was well aware that mountains other than Everest were more difficult and dangerous than anything she had climbed to date. If Sue succeeded on Gasherbrum it would be her fourth 8000-metre summit, and while dozens of women had climbed Everest in the thirty years since the first female ascent, only a handful had climbed four or more 8000-ers. She was now entering an exclusive league.

Sue had spent enough time in the Karakoram to learn how the locals felt about their mountains. To the Baltis, *gasher* meant 'beautiful' and *brum* meant 'mountain', the simplicity of the name stating that there was nothing more to say about such a perfect peak.

But for a mountaineer there was more to it than that. There was mystique in the names of each of the fourteen 8000-ers. With Gasherbrum it came from the sound, not the meaning. The clue with Gasherbrum was to say it aloud. Give it space and the word rolled out with the flash and rumble of thunder …

Gasherbrum, the alluring, the frightening, the all-powerful.

10

GASHERBRUM 2004

The cook smelt like hashish, the food was inedible, the mood at Base Camp was sour. I was suffering from severe cabin fever, and I thought, *Anything is better than this.*

I had been to the Karakoram mountains in Pakistan several times as a trekking guide, but this was my first time as the leader of a mountaineering expedition. Compared with Nepal and Tibet, it was a much tougher experience all round. The local Baltis did not offer the same level of service as the Sherpas, a reminder that the Nepalese were extraordinary in their dedication to their roles and their good spirits in hard times.

There were hard times aplenty here on the Baltoro Glacier. Five weeks earlier, a catering truck had rammed my Singapore Airlines 747 at Sydney airport, and I had to swap aircraft. My luggage did not make the transfer to Rawalpindi. As the leader of the expedition, my role was to handle formalities, coordinate logistics, keep the expedition on schedule and determine the best strategies for success, so I was not able to spend an extra day at the airline offices in Rawalpindi hunting for more information about my missing bags. It was nineteen days before they caught up with me at our Base Camp. I suffered during those weeks of trekking and our first forays up the mountain. There was only a limited amount of gear that I could borrow. I had no rain jacket, no warm clothes, no torch, one pair of socks and one set of thermal underwear. I had my boots because I had been wearing them to reduce the weight of my check-in luggage. Also missing were small but essential items. As a result of a miscalculation in timing, and the fact that I had no sun-protective clothing and sunscreen, I was so severely burnt by the sun reflecting from the fresh snow on the glacier that I had fluid seeping from big blisters on my swollen face. I spent three painful days in my tent. On the fourth day my luggage arrived, when I was at the point of accepting that my gear was lost and I would have to give up the climb.

I figured that things could only get better from that point on, but the Karakoram was a tough place to be. At 8035 metres, Gasherbrum 2 was lower than both Cho Oyu and Shishapangma, but the climbing route was definitely more challenging. Gasherbrum 2 was not a peak where you could simply follow in the footsteps of others, as was the case on Everest. Here you needed more than total fitness and an unshakeable commitment to your goal. You needed a real understanding of the dangers of high altitude mountaineering.

The mountain proved to be tougher than everyone expected. There had been many times on my various expeditions when the obstacles had seemed too great to overcome. But in life I give everything my best shot, and because of this, although exhaustion turned me back on my first expedition to Shishapangma, I have reached the summit on every expedition before and after that.

Here on Gasherbrum 2, I could tell from the snow conditions and the steepness of the terrain that we would need this same attitude of bloody-minded determination if we were to overcome the difficulties. Early signs led me to expect that only two of us would be shooting for the top. Apart from a British climber called Ian Wade, the other members of our team struggled to negotiate the crevasses and other obstacles on the glacier above Base Camp. This was not a good omen. Sure enough, in ones and twos those members turned back before reaching Camp Two, where the difficult climbing began. This mountain was not for them on this occasion. They headed home, leaving only Ian and me still committed to go for the summit.

Ian later confided that he had thought the rest of the team would not get past Camp One at 5800 metres, where the climb really starts, and in fact only one of them did. Ian had been to Pakistan twenty-three times, mostly as a guide for a British company, and he knew exactly how many trips he had led as a trekking guide in Nepal and Tibet as well. Both the Pakistanis and the climbers called him Osama because his full beard created a resemblance with Bin Laden. He was very witty and had developed entertaining ways of passing time in tents, such as joking about menus and doing impersonations. These were trivial pursuits but they lightened the mood when the snow was beating down and we were nervous about the tent getting buried.

After several trips up the mountain as far as Camp Two, carrying equipment and acclimatising, we were now waiting at Base Camp for the storms to subside. By the last week of July the weather appeared to be clearing and we grabbed the chance to escape from the depressing atmosphere of Base Camp. The mountains around us were so magnificent, but the mood at Base Camp soured the experience.

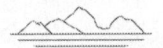

Gasherbrum 2 was a very different project to my climb of Everest, much more reminiscent of Cho Oyu where the decisions had all been up to me. However, there had been many more people on Cho Oyu, including Russell's well-organised expedition. This had created a feeling of there being a climbing community on and around the mountain. Although I had not appreciated it at the time, the crowds on Cho Oyu made it a less daunting undertaking. There was no such atmosphere on Gasherbrum. It was much tougher from the start, beginning with the hike into Base Camp, This was arduous to the point where it was beyond being beneficial for acclimatisation. Base Camp was less comfortable, and even on a good day the 'catering' was average. We ate much better when cooking for ourselves on the mountain than we did at Base and during the walk in, and on every other expedition of mine the opposite had been the case. From a climbing point of view, the Karakoram was even more inhospitable than the Himalaya. Sometimes this made being here exciting, but often the power of nature was so formidable that it was a short step from excitement to fear. Storms of great ferocity and duration dumped huge amounts of snow, but in between there would be a few perfect days, which were magical.

It seemed that a good spell of weather was on the way, which was another trigger for Ian and me to move up the mountain. Among the many expeditions at Gasherbrum Base Camp (some of which were headed for Gasherbrum 1, also approached via Camp One), the accepted timing for the move up to Camp One was to leave at midnight. This tactic saw climbers negotiating the unstable icefall above Base Camp in the early hours of the morning when everything was frozen into place.

Ian and I had planned to leave Base Camp at midnight on 22 July, along with several other teams. But that day, as we waited for the hours to pass, it occurred to me that we could make the climb safely after lunch. I had noticed that temperatures dropped dramatically when the sun moved away from the glacier as the day went on. The icefall would be frozen by late afternoon so we would be able to make the climb safely. We would also have the climb to ourselves and would reach Camp One in time to have a good night's sleep.

'What do you reckon?' I said to Ian. 'Let's go now. Let's go this afternoon.'

It sounded good to him. He was strong, competent and ready for anything.

We packed enough food and equipment to see us through our five-day summit attempt, then we left at around 3 pm. As planned, by the time we reached the treacherous icefall, the sun had long since departed and the loose blocks of ice and the snowmelt rivers had frozen into place again, making passage easier and minimising the dangers. We were making good time despite our heavy packs.

Unfortunately, in our excitement about finally setting off on the final climb, we had forgotten about our headlamps. We had taken these to Camp One on a previous load-carry a week earlier and left them in our tents there. This was a very serious omission which we only remembered when halfway to the camp. It was obvious to us now that by the time we got to the final crevassed section close to Camp One it would be completely dark. We had no rope because the safe route to camp had been well-trodden and was easy to follow during the day. It would have been easy to follow during the night as well if we had not been stupid enough to forget our headlamps.

I was wearing lightweight thermal underwear beneath my wind-suit, which meant I would be cold as soon as I stopped moving. We were in serious trouble, but the only thing Ian and I could do was increase our speed. When the twilight vanished into darkness it was the darkest of nights, and despite our best efforts we had not reached camp. We knew we were not far away. We also knew that the only way to Camp One was along a narrow span of ice between two huge crevasses.

The well-trodden path was frozen into a distinct trail so we followed it carefully. We were moving very slowly now, and both of us were shivering uncontrollably from the intense cold. I feared that we would not make it, that the cold would take us first.

Suddenly Ian turned around and said, 'Sue! I can't find the way! I've lost the trail.'

'It's okay,' I said, which was more than a slight exaggeration. 'Let's go back to our last known point. We'll find it from there. We are very close now. I know it.'

We backtracked slowly, and suddenly Ian spoke again. 'I can feel it! I've found a marker.'

I whooped with delight.

By feeling our way along the trail of footsteps we were finally able to pass safely between the gaping crevasses to the first rows of tents at Camp One. We threw ourselves into our tents, groped for our headlamps, then immediately wriggled into our sleeping bags and lit our stoves. Our tents were only a few metres apart so we exchanged comments about how good it felt to be warm and how lucky we were to have survived our stupidity. We wondered how both of us as experienced guides had made the same potentially fatal mistake. And all of this before a summit bid, when we should be conserving energy! We were making life even harder for ourselves.

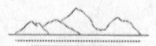

We rested at Camp One for a day, which had been part of our plan. Early that morning the teams which had followed the routine of leaving Base Camp not long after midnight arrived, and among them was Izzat, our high altitude porter. It was an easy place to spend time as the weather was good and the view from the snowfield where we were camped was spectacular. Gasherbrum 1 rose to one side and Gasherbrum 2 to the other, with the daunting granite mass of Gasherbrum 4 rising across the glacier.

At seven o'clock the next morning we set off to Camp Two and climbed steadily. It was steep, exposed climbing but enjoyable, and familiar to us from the load-carrying and acclimatisation forays we had made over this same terrain, which added to the experience. At Camp Two we did not have a good tent site. When we arrived we found that our tent had been completely buried by an avalanche triggered by climbers above. I felt a huge sense of urgency about digging it out, because if it was destroyed our summit chances were gone as well. Our shovel was in the buried tent so we had to use our hands. Izzat asked if I would like him to film the desperate excavation. I told him I wanted him to dig.

The tent was fine but we spent a nervous night wondering if we were going to be buried again. In the morning the weather was marginal, with persistent spittings of snow. We cursed, thinking that we had missed the window of good weather. To avoid getting trapped by heavy snow at this less than ideal camp, we thought we should pack up and head back down. Then we noticed that a friendly German guide with the nickname of Hayo (short for Hans Johan) was starting to climb upwards with his four clients. I certainly respected his judgment and the sight made us pause and think.

Ian had been quite adamant about descending because of the weather. After a tension-filled night of snow flurries building up around our tent, I agreed with him, but now he asked, 'What do you think we should do?'

This 'crossroads' situation reminded me of Shishapangma, when Nima and I had food poisoning and Nima had returned to Base Camp. On that occasion I felt decidedly ill, but then I realised that Pasang and Johan, the leader of the Belgian expedition, were heading up to Camp Three and the summit—that the train was leaving and I had to be on it. I joined them and the three of us summitted together.

The same scenario was unfolding here. There were enough people heading up to create a wave of energy that would help forge the route in the deep snow. We needed to be part of the action. Ian agreed, but Izzat decided to head down. Ian and I packed as quickly as we could, taking a small tent with us. It was hard climbing with heavy packs in thin air and deep snow, interspersed with a series of 'steps' of ice or mixed rock which required good technique. We reached Camp Three at 6700 metres in good spirits and reasonable shape.

The next day we were in no hurry to leave Camp Three because we had been up half the night as part of a foolish false start. The Spanish expedition had wanted to go for the summit from Camp Three in one long day, from midnight, light and fast. I said no at first, that 'light and fast' was a sales pitch. But it was alluring, and neither Ian nor I wanted to miss what could well be a one day window of good weather. We went for it, but soon we were floundering on rock covered with a dangerous layer of fresh powder snow on the edge of a cliff in the dark. When Ian, who was leading, slipped and skated down a rock slab towards me, we both agreed it was time to go back to the tents.

When we set off again in the morning, it proved to be only a three-hour climb to Camp Four at 7350 metres, but the terrain was tricky and much safer when tackled in daylight. The wind picked up but the skies were clear and the scenery spectacular. We realised that staging the ascent in this way—rather than one long push from Camp Three—put us in a much stronger position for reaching the summit.

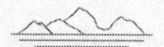

At around 3.30 am in the morning of 26 July, we left Camp Four with a group of Spanish, Italian, German and Austrian climbers, totalling about fifteen people. The snow was deep and there was a lot of post-holing to be done. This technique involves one climber breaking the trail in soft snow by taking high steps and plunging one foot after the other deep into the snow, with the aid of an ice axe for balance. This process creates a line of holes that which is used by everyone behind. It is a very tiring activity for the person up front and still strenuous for the next two or three people in line. After the footsteps are consolidated, it is easier for those who follow. Although we were at the front, I was not able to take the lead. I just did not feel strong enough. Ian did his fair share, but I could not manage better than second or third position, which was still hard work. My tiny saving grace was to offer support and peppermints for the workers doing the post-holing. I had to be careful not to exhaust myself at the beginning of the day because I wanted to be sure I could deal with our descent. It was still pitch dark, so the obvious task was to focus on the effort of climbing and in this way make progress as efficiently as possible.

As the light came, the colours on the mountains were magical. I tried to video the scene but my camera shut down — it was too cold. As we moved up to the gap on the ridge it became very windy. The snow was wind-packed and hard. I was concerned about getting blown off balance because I would have been unable to check a fall. We were not roped so I kept close to Ian.

We rounded the spur and moved away from the worst of the wind. The sun hit our side of the mountain and the environment felt less hostile. Above us was the final snow slope to the summit. The different aspect allowed the wind-packed surface to hold half a metre of soft snow. Again post-holing was called for. It was energetic work at such high altitude. I also battled the sense of lethargy that becomes almost overwhelming at these heights. This time I was sure the sluggishness was worse because we were on reduced rations. We had allowed five days for our summit push, but today was our fifth day and we still had the long descent to go. Nonetheless, I knew we would manage because I had got through the same situation on Everest. As my confidence grew that we would reach the summit, my excitement grew as well—not that I had any spare energy to express it.

Ian was moving ahead. I let him go and stopped to take a photo because my photographer's eye demanded it. I was not making an excuse for a rest as it is a considerable effort to take photos at close to 8000 metres. Up here photography is a definite chore. I needed to take off my mitts, drag my camera out from inside my clothing, push my goggles up my forehead, and try to hold my breath while I pressed the shutter. No matter how tired I am, I pause to take photos, and today the view was so magnificent that it was mesmerising.

Suddenly I was slammed off my feet. A man in a purple down suit had slipped above me and careered down the slope, taking me out like a bowling pin. Now I was sliding as well, but not slowing down. I refused to let this happen. I had put so much effort into climbing this mountain I was determined that I was not going to fall off it, even though gravity had the upper hand. The blow knocked my ice-axe out of my grasp and it was flying on its leash. Without my axe to use as a brake, I had to dig into the slope with my crampons and my arms splayed apart. My arms cut through the soft snow but slowed me enough to bring me to a stop thirty metres down. My purple-suited 'assailant' was still sliding. While I caught my breath, I watched him come to a stop fifty metres below me.

I lay there shocked and winded, then I carefully stood up. I looked up and sighed at the height I had to regain. It was only thirty metres, but it would take half an hour because of the altitude. As I climbed upwards, another man's footing gave way in the soft snow and he slid down as well, from near the top all the way to the bottom. I feared he was going to disappear over the edge. For big men it was harder not to slip in the soft snow. There were quite a few big men above me, and I did not feel like playing any more snakes and ladders.

Ian was well ahead of me now. I thought, *That's okay; put yourself in a different headspace.* If he got to the summit that would be great, and I would get there too, one step at a time. Then I looked up and saw that he had stopped. He had seen what had happened and was waiting for me. I thought, *Man, this is really cool. He's not going to bolt without me.* Nor did he move off as soon as I arrived. Instead he checked I was okay. That was really special.

'Right,' he said. 'Let's stop here for a moment and have something to eat and drink.'

We sat ourselves down carefully so that the snow did not collapse beneath us. He shared his food as I had very little with me, and we drank from our water bottles. We made all the necessary checks before starting to move again, then we continued up the slope as a unit, just as we had on every other day of the climb.

Ian was a guide himself, and although he saw us as equals, he was now encouraging me as if I were a client, thinking I might still be shaken by my fall. I had pulled myself right back in line, but it was still great to have him say, 'Come on, just another five steps and we'll have a breather.'

Five steps is a long way at 8000 metres without oxygen gear, and there was still a lot of 'just another five steps' ahead of us.

It was hard post-holing up the slope while taking care not to let the footsteps collapse. It was easier for me because I was so much lighter, but I also found it more difficult to take the big steps up that were much easier for the men with their longer legs. We climbed methodically, taking only brief stops to catch a few breaths. This method of not taking proper rests put us in front. Suddenly I realised there were only three others ahead of us. I looked behind me and saw climbers all the way down the slope—not an unbroken line by any means, but perhaps two dozen people. Ian and I had drawn ahead because we were aware of the 'big mountain factor', that constant sense of urgency telling us there was not a minute to waste. The sooner we tagged the top the better, as it meant we could head back down to safer altitudes where there was enough oxygen for us to think clearly.

We crested the slope which had led us to the summit, thankful that at last we had to take no more upward steps. At 10.30 am on 26 July we stood on the top of Gasherbrum 2. We had now stopped climbing but still took huge gasps to fill our lungs, even though the air felt empty because of the lack of oxygen. We assessed the summit area, wary of the huge drop all around us. There was a cornice curving over the lip which was the highest point, but neither of us wanted to go there. Hermann Buhl, the most famous European mountaineer of the 1950s, had died when he broke through a cornice on Chogolisa, a nearby Karakoram peak.

For me, Gasherbrum 2 was another big mountain, another 8000-er. At that moment I felt very pleased with my achievement—with what Ian and I had achieved together. More than that, the day had been a great example of different expeditions working together to allow members from every team to summit. In many ways this mountain had been harder than Everest, including physically. During the expedition it had snowed continually, which meant the tracks were constantly being filled in, so the route always had to be replugged. We had no oxygen equipment, so as well as the extra effort involved, the low level of atmospheric oxygen was not enough to keep us properly warm. Without oxygen equipment, frostbite was a much greater risk. There was no security net of Sherpas. Everything was up to us, and, as leader of our team, the buck stopped with me. But we had stuck with it, and we had reached the summit.

The weather was perfect. A slight wind buffeted us, enough to make me conscious that I did not want to be the bird who got blown off her perch. We were very exposed to the heavens where we stood, and it would be easy to overbalance.

There were immaculate views in all directions—of the dramatic pyramid of K2, the world's second highest peak, of Masherbrum, of Gasherbrums 1 and 4, and the huge mass of Broad Peak living up to its name. We looked out over hundreds of peaks stretching as far as the Bilafond and Siachen Glaciers in India. It was a phenomenal sight.

The majesty of the scene absorbed us both and we drank it in like an elixir of life. All our efforts had been rewarded and I felt so happy. I looked at Ian to share the timeless moment and he burst into tears. This big, bushy-bearded bear of a man. On this most beautiful day. On this most beautiful mountain.

EPILOGUE

For me the climb of Gasherbrum 2 was a fantastic indulgence in pure mountaineering. It is a beautiful mountain, and the climbing of it provided real spiritual sustenance. The expedition had a difficult beginning, the climbing was harder than I had expected, and Ian and I suffered an epic journey out from Base Camp. When we came down from the mountain to the Base Camp area, we found that most of the expedition crew and the remaining two climbers had packed up and disappeared. While we were still high on the peak, focused on the climb, they trekked down the glacier en route to the road-head. It was an extraordinary course of action on their part. We had no option but to follow in their tracks. Exhausted by the demands of the climb and the debilitating effects of altitude, we had to make the trek down the valley with only our backpacks, since we could not find porters to carry our luggage. We had minimal food, and when our meager rations ran out we had to rely on the generosity of other expeditions, also on their way out of the mountains. It was hardly a glorious finish to what we felt was a magnificent achievement.

For both of us the important thing had been the climb. For me it had been a relief to escape from the spotlight and the expectations that had faced me continually in Australia since my elevation to 'Ms Everest 2003' status. On Gasherbrum 2 I enjoyed the feeling of freedom that came from climbing a mountain other than Everest. The Karakoram is the realm of mountaineers, but while there are many guided expeditions to the region, no mountain has the same magnetic pull as Everest.

The world's highest mountain continues to attract people for whom the summit is just a trophy. I knew only too well that this 'Everest attitude' brought huge tensions to expedition teams. But despite the problems I encountered, I was deeply satisfied by my success on Everest. I had achieved my goal, and this had empowered me to tackle other mountains—peaks that were icons among mountaineers but ones about which the general public knew little. Gasherbrum 2 was the first of these. Without Everest behind me, I would never have considered accepting the invitation to lead the Gasherbrum expedition.

Every mountain I have climbed has taught me something new, and between times I have returned to guiding treks, selling outdoors gear at Mountain Designs, and using my expertise to develop the World Expeditions adventure travel business. For years I was content with this lifestyle, but post-Everest I found new challenges in broader segments of society. During the slide show tour which took place immediately after I returned from Everest, I had begun to feel like a commodity that was for sale at $10 a ticket, even if the funds did go to charities I supported. When I had been allowed time to recover from the rigours of the expedition, I became excited and motivated by the inspiration I could bring to people with no real experience of adventure and mountaineering. Not everyone was inspired, of course, but at least I had revealed, by example, how a person could achieve dreams which, at first consideration, might seem totally beyond them. Such a message is very powerful, and for me passing it on was a huge reward.

I returned from climbing Gasherbrum 2 with another amazing story to tell, but I discovered that schools and corporate clients only remained interested in Everest-focused presentations. Everest was more than just a mountain to the general public; it had become a symbol with almost universal relevance to the world of non-mountaineers. It was only mountaineers who understood the similarities between climbing Everest and other giant mountains. Only mountaineers knew that greater challenges could be faced on K2, the world's second highest peak, or on other mountains unknown to the world at large. I realised that climbing Everest was a phenomenon about which I would always be asked questions. At first I was surprised that no one expressed more than passing interest in Gasherbrum, but when I thought about the implications I felt relief. Everest would always be 'The One' as far as the mainstream world was concerned. There was comfort in the fact that my future climbs on other mountains would not attract such huge public interest, and that they would remain more personal, my own private journey towards growth and exploration.

My most recent adventure has been the guiding of clients up two mountains in the Everest region. They were both lower than the summit of Mera Peak, with which I was very familiar, but the higher of the two mountains involved terrain that was more challenging to climb. I was in Nepal for five weeks on this trip, and while much of my attention was focused on the climbing, the welfare of my clients, and the roles and responsibilities of the Sherpa guides who were helping me, I still had time in quiet moments to reflect on the course my life had taken. Foremost in my mind was this book, which we had completed the day before I flew to Kathmandu.

As fate would have it, since the completion of the first draft some months earlier, I have crossed paths with many of the people who appear in these pages. Most of those meetings have been by chance, but I have sought out some with whom I have maintained contact and developed strong relationships. Raju, my cook on Makalu 2, whose culinary craft and logistical skills had been rudimentary on that expedition, came with me on the trip I have just completed. He is now my good friend and favourite trekking cook: efficient, talented and a good manager. Zeddy, who almost drove me to distraction on Everest, was very enthusiastic about the prospect of climbing Kosciuszko with me, the last of his Seven Summits, and he continues to send me joyous emails about his latest ventures, and best wishes upon the anniversaries of our climb. Also from Everest, Matt has kept in touch, recalling our good times together in outrageous places.

During my most recent visit to Kathmandu I ran into Hermann at the Radisson Hotel. He was delighted to see me, and I felt the sincerity of his interest in my life since the Everest climb. On my side, I was pleased to see him as well, which surprised me. Unfortunately, our commitments to the respective groups we were guiding did not allow us to catch up for a beer. Whether we had wanted it or not, however, a bond had been formed between us because we had both achieved, in our very different ways, our dream of climbing Everest. Admittedly, not much of what we had gone through together had been pleasurable, but the fact that the experiences occurred on Everest gave that time a special place in our lives. Although within our team we had squabbled among ourselves, we had still been fighting on the same side. We were not fighting against Everest (which is immune to all battles and supposed conquests) but against our own human frailty, with its full gamut of fears, doubts and suffering.

Similarly, some of the people I have spoken to while checking my version of events have shared their thoughts with me for the first time, about 'that expedition' or 'that time back then'. This has been a positive and warming experience, but also a reminder of what I have learned. On Everest and elsewhere I can see now how I might have circumvented some of those pressure-cooker situations, but that is the wisdom of hindsight. I think we can all look back at some time and say we could have handled something differently or better, but we didn't. What matters is learning from those lessons and applying them to the present and the future. For me that means continuing to develop new friendships, to learn what I can along the way, and to 'do something useful with yourself', as my parents often said, until my last day.

The mountains can bring out the best and the worst in people. It is a life-threatening arena, with very goal-focused people, financial pressures, ill health and more all adding further to the tension. It is understandable that people react in adverse ways. Having the final word on safety is critical in staying alive on climbs, but some tolerance of different views and ways of achieving the goal can go a long way. I can't recall how many times I might have said, 'Well, this is interesting

...' when a very different idea has been proposed to me, be it in Russia, Bolivia, Nepal or somewhere else. At those times I have thought, *Okay, let's see where this leads*. I will always credit someone who offers solutions rather than just pointing out problems.

My story features many incidents and challenges of one kind or another. If I had left certain tense moments out of this book, the story would have been diminished. I hope that readers can see the bigger picture for what it is—that life throws all sorts of things at you and you don't always need to respond by backing off. Nor should it be a case of 'the summit at all costs'.

One of the joys of adventure travel and expeditioning is the spontaneity of events and how you adapt to them. Readers may think that after my first trip to Africa I would never want to travel to diverse, unknown places again, yet those experiences sowed some of the first seeds of my maturity. I grew to understand what is good and bad in human nature, and I certainly appreciate how valuable such lessons were. There are huge benefits in being involved with adventure travel, which is why I have continued to work for the same company, World Expeditions, for so many years. As my perspective on the travel business matured, I found that my satisfaction was greatest when I was involved in researching trips and then leading them. This was not only because I went to new destinations, but also because I had to forge new relationships in unknown lands—a huge challenge, but hugely rewarding.

My expedition to Gasherbrum 2 in 2004 had plenty of challenges that left me tired and rumpled, but when I look back at my images of the climb and recall my experiences with Ian on those intense summit days, the value of our achievements and the process is crystal clear. The message is that I should not stop doing what I love because of a few setbacks. This is true in every walk of life, for everyone. Missed opportunities are gone forever. Everything is relative. It's about keeping a balance in our lives. When I look at my life compared with others', I feel very fortunate to have met so many people in my travels and to have shared their world. I have had many opportunities which I have been able to turn into something real—unique adventures, unfamiliar cultures, unknown landscapes, new relationships.

Especially important to me, as part of the 'Everest effect', has been the opportunity to contribute to community and social issues by fundraising for the Fred Hollows Foundation, the Australian Himalayan Foundation and other groups. It is only because I climbed Everest and became someone who has 'done something' that I am able to raise money for charity by selling limited edition prints and posters and giving lectures. I have been particularly excited about how well my contributions have been received at forums about growth and change, notably those attended by girls who are about to face the challenges of becoming women in what is still largely perceived as a man's world—and I am not referring to mountaineering here.

A totally unexpected recognition of my efforts in these areas, as well as in mountaineering, is the very recent honour of being awarded a Medal of the Order of Australia (OAM), a perfect gift to mark the second anniversary of my Everest success.

Many people are amazed that I chose a path that took me to the summit of Everest and beyond. Perhaps this is because I don't look like their image of a mountaineer (whatever that is!); perhaps because they have no conception of the rewards such a life can offer. There are many paths we can take in the world beside the conventional routes of career and family. There are huge rewards to be gained by setting out to discover the world and to explore your own potential in the process. This need not be through mountaineering; in fact, mountaineering is one of the most difficult paths to choose because of the dangers, the discomforts and the degree of commitment required.

But you do not have to go over the top in some way to do something worthwhile. Regular people can do great things, often more easily than those in the spotlight because there is less pressure. While the majority of people are happy to follow the beaten path, at a certain point some realise that it is possible to make a positive difference during their lifetime by deviating from that path. A sense of purpose is an amazing thing, and it can yield unexpected rewards.

EPILOGUE

The last thing my father said to me the night before he died was that I was courageous. He had never said that before and I laughed it aside, thinking that the term belonged to the realm of extraordinary people. Yet now that I consider the word again, I can see that it applies to all those people out there who are not put off easily, who challenge their fears and the unknown, sometimes just to reach the other side. I realise my dad paid me a great compliment, even if he was biased, and I hope the stories told here give others the courage to go on and 'be who they want to be'.

POSTSCRIPT

In April 2006 Sue Fear set out for the Himalaya once more. It would prove to be her last expedition. Her goal this time was Manaslu—another of the world's fourteen mountains higher than 8000 metres. A successful summit would put Sue's achievements on a par with some of the world's best women climbers. Few have summitted more than four of the 8000ers.

At 8163 metres Manaslu is the eighth highest mountain in the world. Situated in the Himalaya it is classified as a remote mountain since access is very limited—it takes around two weeks to trek into the Base Camp before mountaineers can begin their climb. Perhaps because of this remote location, or because of its reputation for heavy snow drifts and avalanches, it is climbed less frequently than other 8000ers. Only about 240 people have successfully climbed Manaslu compared with almost 2000 ascents of Everest. Two Australian expeditions had previously climbed Manaslu. Greg Mortimer, the first Australian to climb Everest (with Tim Macartney-Snape) and K2, summitted just a few weeks after Andrew Lock became the first Australian to successfully reach the peak of Manaslu on 21 April 2002.

As it happens, 2006 marks the 50th anniversary of the first summitting of Manaslu. After three earlier aborted attempts by Japanese mountaineers, the first successful expedition took place in 1956. Japanese climber Toshi Imanishi and Nepali Sherpa Gyalzen Norbu made the summit on 9 May 1956, with Kiichiro Kato and Minoru Higeta summitting two days later. Interestingly, it was not climbed again until 1971.

Sue expected the expedition to take around two months. She had arranged her climb through handling agents Asian Trekking of Kathmandu and was to share a permit and Base Camp with the Golden Jubilee Manaslu Expedition under team leader Chieko Shimada from Japan. They were to follow the regular north-east route. Sue's climbing partner would be her long-time friend, Nepali Sherpa Bishnu Gurung. Sue and Bishnu planned to set their own schedule for the climb. This would be challenging since, as Sue acknowledged before she left Australia, it meant they would 'have to haul their own gear including rope for fixing the route if required and work in cooperation with other climbers in order to open a route to the last camp'.

Opening up the route would be even more daunting than usual because of excessive snowfalls over the previous two seasons that had deterred any would-be expeditions from making an attempt to climb Manaslu. The mountain had a significant history of avalanches. The most devastating incident occurred in 1972 when sixteen members of a Korean expedition attempting to climb the north-east face were swept to their deaths.

A fact sheet circulated just before Sue left Australia gives us an insight into her attitude towards the task ahead:

> Drawing from her experience of continuous snowfalls on Gasherbrum 2 in 2004, [where] Sue found that despite this [the weather], they were still able to be up in position when the small window of good weather appeared to be able to nab the summit. This may well be the case again, however there is additional concern of avalanche-prone slopes around camp 2 that one needs to pay respect to, no mountain is worth a life.

As always Sue was a realist about the challenges that may have lain ahead. She felt that, through her climbs of Gasherbrum 2 and Shishapangma, as well as Everest, she had developed the necessary skills to cope with what Manaslu may throw up at her, and climbing Manaslu had been on Sue's mind for some time. Nevertheless she was not afraid of pulling out if the going became just too tough to continue on to the summit. After all, she had made this brave decision on previous summit bids and then gone on to successfully climb those mountains. This gave her the confidence to seize the challenge of attempting Manaslu.

Sue was looking forward to once more visiting Nepal, a place with which she had long felt a special affinity. She also held the deepest respect for the Nepalese people and their belief that the mountains were sacred places. Sue particularly expected this trip to be 'a real holiday' as Mount Manaslu was located in such a scenic part of Nepal.

Of great interest to Sue was that she would be climbing with Junko Tabei of Japan. Junko overcame incredible odds, having been buried by an avalanche with several of her team, to become the first woman to summit Everest on 16 May 1975, via the south-east ridge route. Now aged 67, Junko had joined the expedition to Manaslu to help celebrate Japan's first successful ascent in 1956. Sue was looking forward 'to sharing experiences with Junko and hearing about her historic ascent first-hand'.

Once under way, Sue kept in touch with family and friends by email and reported on her progress. For now this is the best account we have of the expedition. The first communication was received on 3 May 2006:

> Just a quick note to let you know how things are. Arrived bc [Base Camp] 19 April after trek in. Got bad food poisoning on way in and this seemed to affect my overall acclimatization and performance. But by 28 April I suddenly seem to have come good. (I was starting to think I was too old for all this, but all seems good) we opened way to camp 2 but last few days weather has been terrible with every arvo n [and] nt [night] snowing heavy…so we have to wait. Avalanche danger is a big hazard between C1 n C2, n no summit is worth a life or accident due to rushing, we have to wait a bit. There are mostly Japanese here, our team of 3 women, and a cleaning climb team…

Will be back to u, we hope next visit up, hopefully in a few days, will be summit bid…we have time, we have to be patient.

Hope alls well with u, always more one could say but will save for beers at home,

Cheers mate.

Sue.

There were two teams heading for the summit of Manaslu. As well as the Golden Jubilee Manaslu Expedition with which Sue was climbing, there was a second expedition—the Manaslu Cleaning Expedition—under the leadership of Japanese climber Ken Noguchi who was to reach the summit on 16 May. As predicted, the real danger of avalanches was slowing the progress of both teams.

Almost two weeks later on Sunday 14 May 2006 a second email arrived from Sue:

It's time, after much toing & froing, I am off today to C1 for summit bid, C2 tomorrow, C3 next, C4, then summit—18 May is the plan. The weather has been shocking: wind snow or both and our route destroyed time after time.

Everyone waiting for someone else to reopen the route. Bishnu always up front to be part of it. We had a semi summit go last bit [sic] but things not right, we have established C3 & everything is in place for us now, I think all we need now is a good 4 days, that's all. This mtn [mountain] has proved elusive to get high on…speak to you in a while. Am booked to leave bc 22 May, helicopter to Ktm [Kathmandu] 25 May from Samagoan. So will change flight home, looking forward to getting this sorted and getting back to a life like normal people hey.

Cheers.

A week later another email arrived:

Sunday 21 May

Well, I went for the summit on 17 May fm [from] C4. For varying reasons I didn't quite make the last 150m, the weather was not an issue, I just had no power on summit day due to dramas leading up to it I think…so what a challenge now. To go home as so many do tomorrow, or make a second go to get it right. The latter I am doing and I think it will work. I have to satisfy myself that I could do the whole summit day smoothly as I would do when my strategy in lead up is as I have prepared, not as it was working with all these other people with their dramas. So I will head back up 23 May n try again approx 26 May, Bishnu is keen about it, even though we both are terribly keen to go home. It is a big mtn and a long way to go back up to C4 n be in position to try, especially as the whole route is deteriorating a lot now. The weather is just so unpredictable here, I have never seen it so changeable. There is just me n Bishnu n a Japanese guy Konishi n his 2 sherpas going back so light n quick n uncomplicated is our plan. Konishi can get a helicopter back to ktm from Sama [Samagoan] when we are finished, hopefully around 29/30 May. I feel like I have been here for months. Will be back to you if it changes, n ring when I get down this time.

This last email graphically illustrates the frustration that Sue must have been feeling. As always Sue had let her instincts guide her and had chosen not to push for the summit when things didn't feel right. Instead she had taken the momentous decision to descend the mountain, regroup and make another summit bid. It can often seem an easier option to keep going, even though the odds are against you, than it can be to turn back. Only a mountaineer can fully appreciate the mental and physical stamina required to make another attempt. Only a mountaineer can imagine the energy required to turn around and again head up some 8163 metres to the summit. But, as she had throughout her life, Sue once again demonstrated her determination to go on. She believed she could succeed and so resolved to give this elusive mountain a second shot.

The irony of this moment was that just as Sue's last email was filtering through cyberspace, so too were news reports that her friend and colleague Lincoln Hall had been left for dead after a successful summit of

Everest. For Sue's family and friends this news was very distressing. Not only did they mourn the loss of a great man but their thoughts also turned to Sue. How would she take it? Thankfully, given her remote location, she was unlikely to hear the news until her own summit bid was completed. It was good that she could power on in her second attempt to reach the summit of Manaslu oblivious to the tragic events that had unfolded across the mountain range on Everest. When the unexpected news subsequently arrived that Lincoln had been found alive, spirits soared and everyone focused once more on Sue's challenges.

As we now know, Sue summitted the mountain on Sunday 28 May, becoming the first Australian woman to summit five of the 8000ers. That night, however, first reports began flashing across the airwaves that Sue had fallen into a crevasse during her descent while crossing a relatively level tract of snow with her climbing partner Bishnu. Perhaps spurred on by the miraculous events surrounding Lincoln's rescue, family and friends were determined not to give up hope, but little could be done until Bishnu was located and the true situation revealed. People were optimistic though that a rescue bid could be mounted to save Sue.

After a long two-day wait for news, Bishnu was finally found and able to describe what had happened to Ringi Norbu Sherpa, Sue Fear's friend and agent in Kathmandu.

Sue and Bishnu went for the summit on 28 May in reasonable conditions from their high camp on the edge of Manaslu's great plateau. They reached the summit at 10.30 am. It was cloudy but the wind had dropped. They sat there for thirty minutes, eating some apple and chocolate, taking photographs and drinking juice. At around 11 am they proceeded down, with Sue taking the lead and Bishnu ten metres behind, attached by thirty metres of rope. The weather started to close in as they descended. When they reached the plateau at around 7600 metres, Bishnu heard a loud noise and saw Sue's feet break through the snow crust and her plunging headfirst into a crevasse.

According to the official incident report submitted to Nepal's Ministry of Tourism and Culture:

Since they were both on the same main rope Bishnu immediately ... put the brake on with his ice axe as it was pulling him. He started yelling 'Sue Didi, Sue Didi', and tried to pull her out of the crevasse. There was no reply from her and she seemed to be unconscious.

After arresting her fall, Bishnu tried desperately to pull Sue out. After an hour and a half pulling the rope upwards without success and with no response from Sue at all—no sound and no movement—and with the crevasse opening up further and further, Bishnu tried to arrange a better pulley system to haul Sue out. In order to do this he had to detach himself from the rope. Just as he did this, the crevasse collapsed further. Bishnu managed to jump clear but the rope anchor was taken and with it the rope with Sue on the end. Peering down into the hole all Bishnu could see was darkness—there was no sound at all from Sue.

Totally traumatised and exhausted by the experience, and fearing that the crevasse would open even further, Bishnu reluctantly made his way to the high camp from where he was able to radio Base Camp with a short message. Ang Tshering of Asian Trekking, which equipped the expedition, received the phone call from Base Camp confirming the fall just below the summit.

On 29 May a team of six Sherpas from the Japanese clean-up expedition was dispatched up the mountain by the expedition organisers. They were able to locate Bishnu on his descent and helped him down to Advance Base Camp. On 30 May, shortly before a helicopter was to be mobilised with rescue supplies to Base Camp, a call came through to Ringi Norbu Sherpa from Bishnu who had arrived at Base Camp.

On consultation with experienced mountaineers, it was concluded that there was no hope of Sue surviving such an accident and that relocating the crevasse would be impossible given the wind and snowfall prevailing in the area. Furthermore, among the only people capable of reaching the site within a reasonable time there was a lack of the specialised technical capacity necessary to safely orchestrate the recovery of a body from the depths of such a crevasse.

POSTSCRIPT

Sue loved Nepal and she loved the mountains. While it was never her wish to die in pursuit of her dreams, the mountains were nevertheless her spiritual home. She frequently spoke with reverence about the spiritual nature of the Himalaya. It therefore seems fitting that she should end her days enfolded in the arms of Manaslu. Perhaps it is no small co-incidence that the name of this mountain is taken from the Sanskrit word *Manasa* meaning 'Mountain of the Spirit'. Sue, may you rest in peace in your spiritual home.

GLOSSARY

abseiling To abseil is to slide down a vertical rope using friction to descend in a controlled manner. In its most basic form, the requisite friction is created by running the rope between your legs, then taking it up diagonally across your chest and over your shoulder, and then diagonally down across your back to your hip (or outer thigh) where your hand regulates the speed of your descent by controlling the rope. Your other hand holds the rope in front and provides balance. A descender (or descendeur) is a small metal device clipped to a climber's harness that provides the same degree of friction in a more secure and easily controllable fashion. Descenders are generally used when descending fixed ropes.

Altiplano The high plain in Peru and Bolivia that surrounds Lake Titicaca.

Ausangate An isolated mountain massif on the Peruvian Altiplano. At 6384 metres, it is the fourth highest peak in Peru.

bergschrund The crevasse that separates a glacier from the mountain above it. It is often an obstacle when climbing or descending a mountain.

Changtse The north peak of Mount Everest, which is separated from the main peak by the North Col. At 7580 metres, it is an impressive mountain offering challenging climbing, but it is overshadowed by Everest and virtually ignored by climbers.

Cho Oyu The world's sixth highest mountain (8201 metres). It lies on the border between Nepal and Tibet, west of Mount Everest, with ascents invariably made from the Tibetan side of the mountain.

cwm A Welsh word (pronounced *coomb*) meaning 'high valley'.

Mount Cook Part of the Southern Alps and the highest peak in New Zealand at 3754 metres, Mount Cook poses many technical climbing routes. Only one of these is relatively straightforward, but even so, it definitely requires mountaineering skills.

crampons A frame of spikes that is strapped or clipped onto mountaineering boots to enable a climber to gain purchase on slopes of ice and hard snow.

Eight thousanders/8000ers There are fourteen peaks in the world that are over 8000 metres above sea level. Only a handful of women have climbed more than four of these '8000ers'. The 8000ers not mentioned elsewhere in this glossary are Annapurna (8091 metres), Dhaulagiri (8167 metres),

Manaslu (8156 metres) and Nanga Parbat (8126 metres).

Mount Everest On the border between Nepal and Tibet, at 8850 metres, Everest is the highest mountain in the world. The first ascent was achieved by a British expedition in 1953, when Edmund Hillary and Tenzing Norgay reached the world's highest point. The first British climbers reached the summit twenty-two years later.

expedition In a mountaineering context, an expedition is an undertaking to climb a major peak, which may take anywhere between three weeks and three months. This is not to be confused with the expeditions run by trekking companies, which are basically walking holidays that sometimes include a one- to three-day climb of a mountain. Also, climbs of peaks in alpine ranges (such as New Zealand's Southern Alps, the European Alps or the High Sierra of California) are called alpine climbs, rather than expeditions.

fixed rope The term given to ropes that are attached to difficult or dangerous parts of a mountain to allow climbers safe passage up and down the mountain in all but the most hostile conditions. Fixed ropes are heavily relied upon by commercial expeditions where many of the climbers do not have the experience to climb safely without them. On the largest mountains, several kilometres of rope may be deployed.

Gasherbrum massif This cluster of mountains in the Karakoram consists of five major peaks, three of which are above 8000 metres: Broad Peak (8047 metres), Gasherbrum 1 (8068 metres) and Gasherbrum 2 (8042 metres).

Himalaya A series of ranges running from the Indian province of Sikkim in the east, westwards along the northern border of Nepal, into the Indian provinces of Garhwal and Uttar Pradesh, then tapering into the alpine ranges of Kashmir.

Kangchenjunga The third highest mountain in the world at 8586 metres, Kangchenjunga lies on the border of Nepal and the Indian province of Sikkim.

Karakoram The great Central Asian mountain range, this north-western sister of the Himalaya extends from India, through Pakistan to Afganistan, and is bordered by Chinese territory on its north.

K2 At 8611 metres, K2 is the world's second highest peak, acknowledged among mountaineers as a more difficult and dangerous mountain than Everest. This mountain forms part of the border between China and Pakistan.

Mount Kenya The highest mountain in Kenya, and the second highest peak in Africa, lies one degree south of the Equator. Mount Kenya has twin summits, Bation (5199 metres) and Nelion (5188 metres), the climbing of which requires technical rockclimbing skills. A third peak, Point Lenana (4985 metres), can be reached by trekking parties.

Kilimanjaro Situated in Tanzania, the extinct volcano of Kilimanjaro is the highest mountain in Africa at 5895 metres.

la A Tibetan and Sherpa word for a high pass.

Lhotse The west peak of Everest, separated from the main summit by the South Col and, at 8516 metres, the fourth highest peak in the world.

Makalu The world's fifth highest peak at 8463 metres, located 25 kilometres east of Everest.

Makalu 2 A secondary peak of Makulu (7680 metres), which is separated from the main summit by the Makalu La.

Niyiragongo A volcano on the Rwanda–Zaire border.

North Col At 7100 metres, North Col forms the low point (!) on the ridge between Changtse and Everest. This is where expeditions climbing Everest's north-east ridge set their first camp on the mountain proper (as opposed to Advance Base Camp and Interim Camp, which are on the East Rongbuk Glacier).

Ruwenzori A glaciated mountain range on the border of Uganda and Zaire, also known as the Mountains of the Moon. It is notorious for its bad weather and muddy approaches. The highest peak in the range is Mount Margherita, which is part of the Mount Stanley massif and the third highest peak in Africa (5100 metres).

serac An isolated block of ice formed where the glacier surface is fractured. Seracs pose a threat to climbers because they are sometimes unstable and can topple over at any time. Falling seracs on steep glaciers can trigger avalanches.

Sherpa A people of Tibetan origin who live in the high valleys of the Himalaya. For over a century they have been valued by foreign expeditions as guides and porters. Sherpa Tenzing Norgay was on his seventh Everest expedition when he reached the summit with Edmund Hillary.

Shishapangma At 8027 metres, this is the fourteenth highest mountain in the world and the highest peak in a massif situated in Tibet, 15 kilometres north of the main Himalayan chain.